D0919635

FIAT LUX

ROLLINS·COLLEGE·MDCCCLXXXV

ROLLINS COLLEGE
LIBRARY

A GIFT FROM

John Young Museum
and
Planetarium

THE STORY OF
THE AMERICAN INDIAN

ZAPOTEC GOLD ORNAMENT

The Story of the
American Indian

BY PAUL RADIN, Ph.D.

Author of "Primitive Man as Philosopher", and "The Racial Myth".
Formerly Professor of Anthropology at the
University of California

LIVERIGHT PUBLISHING CORPORATION
NEW YORK

PREFACE TO REVISED EDITION

In the following pages I have attempted to describe the salient traits of the life of the American Indians, as well as their history, in simple language. It is avowedly an interpretation and not a mere narration of the facts. The assumption with which I begin is that aboriginal American history can only be understood in terms of the spread of the great civilizations that developed in Mexico, Central America and along the Pacific coast of South America from Ecuador to Peru. I do not believe that any scholar seriously questions this any longer. Such a view is not original. It has been promulgated by many anthropologists before me.

I have tried to present the facts as authentically as possible and to select for description, tribes representative of every type of culture found in the Americas.

Some critics of the first edition of this book contended that it was unfair to the less complex cultures of America, to attribute all their achievements to the influence, direct or indirect, of the great civilizations of Mexico, Central America and South America. But the investigations of the last seven years have confirmed my general point of view beyond my fondest expectations. Even in the case of the southwest of the United States, although it has become increasingly evident that this culture is much older than we had anticipated, still it is now more than ever apparent that all its initial development was due to influences from Mexico.

For our knowledge of the archæology of the Valley of Mexico and adjacent regions, the last seven years have been revolutionary. We can now retrace the cultures there as far back as 1,000 B.C., and the civilization of the peoples we have called the Toltecs has proved to be but one of many superimposed layers, and a fairly late one at that. But in spite of the added complexity which this gives to our picture it does not materially interfere with the main thesis. It is possible that what I have designated as early Maya influences upon the United States will have to be interpreted more generically, as Southern Mexican. That is all.

With regard to the tantalizing question of what type of culture the Indians of the United States possessed before the spread of the higher elements from Mexico, in the light of recent studies, we can now say this: that although these cultures were on a non-agricultural basis, some of them were clearly more complex than has generally been assumed. It is quite within the realm of probability that, at a very early date, a fairly unified civilization, possessing pottery and a significant ritualistic and political development, stretched across North America from the northwest coast of Canada, across the northwestern plains to the Great Lakes, then along the entire area east of the Mississippi, across the Caribbean, to northeastern South America. Such a culture would be able to react in a markedly individual manner to whatever impulses and influences came to it from the great civilizations to the south, and this may possibly explain, for instance, both the variability of the Mound Builder cultures as well as their special developments.

The question of terminology has been as refractory as such problems are wont to be in a semi-popular book. I have tried to be as consistent as I could. If I have occasionally slipped I hope my readers will be generous and bear in mind the definitions I have, at different places in this book, made of these controversial terms.

PAUL RADIN

Berkeley, Sept., 1934

x

CHAPTER VIII.—THE MOUND-BUILDERS

The confusion of culture—The torch-bearer of the south—
Specialization in borrowed goods—The new style—The loss of
inspiration

192

CONTENTS

x   *Contents*

Contents

Contents

COLORED PLATES

BLACK AND WHITE ILLUSTRATIONS

THE STORY OF
THE AMERICAN INDIAN

THE STORY OF
THE AMERICAN INDIAN

PROLOGUE

THE GOLDEN DAY

On the Fox River where the city of Neenah now stands
and still further north along the southern shores of Green
Bay, once lived a people called by their neighbors the
Winnebago. They were harassed on all sides by enemies
who had but recently emerged from the wilds of Canada.

So long had they already dwelt in this new Wisconsin
home when the French first visited them in the seventeenth
century, that their recollections extended no farther. The
village of Red Banks, situated on the red sandstone bluffs
rising rather abruptly out of the bay and clearly visible for
a great distance, was to their minds their ancestral home.
It was in fact the precise spot where according to legend
their remote animal ancestors had first become transformed
into human beings.

From the bay the approach to this village was extremely
difficult. Certainly no enemy would have hazarded it. But
from the south only the forbidding primeval forest screened
the place from the view of an approaching visitor. Assuming that he could have made his way undetected through
the trails of this enveloping forest, a traveler would have
discovered as the foliage becomes thinner, an artificially

3

cleared space of considerable proportions. He was at the outskirts of the village. As far as this open space the inhabitants might stroll with a certain degree of safety. Beyond it lay the wilderness and probable death.

The houses were clearly visible from this open space, and even a casual observer would have noticed that the village itself was laid out according to a definite plan. It was circular in outline and the houses were grouped in a specific manner, on both sides of a small space that might very well be called a street, which extended right across the entire village. At some distance in the rear, on both sides of this street, stood two gabled houses made of elm and birch bark and obviously more imposing in appearance than were the others.

Inquiry would soon have elicited the information that that on the left belonged to the chief of the tribe, that he was a member of a clan called the Thunderbird and that all the people on his side of the street were prohibited from intermarrying. Furthermore it would have been discovered that he could never embark on a war undertaking and that, in general, whatever powers and influence he possessed were always employed in watching the welfare of his people, admonishing them, preventing quarrels, exerting himself toward reconciling those who had grievances against each other, and practicing the cardinal virtues of his community— hospitality, moderation, and taciturnity. When in summer he gave an annual feast to the assembled villagers, he was acting in his essential capacity of protector of the tribe. He then symbolized, so it was contended, a mother-bird feeding her young. It was his duty to ward off all evil from the community.

"Try to do something for your people," so ran an old

injunction to the chief, "something difficult. Have pity on your people and love them. If a man is poor, help him. Give him and his family food, give them whatever they ask for. If there is discord among your people, intercede. Take your sacred pipe and walk into their midst. Die if necessary in your attempt to bring about reconciliation. Then when order has been restored and they see you lying on the ground dead, still holding in your hand the sacred pipe, the symbol of peace and reconciliation, then assuredly will they know that you have been a real chief."

The house on the right side belonged to a chief equal in importance to the one just described. He was, however, a member of a different clan, the Bear clan, and as in the case of the tribal chief the people on his side were prohibited from intermarrying. His functions were fundamentally different from those of the chief of the Thunderbird clan. Not only could he go to war, for instance, but he enjoyed everything connected with it. In the village he was the chief of police. Instead of a badge, however, he carried as an emblem of his authority, a little stick cut in a curious manner and with which, whenever it was absolutely necessary, he would strike an offender. It was his duty to enforce order, to prevent any individual from behaving in such a way that his action would endanger the lives of his fellowmen, and to guard the village against enemies and disease. All the members of his clan, as well as those of his particular friend-clan, the Wolf, acted as his aides. Every night, leading a selected number of his people, he would circle around the village and make certain that nothing untoward had taken place within or was threatening from without.

But his functions in the village were secondary to those

that fell to his lot when the tribe was on the hunt or on the warpath. In the village, after all, tradition and routine took care of most things. It was different, however, when people were exposed to the danger of the hunt and the attack of enemies. One misstep, one act of uncalled-for bravado, any refusal to obey imperative orders, might lead to fatal consequences. The rules in force in hunting and on the warpath were consequently exceedingly rigorous and they were ruthlessly enforced by the leader of the Bear clan and his aides.

Not far from the lodge of the chief of the Thunderbird clan stood that of the warrior or Hawk clan. In his lodge were kept many of the articles connected with war-weapons, sacred war emblems and scalps, as well as all prisoners preparatory to their torture and death. Scattered over the rest of the left side of the street were the houses of the Pigeon and the Eagle clansman. These three clans together with that of the Thunderbird formed a unit of their own called the Sky or Upper people and were definitely set off against the clans on the right side of the street.

On that side of the street ruled over by the chief of the Bear clan there were in all eight clans. They, too, formed a definite unit and called themselves the Earth or the Lower people. Foremost among them were four clans, the Wolf, the Buffalo, the Water-Spirit and the Elk. These four had certain special and important functions to perform in the government of the village. The members of the Wolf clan, for instance, all acted as reserve policemen. Those of the Buffalo as public criers and messengers of the tribal chief, those of the Waterspirit as representatives of the chief of the tribe, and those of the Elk as the firemakers. Scattered over the rest of this half of the village stood the houses of the three minor clans, the Deer, the Snake and the Fish.

If, upon the first landing of the French in the fall of 1634, the leader of the expedition, M. Nicollet, had been invited, let us say, to spend a fortnight with those friendly people—for they were friendly and received the French in the kindliest of spirits—he would have witnessed an instructive and unusual series of customs, festivities and ceremonies.

In this latitude, even in fall, night comes early and M. Nicollet would have been hustled into the chief's lodge rather hastily, for night to these people had very definite discomforts, dangers and perils, against which an honored guest had to be protected as much as grown-up natives and children. An enemy, for instance, might conceivably manage to slink in and take his revenge for a death of some kinsman. Yet that, however, was not very likely.

The real danger and annoyance came from within. The ghosts of the departed always hovered about at night and while they could not kill an individual, they might frighten him so badly that he would become rigid with fear. Especially was this the case if a person had spoken slightingly of them. Indeed some people had been known to become stark mad after an encounter with a ghost. Much more to be dreaded, however, were certain living members of the community, those specially-gifted individuals who were adepts in the practice of black magic, who, for instance, had the power of transforming themselves into bears and wild turkeys. They would ride through the air at night until they came to the lodge of some one whom they desired to kill. If all the openings of the lodge were not properly closed and protected and if the occupants had not in early life provided themselves with all kinds of medicines to counteract the power of such a bear-walker, they were lost. Fortunately for the community these bear-walkers expended most of their iniquitous energies in fighting one another. Such conflicts were not uncommonly visible at night. Not indeed that the combatants were really visible; the powers they possessed prevented this. But flickering lights showed the onlooker where their eyes were. A gleam of light always gave warning that bear-walkers were about. Victory in such a conflict always meant death to the vanquished.

Night thus had its terrors. Indeed the spirits who were the cause of darkness were not particularly distinguished for their gentleness and leniency toward mankind. Darkness, it must be remembered, was not caused by the mere absence of light, so the sacred myth insisted, but by the coming of Night-Spirits, called in the ceremonies Walkers-in-Darkness. These Night-Spirits were beings, human in shape, and with long white hair. In their hands they carried a small round cane, and woe to him who felt even the slightest touch of this cane! He would die immediately.

On a moderately cold night in northern Wisconsin M. Nicollet would doubtless have been delighted to be ushered into a well-warmed lodge, even had he been entirely unaware of ghosts and bear-walkers and cane-using Night-Spirits.

The fire was in the center of the lodge and a railing made of ironwood encircled it, in order to prevent the ashes from falling outside and possibly causing damage. On either side running along half the length of the lodge, was a slightly raised platform, covered with animal furs and skins. Here the members of the family slept. At the very rear an entirely screened partition was to be seen. An occasional movement of the covering of the partition disclosed a moderately high platform that was apparently being occupied by some one at the time.

The entrance to the lodge was tightly closed by a skin flap whose provenience would have made even M. Nicollet rather uncomfortable. He probably thought that it was the dried skin of an animal, but it was, in fact, the dried skin of a human being, of some enemy who had been flayed, according to the custom of the tribe, after he had been killed. Some of the mats scattered through the lodge had the same origin. And if M. Nicollet could have examined the roof of the house in which he was to sleep, he would have found that human skulls were used as weights to hold the coverings down.

Nicollet was undoubtedly well feasted. Indian hospitality is unthinkable without good food. But the feast was partaken in absolute silence. After the meal the children must unquestionably have pressed some older member of the family to tell them a story, most likely an episode connected with the numerous adventures of that great and mischievous hero, Hare.

Nicollet, we may feel certain, would not have been interested even had he understood the story. What aroused his curiosity was the person hidden behind the partition and the strange monotonous chant accompanied by the rhythmical beating of a drum which suddenly reached his ears as a guest, lifting the door-flap, quietly entered the lodge and spoke hurriedly and softly to Nicollet's host. Thereupon the chief rose, and beckoning Nicollet to follow, they left the lodge.

The monotonous chant and the drum beat were heard very distinctly as soon as they stepped out into the crisp night air. All these noises, in fact, issued from a long lodge only a short distance from the chief's house. They soon reached the lodge and, stooping down, entered. Keeping to the right as they entered, they circled around the interior and finally took their seats near an old man sitting to the left of the entrance. The temple—for this it was to all intents and purposes, in spite of the flimsy nature of its construction—was filled with people reclining on reed-mats and animal-rugs. At the rear, apparently separated intentionally from the rest, sat the women and the children.

Suspended from the ceiling, along the entire length of the lodge, hung twelve dried buck-skins attached to a frame. Each one was painted in a special manner and some of the markings seemed intelligible even to an uninitiated person. One, for instance, had two cross lines, another a green colored crescent moon, a third a blue star, a fourth a series of black lines. Grouped around these buck-skins, along the whole length of the lodge, sat the worshipers. They fell into twelve sections, each one in charge of an elderly man. In front of this man, apparently the leader of each section, there was spread out on a decorated mat of reeds a curious conglomeration of objects—dried bird-skins beautifully decorated with porcupine quill work, bamboo flutes, a war club, a deer-tail headdress, some eagle feathers and magical medicines of the most varied description. All these objects were clearly regarded with profound reverence. The leaders were just then engaged in sprinkling tobacco upon them preparatory to placing them in their buck-skin wrappers.

These objects, of which each clan had one and upon which so much reverence was being lavished, represented the most sacred possession of the tribe. They were called the clan or war-bundles. No man could depart on any war expedition unless ne previously gave a feast in honor of the particular war-bundle belonging to his clan. Such a ceremony was the most elaborate thing imaginable. The possessors of war-bundles had to be invited and fireplaces to be erected in honor of all the great deities. For each bundle there had to be a decorated buck-skin inscribed to a special spirit. The marks on these buck-skins indicated in whose honor each particular one was being offered.

The pantheon of the tribe was extensive. To mention only the most important, there was first of all a nebulous creator of gods and men, Earth-Maker; the powerful Night-Spirits and the equally powerful Thunderbirds; the Sun and the Morning Star, both enthusiastic patrons of war; the terror-inspiring Disease-giver from whose body life or death was dispensed depending upon which side he turned to you; the lynxlike and enormous Water-Spirit whose blessings were so difficult to attain and so dangerous to properly utilize when obtained; the Moon; the Earth; the oldest of all, Fire; the South-Wind and the Eagle. For all these, sacred buck-skins were prepared, tobacco, food and eagle feathers offered, and a dog sacrificed. Now the sacrifice of a dog was not merely the sacrifice of an animal whose food would be palatable to the deities. It represented the symbolical sacrifice of one of their own clan, for the dog and the wolf were synonymous.

But let us listen more particularly to the prayer uttered to the Thunderbirds, those mysterious, divine birds who caused thunder by the flapping of their wings and lightning by the flashing of their eyes:

Oh grandfather, Thunderbird, here I stand with tobacco in my hand. Grant us what you granted our grandfathers! Accept our humble offering of tobacco. We are sending you buck-skins from which you can make moccasins, feathers from which you can make a headdress; we are preparing a meal for you from the meat of an animal who is like ourselves. And not I alone but all the members of my clan and all the members of the other clans present here, beseech you to accept our gifts. Grant us but this favor—that we may be victorious on the warpath, that we may kill an enemy outright, that we may receive the greatest of all honors, return safely with the scalp of an enemy. This, indeed, would constitute a life-honor, this indeed would give meaning to life. We have prepared ourselves fitly and, I and all my kinsmen sit here humble in heart, a sight to awaken pity, so that we can receive your blessing and live a good life.

Numerous prayers have been made, numerous speeches delivered, songs sung. The night is far advanced: dawn is imminent. Suddenly one of the guests arises and taking the first of the suspended buck-skins, that dedicated to Earth-Maker, begins the circuit of the lodge. Others follow, each carrying a buck-skin. Preceding them is an attendant, walking backward and purifying the path by scattering cedar incense as he walks. The singing grows more ecstatic, the dancing more frenzied. The flutes are blowing. Four times the circuit of the lodge is made and then the buck-skins, lifted off their frames, are thrown out through the openings in the roof of the lodge so that the spirits may come down and claim what is theirs. The noise is deafening. Then it stops suddenly and a man steps out from among the ranks and, patting his mouth a few times, gives forth a terrific war-whoop, one that the spirits can hear. The feast is over.

While this dramatic ceremony was taking place here, minor hunting rites were being performed in some of the private lodges. Now the hunting of bears or deer was not simply dependent upon skill in the use of the bow and arrow. The soul of these animals had first to be attracted to the prospective slayer if the animal itself was afterwards to be successfully trailed. So kettles of corn were prepared in the various lodges and dried fruit and maple sugar added in order to make the offering as tempting as possible. The inevitable tobacco and feathers were, of course, always at hand. Then the prospective hunter took two short sticks with very rough edges and rubbed them together, singing songs at the same time and gazing steadfastly into the fire. Suddenly he stopped. A streak of flame has shot out from the fire; the animal is doomed. That streak of fire was the visible symbol that some particular bear or deer had succumbed to the fascination of the offering and to the fervor of the hunter. Soon he was to fall an easy and fascinated victim to the latter's arrow. . . .

Dawn was already breaking as the participants in the warbundle feast hurried home. Nicollet, fairly exhausted, lay down to snatch a few moments' rest. Even in his sleepy condition, however, he still felt an unsatisfied curiosity about what lay hidden behind the partition at the rear end of the lodge. This curiosity was fanned anew when he saw an old man approach the screened-off partition and engage in conversation with some one within. The conversation that ensued was carried on in such a muffled tone that it was difficult at first to distinguish the voices. Apparently, however, the person hidden was a young boy, to judge from the timbre of his voice. The colloquy between the two was short and evidently to the old man's satisfaction, for as he turned his face toward Nicollet, it was beaming with pleasure.

What the young boy had told the old man neither Nicollet nor any other person, white or Indian, was ever to find out. Possibly in later years, when on the point of death, he might entrust it as a sacred trust to his son or his most intimate friend. But even that was by no means certain. The blessing vouchsafed by the spirits to a youth during his adolescent fasting was too holy, too personal a thing to ever be divulged. It meant life. To-day, in these degenerate times, we know what he said. He had dreamt and this was the dream:

To me it seemed that I wandered into the wilderness. Near an oval hill I sat down and wept. Below the hill lay a round lake and there I saw the rising dew coming up in a fog, that spread itself over me and then shrank away and became small. All the time I sat there weeping. I knew that there was something in the lake, but although I looked intently in that direction I could not see anything. Yet the spirits were unquestionably stealthily stealing upon me. Suddenly two flames of fire burst forth extending from the sky to the lake, and then I heard a loud report. The spirits were causing it. Again I heard an even louder report. I remained quiet, crying all the time, for I was trying to be blessed.

There I sat with bulging eyes looking at the spirits. "I must be receiving a blessing," I thought. I continued crying. After a short time it began to rain very hard. "How is this?" I thought to myself, "only a little time before the weather was so pleasant and now it is raining." I looked above and saw that it was very cloudy, yet immediately in a direct line above me there was a blue spot. This blue spot was like a round object and it covered me and only me.

The Thunderbirds were blessing me. With the blue sky they were blessing me. Soon the noise stopped and when I looked above I saw four men standing before me with packs upon their backs. I saw these men killed before me. Then the spirits blessed me with the power of killing. They spoke to me and said, "Stop your crying. What you have longed for and fasted for, that we shall bestow upon you. Just as these four men have been killed so will you be able to kill people. But you will also be able to restore them to life again. Upon your body we shall now place a mark and those whom you, in future years, will wish to bless, will be given an opportunity for selecting life for themselves from you. Even when a person is practically dead you will be able to restore him to health. That which is above you, the blue sky, that we place upon one of your fingers; with that we bless you."

It was light outside now. People were awake. A public crier was passing through the village beating his drum and admonishing all to get up and take their morning bath. The chief of the Bear clan and his aides could be heard making their morning patrol. All was well. Disease, the danger from bear-walkers, attacks of the enemy, all had been successfully averted. The day could be begun aright.

The village was all astir now and people were emerging from their lodges. Out of one of these houses there suddenly stepped a young man with his body painted in the most fantastic manner. One side was a livid green and the other an ochre-red. Red dots were scattered irregularly over the green and green dots over the red side of his body. On either breast appeared a crude drawing of a circle, apparently meant to represent the sun. In one case it was red and in the other green. The face of the young man, likewise, was painted but the designs were quite different. Across his forehead was tied the dried skin of a weasel. In his hands he held a rattle made of a dried gourd. Nothing more fantastic could very well be imagined. Dancing and singing he left his house, keeping time with his rattle. Thus the young warrior danced from lodge to lodge intoning his war song:

Oh, Big-White Wings if he dies, if he dies,
Oh, Big-White Wings if he dies—
Who will weep for him?

Others joined him and soon there was a veritable bedlam
of music as each man sang his personal war-song. The
leader of the prospective war expedition could be heard
above the others:

War leader though I am, war leader though I am
My life I value no more than that of a dog.

A particularly husky volunteer could be heard singing
lustily:

The odor of death, the odor of death,
I smell the odor of death
In the front of my body.

Yet not every one joined. As the increasing number of
volunteers passed these stay-behinds, taunts and jeers were
thrown at them:

Stay with your grandmother, stay with your grandmother,
You woman, you coward!

The leave-taking was over. Led by the war chief and
followed by his nephew carrying on his back the sacred war-
bundle, the hunters and warriors filed slowly across and
through the village over the cleared space encircling it,
slowly disappearing, single file, into the tortuous trails of
the thick forest. Scouts had preceded them by a few hours.
A few days, probably a week, would elapse before they
returned and during that time the routine of life would
have to continue. The women would have to attend to

their gardens of corn and squash and beans, and the men who remained behind would have their chores to perform. They would, in addition, have to be incessantly on guard against surprise attack from an enemy. No festivities would take place. Yet there would be little real anxiety. Hunting and war-parties always returned home victorious. The spirits might conceivably deceive even a mature man, but the leader under whose command this war-party had embarked was too old and too experienced a man to be taken unawares either by a treacherous spirit or an enemy. Walks-In-The-Rain had led many expeditions and rarely had mischance befallen any of those who enrolled themselves under his banner.

Nicollet stayed behind with the chief of the tribe. He would now have ample time to observe the peculiar customs and habits of the people. Indeed, he need never leave the very lodge in which he was staying to obtain a rich reward.

He had already noticed with astonishment the veneration in which everything connected with the fire was held. Fire was indeed a friendly element possessed of articulate wants. Yet only when offerings were made to it, would it function properly. Then its flames rose high and the donated food, tobacco and red feathers would be carried to the deities above. Sacred in its own right, it was at the same time an intermediary between the gods and man. Sweetest of all offerings to its nostrils, however, was tobacco. To nothing did the deities succumb so quickly and so graciously as to a whiff of this delightful weed. In the dim mythical past, so it was told, Earth-Maker the creator, had bestowed tobacco upon man, then weak and uncertain in his hold upon the world into which he had been but lately ushered. From the very beginning, so the clever creator of all things had arranged, the odor of tobacco would be like opium to the senses of all the spirits and they would grant puny man, whom cannibals and giants were then destroying, all his requests. Often, indeed, tobacco meant death for a deity. Should a buffalo spirit, for instance, particularly a young one, stray too near the opening through which the fumes of tobacco offerings reached the sky, overwhelmed and conquered, he would transport himself to the earth, a willing and fascinated sacrifice.

One other custom—or was it merely etiquette?—amazed the French stranger. Certain individuals, apparently, had very little to do with one another. Sisters and brothers rarely conversed and when female cousins came Nicollet noticed that the men refrained from talking to certain of them and yet took liberties with others. Upon inquiry, he would have found out that in one case these cousins were the daughters of a man's paternal uncle and maternal aunt and in the other the daughters of his paternal aunt and his maternal uncle. Indeed, he called the former sisters and they were regarded as related to him as closely as if they had been his real sisters. The other cousins, oddly enough, were not called cousins but nieces.

Etiquette, however, seemed to reach its most ridiculous culmination in the case of a man's mother-in-law. One of the chief's sons was then temporarily living with him, and his mother-in-law had on a number of occasions paid the young couple a visit. Not only did the young son-in-law refuse to greet her when she entered, but he ostentatiously averted his gaze. Whenever possible he sat with his back toward her. Not one word did he address to her nor, for that matter, did she address any to him. Whenever he had occasion to say something that might be of interest to her, he relayed it through his wife. Mother-in-law and son-in-law were manifestly greatly embarrassed at being together in the same room. Had Nicollet realized that these two were, throughout their lives, never to speak to each other, that any relation between them was absolutely unthinkable, he would doubtless have given utterance to one of those forceful ejaculations in which Frenchmen have always been so wonderfully proficient.

And so day followed day or, as his host would have said, night followed night. A week had already elapsed since the hunters and warriors had disappeared into the treacherous wilderness. They ought to return at any moment now; otherwise there might indeed be cause for alarm. Some nervousness was already beginning to manifest itself for the night before a man had dreamt of a snake, a very bad omen.

One day not long after noon, Nicollet thought he heard in the distance the sound of some one wailing. Apparently he had not been the only one to hear it, for soon out of every house rushed men, women and children in evident consternation. The women began to howl, some of them at the same time cutting their hair and blackening their faces. The howling took on a regular and rhythmical character and Nicollet was somewhat puzzled at what appeared to him the rather mechanical aspect of the whole manifestation. This grief could not be very profound! But then, after all, so he thought to himself, these people were savages and no depth of feeling could very well be expected of them.

Near Nicollet stood the chief of the tribe, his features expressionless. The wailing became more and more audible in the distance and soon there emerged from the wilderness the figure of a warrior with his body entirely blackened and his face set and rigid. Some one had been killed, that was manifest. Behind this man followed three others, their faces likewise blackened, and then after an interval, came the rest. Was anybody missing? Nicollet, of course, did not know. If, as was clear, some one had been killed his body had apparently been carried away by the enemy, for there was no evidence of it. Or had his tribesmen buried him hastily in some lonely grave far away from his home and his kinsmen?

The returning warriors were greeted by the continuous monotonous howling of the women as they came forward toward the center of the village. The chief approached the first man and asked him in a scarcely audible voice what had happened.

"The enemy came upon us unawares and we lost four of our bravest men. Our leader, Walks-In-The-Rain, was the first to fall. His nephew, Lone-Tree, followed and then before we could gather ourselves together Comes-With-A-Mighty-Tread and Big-White-Wings died, deceived by the spirits."

The howling of the women grew louder. Their grief seemed to have a peculiar effect upon them because they were almost on the verge of dancing. Suddenly, from the other end of the village, were heard four terrifying war-whoops and then pandemonium broke loose. Every one, the returning warriors, men, women, children, all rushed at four figures just then emerging into full view. And behold there stood Walks-In-The-Rain, Comes-With-A-Mighty-Tread, Lone-Tree and Big-White-Wings, their faces set but joyful. And what is it each one is carrying? The answer is clear to the horror-stricken Nicollet. Suspended from four poles hung four scalps.

The four victors were soon surrounded by their admirers, clansmen and kinsmen. Everybody tried to strike the scalps and even the children were allowed to touch them. One old man who had, of course, stayed behind, after striking the scalp, insisted upon breaking into song, an old and magnificent song:

> Sun and earth are everlasting
> Men must die!
> Old age is a thing of evil
> Charge and die.

So this was the explanation! These people had not really been grieving! On the contrary, the wailing that seemed so ominous as it first struck upon Nicollet's ear, was the most welcome sound imaginable, for it meant that the war-party was returning victorious, and that there would now be round after round of festivities.

When the turmoil had somewhat subsided all returned to their homes. There were numerous things still to be done before nightfall. The victory-pole had to be erected and a thousand smaller things attended to. Above all, the chief was anxious to hear the details of the great encounter. Four scalps on what was only a moderately large warpath, that was indeed an unusual accomplishment!

So not long after the chief and Nicollet had returned to their lodge, Walks-In-The-Rain with a few friends entered and were welcomed to seats of honor. The proffered pipe was accepted and as it was passed around the lodge, each man took a puff. Then Walks-In-The-Rain arose to give his report:

Hanho, grandfather. You know that of ourselves we could never have succeeded. But the spirits who blessed our ancestors and who appeared to us in dreams, accepted our poor offering and, unworthy though we were, gave us success in hunting and victory on the warpath. It is well! Yes, we have killed our friend, the black-furred one. You know, that at this time of the year, it is not so dangerous to go bear hunting as in the spring when the bears are protecting their young. We knew that the bears would be lying in the spaces that have been cleared and in the timber under the trees. We soon saw some from the distance. They looked like tiny black objects. They did not hear us approach. How could they? Did not our medicines give us the power of approaching without sound? And did not their souls come to us willingly that night when the flame leaped out from the fire? Yet we took care not to approach when the wind was with them, for we were afraid they would scent us. We saw them eating acorns in the cleared spaces and we shot and killed them. Their bodies are in the wilderness near the entrance to our village. Soon we will carry them to our lodges where the women can prepare their carcass for us.

That same night we camped on the slopes of a hill overlooking the sacred lake that lies three nights' journey from here. I knew from what the spirits who blessed me had told me, that the enemy was not far. I sent out the scouts to explore the land and they came back with the news that they had discovered the whereabouts of the enemy on the other side of the hill and that they were clearly unaware of our presence. Then we offered tobacco to the spirits and prayed for help. I opened the war-bundle which I had been privileged to carry, took out the sacred objects and practiced the powers bestowed upon men. I rubbed my body with the paint that had been made from the bones of the Water-Spirit and which made my body invulnerable and invisible. I knew that the moment I blew my flute the enemy would become paralyzed and unable to move, and that my eagle-pouch gave me the power of swooping down upon the enemy and tearing him to pieces just as the eagle does its prey. The Thunderbird and the Sun had bestowed upon me and my companions the lives of four men and the spirits had promised that I would return home safely without losses.

It was my intention to creep noiselessly upon the enemy and attack them just before dawn. When, therefore, the last of the

Night-Spirits had departed, we crept stealthily along the ridge of the hill and down to where the small party of enemy were encamped. Then when we had surrounded them we gave the war-whoop and fell upon them. My nephew, Comes-With-A-Mighty-Tread, killed the first man, but it is I who first struck his body and thus gained the greatest of all war-honors. Then Lone-Tree and Big-White-Wings killed two others, one apiece. The rest, cowards that they were, fled, leaving the bodies of their dead in our possession. We scalped the womanly fellows! And now, with the help of the spirits, we are back home. It is finished, grandfather. We thank you, Hanho-o.

Evening had fallen quickly. The victory-pole was in place and the scalps fluttered in the air as they hung suspended from above. The people were flocking from every side to take part in the dance. They stood in circular formation around the pole and giving vent to the most fiendish shouts of glee, they began to dance. Each one danced by himself. Every now and then a dancer would fall foaming to the ground, overcome by his frenzied exertions.

Yet this was only the first part of the festivities. The real pæan of victory was to be sung afterwards. The ceremony at which this was to take place was known as "conquering the soul of the ghost." Its avowed purpose was to transfer to the victor all the bravery and all the courage that the owners of the scalps had once possessed. Nicollet saw the four warriors who had obtained the highest honors sitting in a row with the others ranged around them. An old man acted as master of ceremonies. He arose and addressed the scalp:

Let us eat with our friend the scalp, weak and ignoble though we are! Oh, grandfather, oh, grandfather, surely you were no weakling, surely the spirits gave you great powers! Oh, grandfather, permit us to trample upon your soul, permit us to crush your soul and to transfer to ourselves the bravery you had, the virtues you have possessed and the goods of life that were still your due! For brave man as you were, you were killed before your prime! Let all those present aid us by their dancing to make you more amenable to our prayers. Men, women, children, old and young, dance, dance, dance with all your power! For not in a frivolous mood can the soul of a brave ghost be conquered, not lightly can we dance ourselves into life.

Then a woman seizing the scalp led the dance. Men and women fell in behind her. They danced without resting. Only a few became boisterous. Though clearly filled with suppressed religious ecstasy, most of the dancers held themselves in check and thought only of the purpose to be accomplished—to vanquish the soul of the ghost whose scalp fluttered tauntingly from the victory-pole.

All night they danced and when the sun rose they danced the victory-dance again around the pole. Night after night this lasted. Nicollet was getting weary. Then, finally, early one morning, they marched to the grave of a child who had recently died and there dancing once more with all the intensity that comes before exhaustion, they stuck the scalp in the ground above the grave so that its owner might act as servant to the deceased child. For the parents of the child to mourn after that would be a sin. There the scalp withered and dried up and the father of the child who had died felt happy.

When the exhaustion attendant upon the strenuous dances of victory had somewhat worn off M. Nicollet would fain have returned to his own people who were doubtless uneasy already at his protracted absence. But he still craved to hear something about the Happy Hunting-Ground in paradise of which the first French settlers along the St. Lawrence had told him so much.

His wish was to be fulfilled that very day, for the sacred story of the Journey of the Soul to Spirit-Land was to be told at a funeral wake held in an adjoining house in honor of one who had recently died. He arrived just when the keeper of the sacred story was addressing the soul of the departed:

I suppose you are not far away, that indeed you are right behind me. Here is the tobacco and here is the pipe which you must keep in front of you as you go along. Here also is the fire and the food which your relatives have prepared for your journey. In the morning when the sun rises you are to start. You will not have gone very far before you come to a wide road. That is the road you must take. As you go along you will notice something on your road. Take your war-club and strike it and throw it behind you. Then go on without looking back. As you go farther you will again come across something in your path. Strike it and throw it behind you and do not look back. The objects you are throwing behind you will come to the relatives you have left behind on earth. They represent victory in war, riches and animals for food.

When you have gone but a short distance from the last place where you threw objects behind you, you will come to a round lodge and in it you will find an old woman. She it is who will give you further information. She will ask you, "Grandson, what is your name?" This you must tell her. Then she will say, "Grandson, what did your relatives say to you when you were leaving them?" "Grandmother, as I listened to my beloved relatives they said very little indeed. They said that I was breaking their hearts in leaving them and they hoped that no one would follow me soon. They asked me to make four requests of you: first, I was to ask for life, that the flames from the lodge-fires might go straight upward. Yet they were satisfied, they said, if at my departure the flames merely sway to and fro. Second, whatever fruits had been predestined for me and which I did not taste, my relatives should receive.

Third, they also mentioned nuts, all manner of herbs, all service-able hides and skins, all medicinal roots and grasses. Fourth, they said that if any one had a friend his weapon might have a keen edge on one side. Grandmother, when I started from the earth I was given the following objects with which I was to act as mediator between you and human beings—the pipe, tobacco and food. Then they said you must put the stem of the pipe in the old woman's mouth," and then our grandmother will answer and say: "Grandson, you are young but wise. It is good. Let me now boil some food for you."

Thus will she speak to you and put a kettle on the fire and boil some rice. If you eat it, you will have a headache. Then she will say, "Grandson, you have a headache. Let me cup it for you." Thereupon she will break open your skull and take out your brains and you will forget all about your people on earth and where you came from. You will not worry about your relatives. You will become like a holy spirit. Your thoughts will not go as far as the earth, for there will be nothing earthly about you.

Now the rice that the old woman will boil for you will really be lice. It is for that reason that you will be finished with every-thing evil. After that you must step into the four steps imprinted with blue marks. You are to take these four steps because it is at that place that the road forks. As you journey on, you will come to a fire running across the earth from one end of it to the other. There will be a bridge across this fire, but it will be difficult to cross because it is continually swaying. You, however, will be able to cross it safely, for you have as guides the souls of those enemy whom the warriors at the funeral wake placed at your disposal. They will take you across this bridge safely.

Well, friend, we have told you a good road to take. If at the funeral wake any of the warriors, in recounting his exploits, tell any falsehoods, you will fall off this bridge and be burned. Do not you, however, worry, for you surely will pass across it safely. As you proceed from that place, the spirits will come to meet you and take you to the village where the chief lives. Here you will live happily, for over this country no clouds of ill omen ever pass.

Pre-Aztec Jar

Nicollet's last night with the Indians had come. The following morning he was to rejoin his boat. He sat silently pondering over all he had seen. His host was just then throwing tobacco into the fire and murmuring a prayer and there came to Nicollet's mind the prayer to the fire he had heard at one of the recent ceremonies:

You who stand in the center of our lodge, grandfather Fire, to you I offer tobacco. Here it is! Here it is! You encouraged us to believe that when we called upon your fellow-spirits, it would only be necessary to put tobacco upon your head for our message to be delivered. This is the blessing we ask—that our weapons be sharp and those of our enemies blunt. If, in addition, we are directed to go on a warpath, may the blessing we receive be complete; may the spirits protect us even in the middle of the battle! May we avoid danger: may we be granted long life. To you, oh grandfather Fire, I pour out tobacco. Receive it! Receive it!

As the skin-flap which served as a door and which had once been the covering of a human being, swayed slightly to and fro disclosing a pitch-dark night, Nicollet thought he saw a sudden flash of light and then two points of fire. "Bear-walkers!" shouted one of the occupants of the lodge withdrawing in consternation from the doorway.

CHAPTER I

THE FIRST CENSUS OF THE NEW WORLD

It was, so some historians have claimed, a widespread belief throughout medieval Europe that the world would come to an end exactly one thousand years after the birth of Christ. Yet in the very year when men's thoughts were supposedly turned upon such an end, a new world was revealed, for a Norseman sailing from Norway to Greenland and thrown out of his course by rough seas, came upon land of which he had previously had no knowledge.

There he found self-sown "wheat" fields and "vines."

The name of this adventurer was Leif Ericcson and he had discovered America and a new race of men, the Indians. But like Moses, it was not vouchsafed to Leif to actually set foot upon the promised land. Three years later, his companions Thorfinn Karlsefni, Thorvald, a half-brother of the latter, and a friend named Thorhall, set out to explore the country Leif had discovered, Wineland the Good, as it was called. "Thorhall," so the old saga tells us, "was stout and swarthy and of giant stature; he was a man of few words, though given to abusive language when he did speak. He was a poor Christian and he had a wide knowledge of unsettled regions."

Thorhall lost his life off the coast of Ireland but his followers turning south, after sailing for a long time, came at last to a river which flowed down from the land into a lake and so into the sea. And there as the saga continues,

28

"one morning early when they looked about them, they saw a great number of skin-canoes, and staves were brandished from the boats with a noise like flails, and they were revolved in the same direction in which the sun moves. . . . In these boats were seated swarthy and ill-looking men; the hair of their heads was ugly. They had great eyes and were broad of cheek. They tarried there for a long time, looking curiously at the people they saw before them and then they rowed away, to the southward, around the point."

Such was the first dramatic meeting of the Europeans with the natives of the American continent. Exactly who these Skrellings, as the Norsemen called them, were, we have to-day no certain means of determining. The land on which Leif's kinsmen wintered lay between Labrador and New England and was then inhabited both by Eskimo and Indian. A later and less authentic saga extends the Norse reconnaissance of America as far south as Chesapeake Bay and the Straits of Florida.

Had these daring adventurers stopped to study the strange people they had encountered, the more intelligent among them would have been doubtless impressed by many things, by nothing perhaps so much as by the remarkable differences in culture and in language that existed among them.

The Norsemen were already acquainted with one of them: the Eskimo. Greenland had been discovered in the early part of the tenth century and the Greenland Eskimo must unquestionably have informed the white invaders that they had kinsmen in Labrador. That the Eskimo actually inhabited the whole of the northern part of the American continent, from Labrador to the Aleutian Islands and that, with the exception of comparatively recent intruders along the Pacific coast and in the region immediately to the north

of the Great Lakes, these same Eskimo extended as far
south as the Gulf of St. Lawrence, of that the Norsemen
could have had no inkling.

Over this whole area there is spread to-day an aboriginal
Eskimo population having a very simple culture. That it
was at one time much higher is extremely probable. Yet
whatever it was before, today it remains the classical example of intensive specialization among all primitive people.
Nowhere, certainly not in America, did any aboriginal people
so completely subordinate every phase of their life to a
few clear-cut principles as did the Eskimo. They possessed
none of the basic features of the higher aboriginal civilizations—agriculture, pottery, textiles, a complex ritual and
a complex organization of society—yet with the very little
they did have they achieved a unity to be looked for in vain
anywhere else in America.

To the south of the Eskimo, extending from the Atlantic
Ocean to the western province of Manitoba, Karlsefni would
have encountered a people called the Algonquians, speaking
a language totally distinct from the Eskimo and with a
culture almost as simple, although a little bit more diversi-
fied; a people with some knowledge, rudimentary though
it was, of agriculture and of pottery-making. In the year
1000 A.D. many of these Algonquians had already made the
acquaintance of some of the more refined tribes to the south,
and we may therefore confidently assume that some of them
had by that time advanced to a condition not so very much
different from that which the early settlers in Massachu-
setts and Connecticut discovered six hundred years later.
We can be certain likewise that the Algonquians extended
along the whole Atlantic coast from New England to
Virginia.

In Virginia the picture changes completely. We are in the presence of a new people with a much higher type of civilization. Sign after sign betokens the presence of a richer, more complex, and more varied existence. We find well-defined villages often provided with stockades, and neatly-kept gardens, planted with corn, beans, squash and tobacco. Had the Norsemen made any inquiries they would have been informed that the people living in these villages had numerous and complex ceremonies and that the government under which they were living was organized on an intricate and strange plan. These people were, in fact, we now know, members of the great Sioux family. They did not really belong here, but represented an extension of a group whose original home was much further west and south. In this original home along the Ohio and further south, almost to the mouth of the Mississippi, they had at one time been in contact with a very wonderful race of men, a people whose culture was then already a thing of the past. A thousand years before, however, these wonderful people had played a great rôle, for they had been the recipient of influences that had come from the great and ancient Mexican and Central American civilizations. The Sioux had either borrowed many of the elements of this culture of the ancient inhabitants of the Ohio and the Mississippi or, as some would contend, were their actual descendants.

An interesting people were these eastern Sioux and great must have been the influence they exerted upon their fairly simple neighbors. Some of the Algonquian tribes had probably even as early as the year 1000 A.D., already pushed their way as far south as Virginia, and participated, in no small degree, in the culture that the Sioux had brought from the west. It is even possible that the rather high degree of civilization which the doughty Captain John Smith encountered near Jamestown in 1607, among the people of Pocahontas, goes back as far as the year 1000 A.D.

What was the life these Siouan people led? Let us stop to describe it briefly, for in many ways it is typical of the life led by at least one-half of all the aboriginal inhabitants of the United States. Not that it was the pinnacle of what the Indians had attained north of the Rio Grande. Other regions like the southwest, New Mexico and Arizona, had developed a far richer and far more intricate ceremonialism, and in their architecture, textiles, and pottery had achieved a degree of perfection to which nothing that the Sioux ever accomplished could even be remotely compared. But the very specialization of these southwestern peoples rendered them unrepresentative.

Now two things were characteristic of the civilization of the Sioux: the emphasis upon agriculture and the peculiar way in which society was organized. Whatever stability of organization existed was due to agriculture, to maize. Yet it did not dominate their lives so completely as was the case either among their very remote kinsmen living immediately to the south or among the peoples of the distant southwest. Moreover a new element had entered into their lives—the buffalo. The pursuit of the buffalo had wrought a thorough going change among them, gradually transforming a people whose ancestors were completely agricultural into a nation only semi-sedentary.

Around the buffalo there grew in the course of time innumerable associations. More and more did people's imagination and affection cluster around this magnificent animal. Tribal life fairly reeked of it. Not only did he become the staple of food, but he developed into a whole department store. There was nothing even remotely connected with him that was not utilized in some way or another. Dances and ceremonies sprang up in which he was the center of worship and songs and myths in which he was the glorified hero.

But buffalo-hunting brought other consequences in its train. It often meant encounters with enemies. To guard against this the hunt became a veritable communal undertaking. All the able-bodied members of the tribe banded together and in order to do this efficiently a new type of organization was necessary. Many rules and arrangements that worked well enough in the village were of no use on the march or in the open country. And so gradually there grew up a new regrouping and a new code of laws for the tribe when on the hunt.

Often however it seemed safer to league together with friendly tribes, and then, again, enemies did not always remain enemies. It would therefore be wrong to insist too exclusively on the negative side of these great communal adventures. Instead of scalps and prisoners, frequently enough, it must have been objects, ideas, songs, and ceremonials that were brought back from the hunt. In this way, the buffalo-hunt came to be the center from which radiated new influences, constructive and destructive.

Instead of the one old loyalty, maize, they thus developed another loyalty, the buffalo. One represented an old heritage fully crystallized, unchangeable, and deeply imbedded in the hearts of all; the other, a new revelation, endeared by recollections of narrow escapes and personal prowess and with a continual shifting of scenes from year to year. Half the year was now spent at home, the other on the hunt.   Yet the glamour of this new life on the plains was too alluring.   The buffalo finally conquered.   Maize indeed was never to be displaced but it was to become of less and less importance, to become more and more divorced from the main current of life.

But if the reign of maize was doomed the organization of society and the innumerable dances and rites which had grown up around and together with it, persisted with little change.

Now the manner in which society was organized among the Sioux would seem somewhat strange to us.   The tribe was subdivided into a number of groups much larger than the family, each of which was called after some animal. Thus there was a bear group, an eagle group, a deer group, and other such groups.   No members of the same group were allowed to intermarry, and each individual was regarded as belonging to the group of his father.   In other tribes, particularly those to the south, a person belonged, not to the group of his father, but to that of his mother, and it is not at all unlikely that at one time the same held true for the Sioux.   The individuals in these groups or clans, as they are called, believed themselves to be descended from the animal whose name they bore and this animal was always held in special reverence and honor.   The members of the same clan regarded themselves as related by the closest bonds of blood.

But this was only part of the complexity of the social scheme.   These clans were themselves grouped together to form two larger divisions.   Among the different tribes, these two divisions received different names.   Sometimes, they were called respectively the peace and the war people; sometimes, summer and winter; sometimes, the upper and the lower; sometimes, sky and earth. So fundamental was this twofold grouping that in the villages of the Sioux, all the clans that belonged to one division were placed on one side and all those belonging to the other division, on another side. A number of curious and reciprocal relations existed between these two groups. The members of the same division could, under no conditions, intermarry, and when a man died, he had to be buried by some one belonging to the opposite side. Strangest of all, whenever the favored game of lacrosse was played, the two divisions were always pitted against each other.

The dances, rites, and ceremonies were as intricate as the social scheme. There were dances to maize, of course, and to the buffalo. But in addition, there were numerous dances in honor of the various clan animals, as well as of many other spirits and deities.

Very important were the dances given in honor of those spirits who had appeared in special visions to an individual. Throughout aboriginal America, with but few exceptions, it was customary for people to fast and to pray for some spirit to reveal himself to them. Individuals to whom the same spirit had appeared would then unite to form small secret societies from which all others were excluded. In these societies, there were always four sacred places, named in honor of the deities who presided over the four cardinal points. These deities were worshiped throughout all America from Yucatan to northern Canada and everywhere they were regarded with particular veneration. But most important was the great ceremony given in winter in honor of the whole pantheon of gods. Here religious fervor reached its highest and often its most frenzied expression. Finally there were all those rites and dances clustering around certain sacred possessions, the most famous of which was the sacred pole, the symbol of the health and life of the community.

Such, broadly speaking, must have been the life of these eastern Sioux in the year 1000 A.D. How representative it was of the more significant phases of aboriginal American civilizations, we shall see as we continue in spirit, the early reconnaissance made, so many authorities have confidently believed, by the successors of Leif Ericcson.

South of Virginia, far inland, and wedged in among Siouan tribes lay another people, the Cherokee, speaking a language distinct from any so far encountered, although distantly related to that spoken by tribes within the territory of Texas, the Caddoan, best known to us from such modern representatives as the Pawnee. Indeed, it is even probable that the language of the Sioux was also very distantly connected with that of the Cherokee. Their civilization was not essentially different from that of the Sioux, except that the buffalo played a minor part in their economic life, and had taken no hold whatsoever upon their imagination. The Tuscarora, related to the Cherokee, lived near them, but the vast majority of their kinsmen, the famous Iroquois, occupied the regions to the west and the north. As early indeed as 1000 A.D., they must have already dug themselves deeply into the homes where we find them in the seventeenth century, Pennsylvania and New York.

Throughout all this area maize was still the vital element in people's lives, but here too, among the Cherokee and their kinsmen, a change was taking place. In the energetic, forward movement of the Iroquoian peoples from the southern plains toward the north, the necessity of an organization that would be best fitted for the warlike activities

in which they were continually engaged, shifted the old center of interest. They developed into a warrior civilization
par excellence. War became a pursuit indulged in for its
own sake, and it was not long before we see the Iroquois embarking on a policy of arrogant expansion and imperialism,
comparable to that of the Aztecs in the valley of Mexico.
From these efforts there was to arise in time, if in fact it
had not already developed, that famous confederation of
which the half-historical figure, Hiawatha, was the reputed
founder. All this, of course, meant a change of emphasis
away from agriculture. Here, too, then, as among the
Sioux, we find a divided loyalty. But whereas among
the Sioux, it was the buffalo and hunting that disrupted
the old framework of their culture, among the Iroquois it
was the necessity for a more efficient organization of war and
government.

Continuing our course south we finally reach the coast
of Georgia and Florida where we find new tribes and new
languages. In the year 1000 A.D. the peoples inhabiting
these regions—the Choctaw, Creek, and Timucua—were
very recent intruders, having all migrated from the lower
Mississippi. Their culture was essentially like that of the
Sioux to whom they were also bound by ties of language.
Yet in some ways their life was more like that of the ancestors of the Sioux, for agriculture was still their main and
all-absorbing interest. Town life, too, was more fully developed and there was a tendency for these towns to unite
in loose protective confederations, that is, on those occasions when they were not fighting one another. One thing,
however, would surely have been noticed even a thousand
years ago among the Creek and their kinsmen. In contradistinction to the rather placid life of the eastern Sioux,

they seemed to be infected by a spirit of nervousness and restlessness. And this was little to be wondered at. They had come from a region which was a veritable melting-pot of nations.

But here we must take leave of our early Norse guides, for not even the most poorly authenticated sagas claim that their voyages extended further than the Straits of Florida. In a way this was a great pity, for had these daring Norse adventurers sailed through the Straits of Florida, they would have entered that body of water which was for America what the Mediterranean had been for Europe. Upon the Gulf of Mexico everything converged. Here there was brought to a focus all the cultural movements that radiated from Yucatan, Central America and Mexico, as well as those suggestions and reminders that came from the West Indies and the distant coast of South America. Along its shores and across its waters, culture after culture had invaded the United States.

At what period the first Mexican invasion took place, we have no means of determining. This much, however, is quite clear, that in the year 1000 A.D. the force of most of these Mexican invasions had long spent themselves.

The turmoil that we find around the lower Mississippi was not due to any confusion wrought by the Mexican conquerors. The confusion that existed there was produced by something entirely different, by the attempts of recently civilized barbarians to participate in the new heritage and to adjust their lives to the new dispensation that Mexico had given them.

In this comparatively small area around the lower Mississippi, tribe jostled against tribe, culture against culture, language against language. Here we find the inevitable

Sioux, the Adai, and Kadohadacho—close kinsmen of the Pawnee—the Creeks and the Choctaws, the Natchez, and numerous other tribes who had close affinities to the people of Coahuila across the Rio Grande in Mexico. Yet one interesting fact stood out from all the others. Different as these peoples may have been in language and even in physical type, the divergence in culture between them was slight. On the whole what they possessed was more elaborate than that which we have described as typical of the Sioux, but it seemed definitely to be at a loose end. When in the sixteenth century, the Spaniards first discovered them, they found many things for which there was no parallel, certainly among the eastern Sioux. There were real temples, idols, and a definite caste system.

Whatever the case may be, however, we are certainly in the presence here of a culture higher than that of the Sioux. We now know, in fact, that these people were living amidst the ruins and debris of a still higher civilization. We have only to proceed northward along the Mississippi and make an occasional side-trip to the east of that great river to find the great monuments of this departed people. In the sixteenth century when De Soto discovered the Mississippi, a traveler would probably have found conditions much as they were in the year 1000 A.D. He would have come upon a larger number of mounds and enclosures, some round, some terraced, and some in the shape of animals. Not infrequently in modern excavations to-day we come across the most skillful modeling of the human head. Here, too, are found indications of an extensive use of copper and even occasional attempts at working gold. All this was quite beyond the powers of any of the peoples who have lived within the immediate vicinity of the mounds for the last thousand years.

Who were these mound-builders? Unquestionably they were Indians, possibly even the ancestors of the Sioux and the Creeks. Yet they clearly possessed a civilization immeasurably superior to that of the latter tribes. We have no means of ascertaining to-day what type of government or what type of ritual the mound-builders had, but recent excavations have shown that some of the mounds were used for ceremonial purposes and for ceremonies possessing an elaborateness for which we can find no counterpart among the Sioux or the Creek to-day, or in the days of their greatest glory. The Caddoan culture may have approximated to it.

This mound-builder civilization had a very wide distribution. Its monuments are to-day scattered from the Atlantic to the Mississippi and beyond, and from Florida to central Wisconsin and Michigan. Some of its influences must have radiated even further west, for their reverberations were still felt in southern Kansas among tribes such as the Pawnee, and even across the Rockies into New Mexico. In fact all aboriginal culture east of the Mississippi merely represents what has been salvaged from the great mound-builders.

To the west of the Mississippi, more particularly along its southern course, the situation was somewhat different. Here, as we have seen, dwelt the Pawnee. Now whatever be the degree of influence the mound-builders exerted upon the Pawnee, it was not for a moment to be compared with that which the Pawnee received from other directions, the very latest coming from the peoples living along the Rio Grande River in New Mexico. The culture of the Pawnee is unfortunately so specialized to-day that no safe conclusions can be drawn as to what it must have been a thousand years ago. We can be certain, however, that they once had a clan system and a division of the tribe into two broad groups. We find these two divisions also among the Sioux and the Pueblo Indians of the Rio Grande. The rest is only surmise, but one thing it is safe to assume, that the center of interest was then as to-day—maize, and that there were elaborate rituals, steeped in gorgeous symbolism, clustering around star-deities, and sacred objects called bundles.

From our present knowledge of the culture of the Pueblo Indians of the upper Rio Grande it is clear that the Pawnee had taken some of the features of their religion and ritual, as well as the symbolism which plays so great a part in their lives, from this source. Other elements they owed to their own initiative and originality, and still others to influences that reached them from distant Mexico. And out of all this, the Pawnee and their kinsmen succeeded in welding together what was essentially a new culture and this in its turn exerted the most far-reaching influences upon all the tribes with whom the latter came into contact, principally however upon the Sioux.

A few centuries later, kinsmen of the Pawnee together with the Sioux, were destined to move northward into the great plains between the Mississippi and the Missouri, and there in conjunction with crude Algonquian tribes who had been pressing southward from Canada—the Blackfeet, the Arapaho, the Cheyenne—to elaborate a new and a strange medley, known to us as the civilization of the Plains.

The Pawnee and their kinsmen have thus indirectly brought us into contact with the most remarkable, most elaborate, and most distinctive type of civilization of which we have any record north of the Rio Grande—that represented by the present Pueblo Indians of New Mexico and Arizona.

Here, all phases of culture, agriculture, the organization of society, ritualism, the arts, and oral literature attained an equally high development. To a certain degree this Pueblo civilization did not really exercise as great an influence upon the rest of the United States as might have been expected. Their influence upon the Pawnee was unquestionably extensive and they did, of course, give the immediate circle of wild tribes who came in contact with them, like the Apache and the Navajo, all the culture they ever possessed. The same is true for the tribes of the southern part of California. But one might have expected even more of so remarkable a civilization. The reason for this relatively weak influence is to be sought in the fact that they were essentially a very peaceful people, introspective, with no interest in proselytizing, rarely embarking on war expeditions, and almost always on the defensive. The leisure thus gained they seem to have spent in perfecting their arts and in developing a ritual as rich, as definite, and as rigid as that of the early Egyptians.

Yet integrated and unified as was this Pueblo civilization we now know that it represented but the end of a long and tortuous history. From the affiliations of the languages spoken by the tribes who took part in its development and from the presence of certain customs, we know that here we have the result of a long series of accretions. There are at least four distinct languages spoken to-day among the Pueblo Indians and each one of these languages is connected with some language known outside of the region. The conclusion is therefore inescapable that we are dealing here with a gradual absorption and adjustment of different and distinct peoples to some old basic civilization. What was this old civilization and where can we find any trace of it?

Fortunately the material is at hand. In this very region, the excavations among old ruins have revealed layer upon layer of deposits, mainly in the form of pottery. When we arrange this pottery in its proper sequence, a strange fact emerges. The pottery at the very bottom of the series, that is, the oldest, is identical with that found among ruins that had already fallen into partial decay when the Spaniards first found them in the sixteenth century. Now these old ruins were discovered not merely on the open mesas but very frequently on inaccessible cliffs and in caves, and they extended over a very wide region, from southern Utah and southern Colorado far to the south beyond the Mexican frontier, into the states of Coahuila, Chihuahua, Jalisco, and probably even farther south.

There can be no reasonable doubt but that these cliff-dwellers, as they are generally referred to, were the predecessors and the ancestors of the present Pueblo Indians. All who have visited the famous Mesa Verde Park in southern Colorado will have a clear idea of what these magnificent cliff-towns really were like. The ruins of Mesa Verde, for instance, are built into a cave four hundred and twenty-five feet long, eighty feet wide, and with an extreme height of eighty feet. Here are found the remains of a building, an enormous community house, that must once have enclosed a hundred and seventeen rooms, not including those in the upper stories. The people living in these and similar houses practiced a most extensive agriculture in which artificial irrigation played a dominant rôle. It has been estimated that near the ruins called Los Muertos in Arizona, there were ditches providing for the irrigation of at least two hundred thousand acres. Among other things cotton was planted and extensively used. Beautiful pottery has been found in a great variety of forms and of all degrees of excellence. Some have exquisitely wrought designs in color; and beautifully executed human and animal figures are not uncommon. We come upon turquoise beads and evidence of turquoise mosaics. In short, everything points to the fact that a very high civilization had once existed here of which the present Pueblo people are the inheritors and descendants.

Where, it may now be asked, did this civilization come from? Did it originate here in this beautiful but somewhat inhospitable area, or must we look for its source somewhere else? Fortunately there are clues. In one of the ruins copper bells and copper ornaments have been found, in another cloisonné work of a very specific kind. There is no question where these have come from. There is only one place in North America where they could have been made, and that is southern Mexico and Yucatan. But there are other clues pointing in the same direction, such as certain specific details of architecture. And then, of course, we have the outstanding fact that maize was used. Maize, we know, was first domesticated and cultivated somewhere in southern Mexico or Central America.

The only question indeed is when and in what way these Mexican influences came to the Pueblo peoples, a problem into which we need not enter here. The one thing to be emphasized is that the highest civilization attained by any native people north of the Rio Grande was built on the broad and rich basis furnished by people living far to the south.

But let us pause for a moment to take stock before we proceed on our journey to this distant south. Great as have undoubtedly been the accomplishments and achievements of the aboriginal cultures of the United States, no really fundamental contribution was ever made by these tribes. From the great heritage which reached them in different degrees and at different times, they made their selections, remodeling, recombining, specializing, elaborating, and at times originating new details. But nothing new of a fundamental kind was ever added. In the main it was deterioration; and the history of the peoples north of the Rio Grande is essentially the story of how they lost touch with their great motherland far to the south. The barbarians from the north swarmed in from all sides and in the upper Rio Grande it was only with the greatest difficulty that the Pueblo peoples held them at bay long enough for some of the ancient glory to be passed on to them. Then the Pueblos were overwhelmed.

When the Spaniards discovered New Mexico and Arizona they found the inhabited Pueblos restricted to a very small area. Utes, Comanches, and Apaches, virile and warlike, but totally uncivilized, roamed among the deserted cliff dwellings and citadel-cities on the mesa.

Now these barbarians had originally all come from the country to the west and to the north, from central and northern California, from Oregon and Washington, and from the plateaus and plains of western Canada. Strangely enough, although in this whole region there was no sign of any higher culture, tucked away in the extreme northwest, in northern Washington and in British Columbia, there had arisen a curious non-agricultural civilization of a unique kind. It had a well-developed caste system, laid great stress upon the accumulation of material wealth, had formulated a strange social and ceremonial system and showed remarkable proficiency in wood carving and the manipulation of slate. In time, the influence of these people was to extend in every

direction, toward the north, the west, and the south as far
as northern California. Yet that was all still in the dim
future.

But to return. Maize, cotton and the architecture of the
cliff-dwellers and their descendants, turquoise mosaics, copper bells, cloisonné ware—these were all Mexican in origin.
There were two routes, one along the shores of the Gulf of
Mexico, the other along the west coast. Both take us to
southern Mexico, the first more specifically to the Maya, the
other to the Valley of Mexico and Oaxaca. And yet when
we reach the Valley of Mexico, we find to our dismay that
we have only entered the threshold of a maze.

The Aztecs and their kinsmen who inhabited the valley
of Mexico and the adjacent territory at the time of the
conquest in 1519, turn out to be newcomers, intruders whose
connections were all with the north. As we proceed from
south to north, for instance, we find the culture gradually
tapering down from that of the semi-barbarians north of
Guadalajara in Jalisco, to that of utter barbarians like the
Utes and the Shoshone of Utah and Nevada.

Had a reconnaissance of that region been made in the
year 1000 A.D. a traveler would have found no City of
Mexico. Instead he would have come upon a small, inde-
fatigable and only partially civilized people called Aztecs,
living to the north of the valley of Mexico and fighting with desperation against their more distant but highly
civilized kinsmen, to retain the hold they had won upon
their newly conquered home. Civilized as were these kinsmen, they themselves could not boast of a very old civilization, for at best they had preceded the Aztecs by three hundred years. On one subject, however, they could have
enlightened an inquisitive traveler: they did possess certain

semihistorical accounts of what manner of men and what manner of civilization their ancestors had encountered when they first approached the historic valley.

Let us assume that these kinsmen of the Aztecs had stormed the valley from the east. Within about thirty miles of the present site of Mexico City, at a place the Aztecs called Teotihuacan, they would have found rising out of the valley, three enormous pyramids and a region teeming with small towns, all showing obvious indications of wealth and prosperity. All that these newcomers could do at first was to destroy. Yet, great as must have been the havoc they wrought, nothing was irretrievably destroyed and, as is so often the case, these intruders from the north soon settled down and adopted the culture of the people they had vanquished. It is extremely doubtful whether they altered very much of what they had taken over and it is fairly reasonable to suppose that they added very little. When the Aztecs arrived, they adopted their civilization at second-hand from the kinsmen who had preceded them. If then Aztec Mexico seemed to Cortez and his soldiers an impressive and wonderful achievement, one can well imagine what must have been the civilization of the people who had built the pyramids of Teotihuacan.

Modern excavations at Teotihuacan have shown that it would be erroneous even to assume that the culture of Teotihuacan was either indigenous or even the very oldest. Southward, ever southward, are we pressed until in the state of Oaxaca, we come upon a people speaking a language quite distinct from the Aztec and with a culture as different. Here in towns scattered through fertile valleys, we find a highly centralized monarchy where the head of the state is both king and high-priest and where class distinctions are so sharp that special pronouns are used by the common people when addressing the nobles. Everything here bespeaks an old culture. With these people, the Zapotecs and Mixtecs, our problems properly begin. Is this the goal, or are we merely near the goal? If not the originators these Zapotecs and Mixtecs are at least the intermediaries between the founders of the GREAT CIVILIZATION and the rest of North America. Surely they must have participated in its foundations. But let us continue our journey and turn to the northwest. The signs multiply. We come upon a crudely carved idol with archaic hieroglyphs and at last in the state of Chiapas right near the present borderline between Mexico and Guatemala, we are face to face with the long-sought goal among the ruins of the temple of Palenque.

Here at Palenque surrounded by densely wooded hills and overgrown by tropical vegetation, had once stood an imposing and fascinating city, one of the maturest expressions of Maya and Central American civilization. It had already been abandoned in the year 700 as its builders pushed northward toward Yucatan. Why it had been abandoned we do not know. The desertion of this as well as of many other Maya sites is shrouded in as much mystery as are their beginnings.

Nothing comparable to this Maya civilization is found anywhere to the immediate northwest. On the southeast, however, high civilizations extend practically as far as the Isthmus of Panama. Here in this tropical forest where mountains alternate with the jungle, all that was basic in the culture of the aborigines of North America originated. This was, above all, the original home of maize, without which there could have been no agriculture, little stability of organization, no concentration of population, no stone palaces, no complicated organization in government and ritual, and no perfection in the arts. Though the original interest in maize was somewhat lost sight of as Maya civilization became more and more complex, it regained its ascendancy as their culture spread to the north. Beyond the Rio Grande and the Gulf of Mexico, all social, economic, and religious activities were to center completely around it. Where the cultivation of maize stopped, civilization stopped.

At the Isthmus of Panama we come to a break. On the analogy of conditions in North America, we might have expected to find the civilization south of the Isthmus of Panama gradually deteriorating as we penetrated further and further into South America. Yet here we must be prepared for a surprise, for in Colombia, Ecuador, Peru, and Bolivia the level attained by the Mayas was almost everywhere maintained. The stresses, however, were quite different. Just as all roads in North America seem to have converged upon the valley of Mexico and so ultimately upon the Mayas, so here in South America all roads seem to have converged upon the Incas of Peru and so ultimately upon the great civilizations which the Incas had conquered. And just as in the case of the Aztecs and their immediate predecessors, so here in Peru the Inca conquerors were in their turn to be absorbed by their victims.

It is, however, ridiculous to speak of any gradations in the achievement of the civilizations that stretched from Panama to Peru. Everywhere the same high level persisted. In many ways, the culture of these people was characteristically different and distinct from that of the Mayas. In only one way can it have been said to be inferior: namely, in the total absence of any system of writing comparable to the Mayan hieroglyphs. In architecture and in pottery it was the equal of the Mayas; in the working of gold, silver, and copper, in the weaving of textiles, immeasurably their superior. As in North America, maize was extensively cultivated, but here it had to share its rule with the potato which was indigenous to Peru. The potato, indeed, had a much greater hold upon the life and the imagination of these peoples than did maize.

It is unthinkable to imagine that between Central America and this South American civilization there should have been no intercourse. Indeed of late years it has been abundantly proved that the interchange of cultural goods was fairly extensive. But this seems always to have been an interchange between equals. South America, on the whole, borrowed more from the Central American civilizations than these latter did from South America.

The great South American civilizations played for the rest of that continent a rôle analogous to that which the Maya had done for most of the North American continent. To the south, the Incas and their predecessors extended their influence into Chile. Then crossing the Andes into Argentine, they founded a very remarkable culture, that of the Calchaqui. The inhospitable plateau of the Gran Chaco stopped further progress. In the north, the ancient Colombians and Ecuadorians profoundly influenced the tribes of Venezuela and some of this influence unquestionably extended as far as the Amazon itself. There, however, the jungle effectively barred all further entry.

Apart then from the thin fringe along the Pacific coast there were no distinctive or complicated cultures in South America. The area occupied by barbarians was enormous, much larger than was the case in North America. Yet we must not dismiss these barbarians too contemptuously. They

INSCRIPTION ROCK IN SOUTHWEST

RUINS OF MESA VERDE

MAYA PALACE (*Upper*)   TEMPLE OF THE CROSS, PALENQUE (*Lower*)

had many interesting rites and customs, some of them very significant and pointing to a far off clime beyond the Pacific Ocean, in the Islands of the South Seas.

Here in the Brazilian jungle all trails peter out, just as they had disappeared on the great plateau of Utah and Nevada. But the aborigines of the United States were more fortunate than those of Brazil and Argentine. Faint echoes of the parent civilization found their way even as far north as the marauding Modocs of Oregon. True enough the Mayan culture became contaminated and transformed beyond recognition as it passed from one torch-bearer to another, but some little detail would still linger even in the most outlying tribes.

Aboriginal United States possessed another advantage. Tribes that had at one time been living close to the fountain-head of inspiration migrated in the course of time to new and distant regions. And thus it came to pass that a people whose ancestors had at one time been the neighbors and inheritors of the mound-builders and so distant inheritors of the Mayan tradition, finally found themselves stowed away among simple and alien tribes in northern Wisconsin, on the shores of Green Bay.

CHAPTER II

THE GLORY THAT WAS MAYA

In the year 1524, five years after he had stormed the City of Mexico-Tenochtitlan, the great *conquistador* Hernan Cortez, pushing far to the south, passed through the present little republic of Honduras. A difficult country to traverse it was then as now. A dense and impenetrable forest barred progress at every step. The vegetation was luxurious and magnificent, and odors of all descriptions permeated the humid air, from the most delicately scented flowers to the stench of putrid and decaying matter. The climate was hot and moist. Malaria lurked in the air and enormous snakes and reptiles made any lengthy sojourn impossible. Clouds of irritating and pestiferous insects prevented whatever sleep could be snatched from night to night.

Through this jungle, Cortez and his adventurers plunged slowly, hewing their way as best they could, foot by foot. Apart from the discomfort the journey was without incident. At one point of his march, he passed within three leagues of a certain little river. Not for a moment, however, did he rest at this place nor was his interest aroused in any way. Yet, he had only to turn aside and make his way to this little stream, to find there the moldering ruins of what had once been a glorious city, to which nothing he had seen on his memorable march from Vera Cruz to Mexico-Tenochtitlan could be remotely compared.

Here at one time had stood one of the glories of Maya civilization, *Copan*.

On a level plain within an area seven or eight miles long and two miles wide a resplendent vision had once met the eye. The streets, courts and courtyards were paved with stone or with white cement made from lime and powdered rock. An extensive system of drainage ran through the town, consisting of covered canals and underground sewers built of stone and cement. On the right bank of the river, in the very center of the city stood the principal group of structures—temples, palaces, and buildings of a public character.

Here in this maze of structures we, in fact, find the first civic center of America. It was approximately eight hundred feet square and so constructed as to face the four cardinal points. Within the main building, at an elevation of sixty feet, was a court one hundred and twenty feet square and this with the surrounding architecture must have presented an unusual spectacle.

The court itself was enclosed by ranges of seats, rising to a height of one hundred and twenty feet in the form of an amphitheater and built of great blocks of stone neatly cut and regularly laid without the use of mortar. In the center of the western part stood a staircase and to the north of the court rose two magnificent temples. The interior walls of one of these temples were covered with a thin coat of stucco on which were painted figures and scenes in various colors. The cornices were adorned with stucco and ornaments having the same lurid colors. The outside of the building was profusely decorated with grotesque figures, and around the four sides ran an elaborate cornice having a foliated design of feathers beautifully carved. Higher up, a row of portrait-like busts extended along the entire building.

The northern wing of the main structure had a high pyramidal elevation and facing the plaza of the southern end stood a beautiful stairway covered with hieroglyphs. This stairway extended from the floor of the plaza to the entrance of the temple, a height of three hundred feet. On it, at regular intervals, were placed seated human figures.

Such was Copan and Copan was only one among many. The civic center that we find here was typical of Maya civilization at its highest. The general plan of most of the Mayan cities was always the same. On an artificial acropolis consisting of a large terraced mound forming the separate bases of a number of temples, there would be built courts and plazas of varying size. The buildings generally fell into two well-defined types: one, a temple and the other, a "palace." The temple was rectangular in outline and crowned a fairly high pyramid which rose in successive terraces. A broad stairway always led to this temple. The pyramid itself, as a rule, was a solid mass of rubble and earth faced either with cement or cut stone. The palaces—if they can be said to have been such—were clusters of rooms on low and often irregular platforms and may have served as the habitations of the priests or the nobility.

We know enough of Mayan construction to form a fairly adequate picture of what were its essential features. Limestone was burnt into lime, slaked to make mortar, and then applied to a broken mass of the same kind. The facingstones were smoothed on the outside and left roughhewn and painted on the inside. They were held in place between forms. Lime, mortar and rubble filled the interstices.

The rooms were vaulted in a characteristic way, but the roof thus formed was not what we understand by an arch.

The true arch was in fact quite unknown to the Maya, for they were unfamiliar with the idea of a keystone. This ignorance of the true arch had some very momentous consequences for Maya architecture, since the walls had, as a result, to be very thick if they were adequately to support the heavy roof.

Not infrequently a superstructure was erected on the top of the building proper so that some Mayan structures attained considerable heights. The famous temple at Tikal, for instance, reached the imposing height of one hundred and seventy-five feet, counting pyramid and superstructure.

Seen from the distance many of these towns must have presented something of the appearance of diminutive New Yorks with little skyscrapers towering at irregular intervals from a mass of much smaller buildings. Such a comparison is really not far-fetched, for taken vertically there were three parts to every Mayan building of any pretensions: first, the substructure or pyramidal base; second, the structure proper; third, the superstructure. In the larger palaces two and three stories were not uncommon and these stories were generally not built over the rooms of the lower stories, but directly over a solid core. Thus the upper stories receded and the buildings presented a terraced or pyramidal profile. Although the general height of a building was three stories, four or five stories are known. One building at Tikal rose to the imposing height of five stories in three receding planes, the three uppermost stories being one above the other.

Unusual and remarkable as were some of the more famous Maya temples from a purely architectural viewpoint, Maya architecture derives much of its peculiar flavor not so much from the architectonic balancing of the different parts of a building as from the nature of the decorations used. Sculpture was in fact largely subordinated to this purpose and we find comparatively few examples of sculpture separated from architecture or in the true round.

Such sculptural decoration was used everywhere, in the interior of the buildings, along the façades and on altars and slabs of stone carved on one or more sides called *stelæ*. The sculptural decorations along the façade are perhaps those best known, because so many beautiful examples of them have survived. The best date from the earlier Mayan structures where the style was freer and more realistic. The façades on these earlier and less elaborate buildings always consisted of figures of men, serpents, etc., modeled in stucco or built up out of blocks of stone nicely fitted together.

Fundamentally, all the sculptural decorations were based on relief. Rarely has any people succeeded in equaling or surpassing the achievement of the Mayas in this regard. In the delineation of figures in profile the Maya artists were well-nigh perfect and their skill in representing the human body in the "three-quarter view" was almost as remarkable. Nothing that the ancient Egyptians or Assyrians did is really comparable. We have here a complete mastery in the depicting of limbs in all possible positions. The technical skill attained in this regard is perhaps best illustrated by some of the sculptured hieroglyphs at Copan where figures are represented interlaced and contorted in the most intricate manner imaginable, without any loss of harmony or proportion.

Now the purely decorative use to which sculpture was put led to the very natural result that the figure as such was often completely lost sight of in the superabundance of detail, and this tendency took on unusual proportions as time progressed. The final consequence was that an art that originally began with a fine feeling and appreciation for the human and animal form in relief, degenerated, after a while, into one where the representation of the human and the animal body became merely one part of an intricate ornamental pattern covered with all sorts of scrolls and curlicues. Sculpture having thus become simply the handmaid of decoration was markedly retarded in its development. That the Maya stone-carver, however, did finally succeed in mastering the block and producing sculpture in the true round, certain of the figures at Palenque clearly demonstrate. For the future history of art in aboriginal North America, as is so often the case, however, the peculiarities and eccentricities of the Maya style were to be of more importance than its virtues. Nowhere in the region directly affected by Maya art do we find the true arch, or is there any appreciable advance in the freeing of sculpture from its architectural or decorative entanglements.

To an outsider, therefore, Maya art, with all its unusual merit and attainments, does seem to be largely dominated by the decorative instinct. The themes used in the decoration of surfaces were of course numerous. In contradistinction to the art of many aboriginal peoples of the two Americas and of other parts of the world, geometrical patterns were rarely used. Instead we have the profuse employment of human and mythological figures. Among these there is one that stands out with unusual prominence, namely, the so-called feathered-serpent design. As the name indicates, this animal is not to be regarded as a real serpent. Nothing was really farther from the minds of these early American artists than this. The serpent depicted by them was a most amazing conglomeration of traits of the most fantastic description. He was a symbol, first of all, of a god, indeed of one of the greatest of all Mayan deities, Kukulkan, known to the Aztecs as Quetzalcoatl, that is the *quetzal*-snake, *quetzal* being the name of a certain bird. To this great deity the famous city of Chitzen Itza, now being excavated by the Carnegie Institute, was dedicated.

We no longer understand all the religious significance that went into the making of this peculiar and rather dismaying divinity. He had the body of a serpent, the plumes of the *quetzal* bird, the teeth of jaguar, and ornaments belonging to man, such as ear-plugs, nose-plugs and a head-dress. In his distended jaws was placed a human head.

So curious a combination of features is not likely to arise more than once and we may therefore assume that wherever an animal of such a type is to be encountered either in the art or mythology of any American Indian tribe, it is to be explained as due to Maya influence. Now a feathered-serpent of this kind is to be found far and wide throughout Central America and Mexico and, in increasingly more attenuated form, as we proceed north across the Rio Grande River. The distribution of this figure in art, mythology, and religion thus becomes one of our best guides for determining the extent to which Mayan culture influenced the rest of aboriginal North America.

The dangers of the decorative instinct running amuck and leading to a specific type of conventionalization are very well illustrated by what happened to the feathered-serpent design in the course of time. A reference to the illustration shows what, to the unitiated eye, must appear a perfectly meaningless interlacing of scrolls and hooks. Nevertheless it is our serpent distorted beyond recognition. Yet though the serpent motive spread from the Mayas to the rest of North America the peculiar type of conventionalization that developed in connection with it among the Mayas, was

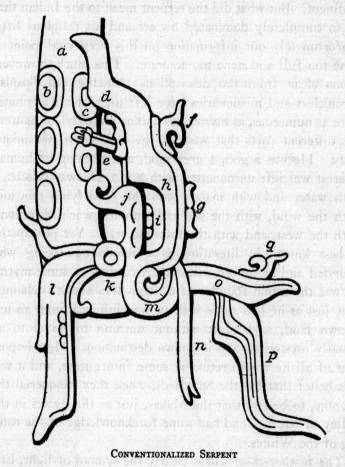

CONVENTIONALIZED SERPENT

largely limited to themselves. Conventionalization and symbolism play a great rôle among many of the tribes north of the Rio Grande but they are of an entirely different kind.

The trail of the feathered-serpent with outstretched wings is found everywhere and, in a manner, it represents the symbol of the Mayan cultural conquest of the rest of the continent. But what did the serpent mean to the Indian that he so completely dominated his art and his religious life? Unfortunately our information on this very vital point is none too full and none too accurate. This much, however, seems clear from the descriptions that the old Spanish chroniclers and missionaries have left us, that his attributes were as numerous, as mysterious and as multifarious as were the different parts that went to the making of his unique body. He was a god, a great god, and nothing of human interest was left unconnected with him. He was associated with water and with maize, with the fructifying rain and with the wind, with the sky and with the world-directions, with the west, and with the morning star. Yet perhaps he is best known in literature as a semihuman being who founded and organized culture. According to some myths, he was the actual founder of Chitzen Itza and it is claimed that just as he had come without warning and from an unknown land, so he left without warning to travel to an equally mysterious and unknown destination. Most important of all he was to return at some future time, and it was this belief that led the Spaniards, when they conquered the country, to believe that the Mayas, just as the Aztecs in the valley of Mexico, had had some foreknowledge of the coming of the Whites.

The feathered-serpent is clearly the symbol of light, life, and motion. His primary association was probably with water in all its manifestations. A well-known Mayan scholar, taking as a starting-point the name under which he was known among one of the Maya tribes, namely, as the "feathered-snake that goes in the water," has suggested that he typifies the ripple born both of wind and water, the aspect of which suggests feathers and the motion of a serpent. According to this scholar, the feathered-serpent represents both primordial motion and wind, i.e., breath and life. His snake and water aspect bring him into close relationship with the rain god and in his bird manifestation he is Lord of the Sky and the World-Directions.

An interesting problem arises in connection with this vague and unusual deity. In Mexico proper and among many of the more complex tribes north of Mexico, the attributes and functions that are found united in this one deity among the Mayas, are there distributed over a large number of gods. Are we then to suppose that as the great serpent-god spread to the north, like everything else about Maya culture, his unity was lost, or, on the contrary, are we to assume that it was the Mayas who artificially constructed him by merging other deities into his person? Some of his attributes may conceivably be due to a secondary accretion, but in the main we are likely to be on safer ground by assuming that his true nature was lost sight of as his cult spread to Mexico proper and beyond.

Two of his traits certainly have an almost universal distribution in North America: His primary association with water and the belief that he holds a head in his distended jaws. Now this head is to the present writer the symbolical representation of the great conflict which he is always represented as having with another deity. What is perhaps the classical expression of this conflict is to be found among the ancient Aztecs. There the feathered-serpent or Quetzalcoatl, as he was called, is being continually thwarted by his arch-enemy Tezcatlipoca, the Smoking-Mirror. It is

Tezcatlipoca who finally wins and drives Quetzalcoatl from his home.   In this version of the far-flung myth we have the reflection of a great historical event, the conquest of the valley of Mexico by invading barbarians, the early kinsmen of the Aztecs.   Quetzalcoatl represents the great civilization these barbarians found there and Tezcatlipoca, the barbarians themselves.

Strangely enough a parallel to this victory of the enemy of the feathered-serpent exists in a myth famous throughout the region of the Great Lakes of the United States.   There, likewise, the counterpart of Tezcatlipoca, the Thunderbird, triumphs over the Water-Spirit, who is the counterpart of the feathered-serpent and Quetzalcoatl, and there, likewise, the Thunderbird represents a barbarian invasion from the north and the Water-Spirit, the higher civilization.   On the whole, however, north of the Rio Grande, the conflict between these two deities is represented as a draw, or better, each one wins for a time.

Another version of this same fascinating story has found its way over most of aboriginal America.   In this version the Water-Spirit, who has now become simply the symbol of evil, conquers his enemy, who has now become identified with the Morning-Star, and carries his head as a trophy. But the victory is short-lived, for the Water-Spirit is finally conquered by the nephews of the defeated hero.

That we are in all these cases dealing with variants of the Quetzalcoatl and Tezcatlipoca myth there can be little doubt.   One of the attributes that is fairly prominent in the Maya version seems, however, to have been completely lost as the deity and his symbolism spread northward from his original home, namely, his bird characteristics.   Yet a curious echo of even this phase of his nature seems to have survived among a simple tribe in northwestern Michigan, in the country known to all Americans as the scene of Hiawatha's exploits. There we find the belief in a water-serpent, who is continually being guarded by little birds who

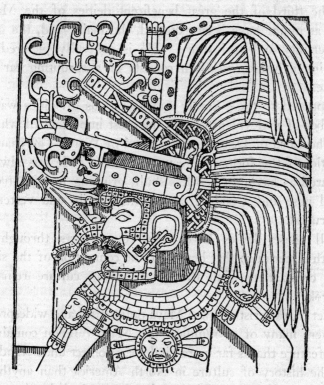

SCULPTURED FIGURE SHOWING MAN WEARING MASK OF TURQUOISE INLAY AND ELABORATE HEADDRESS

hover about him in order to give him ample warning of the approach of his dread enemy, the Thunderbird.

Fundamental as was the feathered-serpent, however, he was not regarded as the true creator of the world. This position was assigned to another god whom the Mayas called

Itzamna and who was always represented as an old man with a Roman nose. He was the god of the east and the rising sun, the inventor of writing and of books and the great healer.

The third of the great beneficent deities of the Maya was, as might have been expected, the maize-god, the god of fertility and agriculture. He is generally pictured as wearing a headdress which consists of a sprouting ear of maize.

Opposed to these kindly and propitious divinities was a number of malevolent deities, the most important of whom are the Lord of Death and the Lord of War. The characteristics of the former were unmistakable. He was always pictured as having a fleshless skull, grinning teeth, a truncated nose and a body from which the ribs and vertebræ protruded.

All these deities have their counterparts throughout North America so that here, too, the connection of the simpler civilizations with the great Mayan culture remains unbroken.

Yet characteristic as was Maya polytheism and widespread as were many of its ramifications, Maya religion contained one feature that is far more vital for a correct understanding of the history of culture in North America than anything we have so far discussed, namely, the marked development of religious dualism.

Connected with the creator god Itzamna—if indeed we are not merely dealing with a malevolent aspect of this deity himself—was a goddess the very opposite of beneficent and whose function was to destroy. She was the deity of destructive floods. Similarly we find associated with the feathered-serpent a god who is represented in art with a fleshless jaw and who brings drought. The third of the great beneficent deities, the maize-god, has no malevolent counterpart, but he is always described as so weak that he would have been completely conquered by the evil spirits were he not protected by the good ones.

Now this type of dualism is the chief characteristic of all aboriginal religions in North America. Itzamna and Quetzalcoatl still persist, as we have seen, in the forests of the northern part of the United States. There among the Winnebago, a Siouan tribe, we encounter two interesting deities with a dual nature, both of them the oldest and most sacred divinities of the group. The first has a body divided into two parts, one part dispensing death and the other life; the second is described as putting his "bones" at the disposal of mankind and from these bones either good or evil medicines can be prepared. In other words, he is ambivalent. In this same region we also find that the agricultural spirits have always to be protected against the machination of the evil spirits, exactly as was true for the Maya maize-god.

The best known expression of this dualism was perhaps to be found among the tribes east of the Winnebago. Here there prevailed a widespread belief in a great good spirit and a great bad spirit. It was this belief that led the early French missionaries and travelers to the erroneous supposition that the Indians of this region believed in God and the devil. As a matter of fact, of course, these two very generalized deities are all that these comparatively simple tribes had still retained of the great impulse that started in Central America.

As was to be expected in a civilization where temples played so great a rôle and deities were so well and clearly defined, the number of ceremonies was legion. There were, roughly speaking, four great classes of rites, the ceremonies performed in honor of specific gods, those performed at the beginning and the end of the year, those connected with the various guilds and occupations, and those performed for special occasions.   They were all carefully adjusted to a complex calendar.   From the viewpoint of the rest of North America, the most significant of these rites were those performed at the beginning of the year and those given in honor of the deities of the four cardinal points—the south, the east, the north and the west.

The characteristic features of the New Year's ceremony were the cleansing of the houses, the renewal and repainting of utensils, the purification of the temple courts with incense and, above all, the remaking of the fire.   Many of these traits are found as fundamental elements in the ritual of a large part of the tribes along the Gulf of Mexico and far to the north.

The ceremony to the four cardinal points has an even wider distribution: it is in fact the ceremonial unit *par excellence* for all North America, for it is based upon what is apparently the fundamental cosmological myth of the new world.   According to Maya cosmology the earth was a cube, from the center of which emerged a tree, the tree of life. The earth was held in place by four deities, the four cardinal points.   With each cardinal point was associated a definite color.   It is difficult to overestimate the significance of these deities.   Indian ceremonialism is almost unthinkable without them.

We know less about the social organization of the Mayas than about any other feature of their culture.   In general, however, it seems fairly evident that nothing approaching the closely knit organization that prevailed among the

STONE STELAE FROM COPAN

Representation of Ordinary Human Sacrifice

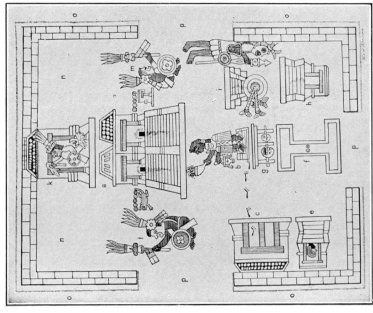

Plan of the Main Temple of the Aztecs

Aztecs and their kinsmen and among the great civilizations that lay between the Maya and the valley of Mexico, existed among them. The city-states remained the characteristic governmental unit and while the possessions of such a city-state might at times grow to such large proportions that it necessitated a well-regulated control, centralization of power never progressed to the point where we can justifiedly speak of the existence of real kings or of a true caste system. This was at least true for Yucatan. Possibly the situation in the southern part of Central America may have been different.

A typical clan organization existed with all its rigors and with descent in the male line. There is a certain amount of evidence likewise for the existence of a twofold grouping analogous to that found among so large a part of the tribes of the United States.

The only really elaborate centralization to be found developed, as was but natural, among the priesthood. The office of the main priest, like that of the chief of the tribe, was hereditary and the rôle played by this chief priest even when the Spaniards first arrived was very great. The monuments and aboriginal manuscripts that have come down to us would seem to indicate that in the early days his rôle was even more important. It would, in fact, not be too farfetched to contend that his office was as definitely contrasted with that of the civil chief as was the case among the Aztecs and their kinsmen, the Nahuatl tribes of Mexico proper. If this assumption is correct, then we have, among the Maya, the prototype of one of the main features of government throughout three-quarters of the region to the north, as far as Canada. This dual chieftainship, in fact, finds its most significant expression among the Iroquoian, Siouan and certain Algonquian tribes, where we encounter two hereditary chiefs, one whose function is connected with peace and the other with war.

As we have pointed out it is hardly justified to speak of kings among the Maya or of any true development of rank. Yet it would be quite erroneous to underestimate the sharp distinctions that prevailed between the rich and the poor or between the leaders and the priestly caste, and all other individuals. The priests included among their ranks all the *intelligentsia*. There could be but few lay thinkers and certainly no lay artists in a civilization so completely dominated by religion as was the Maya. And if priest and thinker, therefore, are synonymous, it is to the priests that we must attribute two of the most remarkable achievements to the credit of any nation, civilized or uncivilized: the invention of a system of hieroglyphs and the devising and elaborating of an intricate calendar based upon astronomical calculations of a very complex kind.

The Maya hieroglyphs resemble no other system of writing known to us. Like the ancient Egyptian these are overwhelmingly pictographic in character and as far as we can make out to-day, were originally meant either to be pictures of the object it was sought to express or something connected with it. In the course of time one portion of this object came to stand for the whole and as these part-symbols themselves became transformed, there developed a series of signs or glyphs that could only with the greatest difficulty be identified as having anything to do with the object originally intended.

In fact this gradual wearing down of the glyphs proceeded so far in some cases that all parts, except those regarded as the absolutely essential elements, were eliminated. Such an essential element might, for instance, boil

INTRODUCING GLYPH

Initial Series

1. 9 baktuns (cycles).
2. 14 katuns
3. 13 tuns
4. 4 uinals
5. 17 kins
6. 12 caban (day)

Supplementary Series

7. glyph F
8. (a) glyph D, (b) glyph C
9. (a) glyph X, (b) glyph B
10. (a) glyph A (30 day lunar month)
10. (b) 5 kayab (month)

Explanatory Series

11, 12, 13 and 14a, possibly explain the dates

Secondary Series

14b. 3 kins, 13 uinals
15a. 6 tuns (to be added)

Period Ending Date

16. 4 ahau 13 Yax

A TYPICAL MAYAN INSCRIPTION

down to two small cross bands or simply an asterisk. A further difficulty was introduced by the fact that the Mayas, like the Chinese, never forgot the purely artistic side of their writings and went to great lengths to produce a balanced and harmonious design, irrespective of the modifications and the distortions this might produce in the form of the glyph itself. So great, indeed, is at times the lack of relation between a word and its glyph that some authorities have even been led to question whether all glyphs could possibly have been pictographic in origin. In spite, however, of this tendency toward abbreviation and wearing down of a glyph, many retained their pictographic character to the end.

Side by side with this development away from the actual pictographic portrayal of an object, there existed a marked tendency to use some of the glyphs as phonetic elements. The glyph for sun, for instance, is *"kin."* But *kin* enters into the composition of many other Mayan words that have nothing to do with the original word for sun, i.e., it came to be employed as a purely phonetic syllable. Of such syllables quite a number probably exist and it is in their determination that our only hope for eventually deciphering the Mayan hieroglyphs lies. These phonetic elements, however, seem to correspond to syllables and not to individual sounds, a fact that adds perceptibly to the difficulty of complete decipherment.

We know the hieroglyphs in two slightly different forms, one associated with the monuments and the other with certain old pre-Colombian manuscripts or codices. The glyphs themselves fall into two well-marked groups: the first including those used in computing time and the second, those found associated with the former and probably containing an explanatory character of some kind.

By far the largest portion of glyphs deals with the computation of time, but it is quite clear that there is a large number recording historical happenings. Not only do such glyphs record the date on which a particular monument was erected, but they apparently record certain contemporaneous events as well. Some of the early Spanish chroniclers even contended that certain of the ancient books were used for a wide variety of purposes such as the determination of good and bad days, how to avert them, prophecies, and the times appointed for the fulfillment of these prophecies. There seems ample justification for such an assumption. Indeed there is reason for believing that with the increase of our knowledge we shall find the glyphs recording such varied matters as the names of individuals, cities, political divisions, feasts, sacrifices, tributes, birth, death, conquest, and numerous other subjects connected with the life of the people.

All this, however, only the future will reveal. To-day our knowledge is unfortunately limited to a small number of glyphs. We actually know only the signs for the names of the days, months, certain time-periods, the numerals from zero to nineteen, the symbols of the four directions and the four colors associated with them, the glyphs of certain gods, of the sun, moon, Venus, Mars, Jupiter and a few other heavenly bodies and, finally, a few representing certain natural objects.

The notation used for the numerals from zero to nineteen is very interesting because it consisted simply of the faces of twenty gods. This was, however, only for the more elaborate notation of numbers. A simpler system also existed, in which 1 was represented by a dot, 2 by two dots,

5 by a bar, 6 by a bar and a dot, 15 by three bars, etc. **Zero** was represented by a shell. How frequently numerals had to be used will become apparent when it is remembered that the Maya had a system with eight units, each of them multiples of twenty. Beginning with 1, there was an ascending series 20 × 1, 20 × 20, 20 × 400, 20 × 8000 and so on to the rather respectable number of 1,280,000,000.

The greatest advance in the decipherment of the glyphs has, of course, been made in connection with the Mayan computation of time and the calendar. What has thus been revealed to us concerning the knowledge the ancient Mayas possessed of astronomy is almost beyond belief. We must naturally bear in mind always that the hieroglyphic writing was sacred and that it was exclusively in the hands of an hereditary caste of priests specially prepared from generation to generation to deal with the subject. The ordinary man knew absolutely nothing about it.

Two general points in particular emerge from the study of the Mayan efforts to harness time, for it was a real harnessing of time that was here attempted; first, that they knew the lunar year of twelve months and thirty days to the month and secondly, that they had arbitrarily invented another time-cycle, a year consisting of thirteen months, each having twenty days. It is this latter year that constitutes the fundamental feature of the Mayan time-count and it reappears among all those nations who were directly affected by Mayan civilization.

Now not only did the Mayas correctly determine the ordinary lunar year but they learned how to correct it so as to make it correspond to the solar year, by adding five days at the end of every year. Allowance likewise was made for the leap year, although a day was probably not inter-

polated. Furthermore, they reduced the number of days
from thirty to twenty probably in order to obtain a number
that fitted better into their system of counting which, as
we have seen, was the vigesimal, that is, based on twenty,
and they raised the number of months from twelve to
eighteen.

We are now prepared to enter into the wonderful and
eccentric calendrical maze devised by the Maya astronomers.
It was made possible by three facts: a knowledge of astronomical time-periods; the existence of a suitable notation
system; and the discovery of the peculiar ritual year of 260
days.

This last mentioned year, a peculiar and utterly arbitrary
cycle of 260 days, was made up of two factors, a series of
numbers (1–13) and a series of twenty names that in origin
were probably the names of days. In the words of a well-
known Mayan authority, Dr. Spinden: "These two series
revolve upon each other like two wheels, one with thirteen
and the other with twenty cogs. The smaller wheel of
numbers makes twenty revolutions while the larger wheel
of days is making thirteen revolutions, and after this the
number-cog and the name-cog with which the experiment
began, are again in combination. Thus a day with the same
number and the same name recurs every 13 × 20 or 260
days."

In addition to this artificial year there are three other
specific peculiarities of the Mayan calendar that are truly
remarkable, the so-called Calendar-Round, the Long Count,
and the Venus calendar.

In order to understand this Calendar-Round we must
keep clearly before us the fact that, due to the necessity
of adding five additional days every year, any day-name

occupies the same month position during the course of an entire year, and a position five days in advance of it during the course of the following year. Every fifth year will therefore show the same arrangement as the first. The month positions of each day during the changes of four consecutive years are consequently very important and we find them frequently recorded on the monuments. Now the Calendar-Round is arrived at by remembering that the day-numbers associated with the day-names entering into the ritual year of 260 days can run the whole gamut of thirteen changes. As a result a particular day with a particular number can occupy a particular month-position every 13 × 4 or 52 years, that is 18,980 days. This period the Mayas called the Calendar-Round and it is of vast importance both among the Maya and the Aztecs in connection with their astronomy and their whole ceremonial life.

We are now in a position to understand what a Mayan date means. It contains four parts. Thus, for instance, the date 11 *Ahau* 18 *Mac* is to be read, "the day *Ahau*, being the eleventh day in the thirteenth week is found in the eighteenth position in the month *Mac*." Now, as Dr. Spinden has pointed out, though such a way of figuring seems at first blush very strange to us it really amounts to nothing much more than saying that Tuesday, July 4th, should be read, "Tuesday, the second day of the week, falls on the fourth day of the month of July."

Curiously enough the time-period which plays perhaps the greatest rôle in the Mayan calendar is one connected with a purely hypothetical time, long before the actual beginnings of Maya history. The starting-point is a fixed day, that on which presumably the world began, and the date given in a long-count records not only the days that have elapsed since the starting-point but, likewise, the name and number of the resulting day and its position in the month, the year of 260 days and the Calendar-Round.

But the culminating achievement of Mayan astronomy was the calculation of the apparent revolution of the planet Venus, upon the basis of which they devised their Venus calendar. They divided the mean synodical year of Venus, which is nearly 584 days, into four parts of 236 days (morning star), 90 days (superior conjunction), 250 days (evening star), 90 days (inferior conjunction), divisions that agree fairly closely with the actual divisions of the Venus year. In addition they recognized the agreement in length between eight solar years of 365 days each, and five Venus years of 584 days each, using this fact both in their calculations and in their ceremonies. There is even ample justification for believing that the slight discrepancy which actually does exist between the mean Venus year and the actual Venus year, namely, .08 of a day, was apparently adjusted by a marginal subtraction of two days in twenty-five revolutions.

Two more short examples will suffice to indicate the re-markable accuracy and the complexity of the calculations indulged in, as well as the terrifying span of years with which the Maya astronomers not infrequently dealt. In one of the famous codices that has come down to our time, 405 revolutions of the moon are set down, and although the period embraced is thirty-three years (11,959 days) the error as computed by the best modern method is nine-tenths of a day.

In this same manuscript the end of the world is repre-sented and periods of 34,000 years (12,500,000 days) are recorded repeatedly without so much as the blinking of an eye. Small wonder then that we have at the end of this manuscript, after these tremendous numbers have been recorded, a representation of the destruction of the world. The rain-serpent is seen stretching across the sky and inundating the world with torrents of water. From the sun and the moon tremendous streams of water also gush forth. The malevolent goddess of floods and cloud-bursts is represented overturning the bowl of the heavenly waters and the malevolent black god surrounded by symbols indicating universal destruction, stalks abroad in the guise of a screeching and raging bird with a terror-inspiring head. For such numbers that is the only fitting end!

Certainly this is a dizzy spectacle that we here behold and our dizziness increases when we remember that these same people had invented a sign for zero and used the zero in their calculations possibly as much as 800 years before it was known anywhere in the Old World!

Who were the people who could accomplish so much, and what light can be thrown on the origin of this incredible culture? Their culture seems to have arisen suddenly and to have disappeared in as mysterious a fashion. Hypothesis upon hypothesis has been promulgated to account both for its rise and its eclipse. What we actually know, however, is simply this:

As early as the year 100 B.C. the hieroglyphic system had already been fully developed although it was somewhat more archaic than that which prevailed a century later. Where and when this hieroglyphic system developed, of that we have not the remotest idea. The earliest hieroglyphic date is found on a little statuette and it is not until two hundred years later that we find monuments with inscriptions and dates. Then without warning or preparation we find enormous mounds with elaborate temples built upon them, public squares, stelæ and altars. No excavations have ever revealed to us any civilization of a simpler nature from which this very elaborate culture could possibly have been developed. It is true that on the margins of this great culture indications of a simpler civilization have been discovered but never directly under the ruins of the Mayan monuments. In short, we have as yet no reason for believing that this simpler civilization was the predecessor of the higher cultures of Central America and Yucatan.

Owing to the present total absence of all indications pointing to an evolution of Mayan civilization in Central America and Yucatan and due to certain resemblances between the monuments and the culture of Central America and certain old Asiatic civilizations, a number of scientists have postulated an Old World origin for Mayan civilization. The difficulties in the way of accepting such an hypothesis are as great, if not greater, than those which confront us when we attempt to account for the origin of Mayan civilization in America. What completely invalidates all Old World origins at present, is the question of chronology, for the civilization from which the ancient Mayas are supposed to have borrowed many of their traits did not exist until 600 A.D., at the earliest, and the Maya civilization as proved by actual dates found, goes back to 100 B.C. on a conservative estimate. For an Old World origin of Mayan civilization this difficulty must first be eliminated either by proving that the present system of calculating Maya dates is utterly wrong or that the Asiatic civilization from which the Mayan has come is much older. For the present, the problem must remain insoluble.

The history of Mayan culture is dominated by one outstanding fact, namely, the small period of time during which any city was occupied. Cities and even regions were abandoned apparently without any cause that can now be

SEATED DEITY FROM PALENQUE

assigned. Nothing is more baffling and puzzling than this continuous shifting from place to place, this abandonment of one town and founding of another. Every imaginable explanation has been advanced to account for it from malaria or an abrupt change of climate to the pressure of conquering hordes or some catastrophic cataclysm. All are unsatisfactory. The enigma persists.

Scholars have divided the history of Mayan civilization into a number of fairly well-marked periods characterized principally by their artistic style. The first great period extends from 176 A.D. to 373 A.D., and the sites that belong to it are all south of Yucatan. The carving of this period is crude and angular and the profile presentation of the human figure is better than the front view. All the essential conventions of the Mayan art were already fixed and the serpent motif had already begun its momentous journey. But it seems likely that all these conventions had already been fixed long before this earliest of Mayan historical periods can properly be said to have begun. The next period, the so-called middle period, extended from 373 A.D. to 472 A.D. and some of the most beautiful works of art belong to it. It is characterized in sculpture by purity of style and a straightforwardness of presentation. The flamboyancy, so conspicuous in later periods, has not yet begun. The great period follows. It lasted for 150 years, from 472 A.D. to 620 A.D. During this epoch architecture made great strides; rooms became wider, walls thinner and forms more refined. The calculations in the inscriptions deal increasingly with complicated astronomical subjects.

The years between 472 A.D. and 620 A.D. constitute the most brilliant epoch in Mayan civilization. It seems to have come to an end suddenly. An overwhelming catastrophe seems apparently to have swept over all the cities where this civilization had flourished. Some scholars have invoked a tremendous civil war, others a devastating epidemic, and still others social decadence. But we do not know, for even the references in the chronicles bearing upon this early period are excessively brief.

All the Mayan cities were abandoned about 600 A.D. and a general shift towards the north took place. This transition-period lasted from 620 A.D. to 980 A.D. Architecture still persisted but an important element, namely, pictorial sculpture, practically disappeared.

From 980 A.D. to 1200 A.D. something in the nature of a renaissance can be said to have occurred. There was a noteworthy revival of architecture in northern Yucatan. The architectural styles of decoration throughout this epoch are, however, far more formal than those of the earlier times. New decorative motifs spring up, such, for instance, as the mask panel, a face reduced to a rectangular area and built up in mosaic fashion out of separately carved blocks, and geometric figures such as fret-meanders, banded columns and imitation diagonal latticework.

The period that followed represents the down-grade and lasted from 1200 A.D. to 1450 A.D., ending with the final destruction of the city which had played the foremost rôle in the period before. The interesting feature about this last epoch is that the Mayan culture seems to have been very profoundly influenced by a civilization that came from the north and which represented, essentially, merely a new remodeling of cultural traits that had many centuries before actually spread from the Mayas themselves. In other words, Maya civilization was being overlaid and transformed by a culture which the ancestors of the Maya, in the remote past, had themselves originated and in the building up of which barbarians from the north had participated.

Such was the glory that was Maya. Its splendor was past more than half a century before the Spaniards began

their nefarious work of destruction. The eclipse of this
aboriginal civilization, however, cannot be laid at their door.
If, indeed, like the ancient Greeks, its disintegration is not
to be ascribed to inner political weakness, we must look to
the north of Central America and Yucatan for the destroyers. There the land swarmed with barbarian hordes.
And it is one of the ironies of history that the great *conquistador*, Hernan Cortez, passed within three leagues of
Copan without knowing that there had ever been a great
Mayan civilization and yet gained his renown from conquering a city that was built on the ruins of the glory that
once was Maya.

CHAPTER III

THE REIGN OF THE WAR-GODS: THE ANCIENT MEXICANS

AFTER Cortez had captured the city of Mexico he sent home to Spain some of the strange objects that had once belonged to the household of the unfortunate Montezuma. The choicest pieces naturally went to the Emperor Charles the Fifth. Yet not even that cynical and somewhat pessimistic ruler could have surmised what misfortunes and tragedies were to result from this intertwining of the destinies of the royal lines of Hapsburg and Montezuma. For three centuries Mexico was never to lose its gloomy fascination for the descendants of the great emperor. And so it came to pass that in the year 1866 a lineal descendant of Charles the Fifth was shot to death by a detachment of soldiers under the command of a man who was himself a descendant of those very Indians Cortez had butchered so mercilessly.

The unfortunate Aztec chief, Guatimotzino, tortured to death by the loyal subjects of Charles the Fifth, and blond Maximilian, the brother of Franz Joseph, Emperor of Austria, led blindfolded three hundred years later to summary execution on the fields of Queretaro—what a glorious theme for a great tragedy! Yet only one great poet noticed it, the Italian Carducci. In a magnificent poem entitled *Miramar* he surveys the fortunes of the house of Hapsburg from the crazed daughter of Ferdinand and Isabella, through Marie Antoinette to Maximilian. He sees the

MAYA SCULPTURED LINTELS

POTTERY INCENSE BURNER FROM SALVADOR

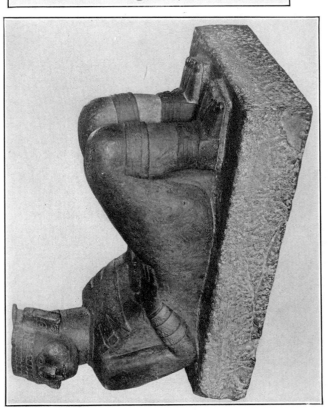

STONE FIGURE OF DEITY

tropical jungles enticing the proud and ambitious Maximilian
to fall a belated sacrifice to the ancient Aztec gods and he
pictures the most ferocious of these gods, the terror-
inspiring Huitzilopochtli, exulting that at last he has obtained a sacrifice worthy of his importance—the blond
descendant of Charles himself.

Who is this Huitzilopochtli that still lives in the verse of
a nineteenth century poet? To understand him is to understand the basis of ancient Mexican civilization.

After the conquest the Aztecs themselves could think of
him only as a destroyer and an illusion and they sang of
him:

> Huitzilopochtli was but an ordinary man;
> A sorcerer, an evil premonition;
> An instigator of discord, a breeder of horrible visions.
> He created war: he gathered the warriors, he commanded the
> warriors.
> Of him is it said that he threw upon the people
> The turquoise-snake, the fire-borer, i.e., war.
> And when his feast is celebrated
> Prisoners are sacrificed,
> Ritually bathed prisoners are sacrificed.

But before the conquest this was different. We see
him sitting on a blue-colored bench from the four corners
of which issue four snakes. Upon his head rested a beautiful crest, shaped like the beak of a bird. Around his neck
he wore a collar made of representations of the human heart.
An eighteenth century historian, Clavigero, thus describes
him: "His forehead was blue but his face was covered with
a golden mask while another of the same kind covered the
back of his head. In his right hand he carried a large blue
club and in his left hand a shield in which appeared five

balls of feathers disposed in the form of a cross. From the upper part of the shield rose a golden flag with four arrows. His body was girt with a large snake and adorned with lesser figures of animals made of gold and precious stones."

According to legend he had no father and he was conceived in terror, for the brothers of his mother conspired to kill their pregnant sister when he was still in his mother's womb. But before they could execute their purpose, the god was born, fully armed like Athena, with a shield in one hand and a spear in the other. Infuriated he threw himself upon his mother's detractors and when he had wreaked his vengeance he had earned the right to the names by which he was subsequently known—the Terror, the Terrible God.

God of war and pride of the Aztecs in the long journey from their ancestral home in the Seven Caves, the grateful people erected a magnificent temple in his honor when the city of Mexico-Tenochtitlan had come into its own. This temple was built of enormous stones that had the shape of snakes tied together and forming a circuit, fittingly called the snake-circuit. Through its rooms idols were scattered everywhere. Battlements artificially wrought in the form of snails, crowned the whole. Four magnificent gates facing the four cardinal points led to as many causeways, each two to three leagues long. Thirty steps brought one to a walk in the midst of which was a palisade artfully contrived of high trees. Between the trees, on bars running from one to the other, were tied human skulls. It is not strange therefore if the famous Spanish chronicler Acosta should have been horrified and that in the quaint translation of his work by the Elizabethan Purchas he should have been made to exclaim that this palisade "was full of dead sculls from one end to the other, the which was a wonderful mournful sight and full of horror. These were the heads of such as had been sacrificed; for after they were dead and had eaten the flesh, the head was delivered to the ministers of the temple who tied them to these bars until they fell off by morcels." At the very top of the temple stood two chapels in one of which was to be found the idol of Huitzilopochtli described above.

His main festival was the occasion of universal rejoicing. Numerous individuals were sacrificed and the priests began their penitential exercises fully twenty-four days prior to the fiesta itself. The unfortunate people doomed to death were painted in the colors of the god and shortly before their actual sacrifice they donned the richest of attire. Processions marched from one end of the city to the other and even from one town to another. The slaves who were to be killed had to divide themselves into two groups and engage in a bloody skirmish. Finally one of the numerous parties that had been parading through the various streets of the city rushed breathlessly to the top of the great temple of Huitzilopochtli and after the ears of the men had been pierced, descended, bearing in their arms a paste image of the god. This was then broken up into pieces and apportioned among the worshipers to be taken home and eaten. The feast ended amidst great revelry, as prisoners and slaves were sacrificed to the accompaniment of music played on conch shells.

Such was the patron god of the Aztec city of Tenochtitlan. Horrified as the Spanish priests were at the gruesomeness of his worship they were nevertheless not slow to detect certain similarities in his ritual that could be put to good use in their missionary endeavors such, for instance, as the ceremony of partaking of the paste image of the god, a rite which the Aztecs themselves denominated "god is eaten."

Now Huitzilopochtli, like the Aztecs, was a newcomer in the valley of Mexico. He had, according to legend, come from a distant region possibly to be identified with the southwest of the United States. Indeed it was supposed that like a second Moses, he had led his worshipers over the inhospitable deserts of the southwest through the still more arid uplands of northern .Mexico, to the fertile valley of Anahuac where the future city of Mexico was to arise. Hardships, defeat and temptation was the lot of the weary travelers time and time again, but through the vigilant and ever-solicitous care of Huitzilopochtli the Aztecs were enabled to triumph over all difficulties. The story of their wanderings has been preserved. Not only does it epitomize Aztec history but it affords an unusual insight into Aztec psychology and the evolution of Aztec ideals.

The Aztecs, in all probability, did not leave their ancestral home much earlier than 800 A.D. At that period they were already a fairly civilized people, for they had, as we have seen, been subjected to all the numerous cultural influences that had swept over the United States by land and sea from the south. The fructifying warmth of the great Mayan culture and possibly even that of the great civilizations of South America had reached them and transformed them from wandering marauders to a nation living a sedentary and well-regulated life.

From their half-legendary home in the Seven Caves the Aztecs were the last to emerge. They were preceded by the six great Nahuatlan tribes, their near kindred, but with whom they were destined to fight for the supremacy of the valley of Mexico. The first to start on the long journey south were those called the People-of-the-flower-plantation. They were followed by the People-of-the-mouths, the People-of-the-bridge, the People-of-the-winding-passages, the People-toward-the-land and the Corn-people.

The Aztecs were the last to start from the mystical Seven Caves, taking with them their god Huitzilopochtli. They affirmed that it was this god who had commanded them to leave their own country, promising that they would be the rulers of all the provinces which had been settled by the other six Nahuatlan tribes, that they would become the chiefs of a land abounding in gold, silver, precious stones and every imaginable costly thing.

With this promise ringing in their ears they began their arduous journey and even at the time of the conquest, such was their claim, numerous ruins still showed where they had once rested from the storm and stress of their adventures.

Whenever they stopped for any length of time they always did two things: erected a temple to their protector-god and sowed maize. The latter did not always thrive very well for there was little water and they had often to depend upon the dew and occasional storms for the necessary moisture. In fact they seem to have been rather indifferent in the matter of agriculture for they harvested their crops only when directed to do so by their god.

Finally they reached that part of Mexico now called Michoacan. Here occurred the first division of the people. It came about thus. So enamored did some of the priests of Huitzilopochtli become of this place that they begged the Terrible God to permit them and a few others to remain there. This request was granted and the others moved on. They were now measurably near their final destination, but hardships of a kind quite different from any they had yet known, were still in store for them. Troubles were now to assail them from within, of which the sister of the god himself was to be the instigator. This woman was unbelievably beautiful and a sorceress to boot. Few could or dared resist her. When Huitzilopochtli saw all the misfortune and unrest which she was causing he became sad, for when he had sent her among his worshipers he had, on the contrary, thought that her presence would serve as a spur and an encouragement to their hearts and arms. In desperation he counseled the people to secretly desert her and this they accordingly did. The city of Malinalco was eventually to be founded by her seed and even at the time of the conquest the people of that place were renowned for their proficiency in black magic.

Eventually they came to a place called Tula. Though they had already been greatly reduced in numbers from the effects of their long and difficult journeys Huitzilopochtli decided once again to test their constancy. He caused the water of a very full stream, flowing through the region, to be deflected so that it might spread over the whole valley and then he had this stream conducted to the middle of the mountain on which they were living, for he wished to show them the appearance of the land he had promised them. But as was perhaps to have been expected, the spot turned out to be so delightful and pleasant that the Mexicans, quite oblivious of the fact that they had been forewarned that what they saw was but an imitation of the promised land, desired to stay there, some even going to the length of insisting that this was really their destined home.

Dreadful was the vengeance which the Terrible God exacted. One night a frightful noise was heard in the camp and in the morning all those who had counseled the people to stay in this most delectable of places were found dead with their breasts torn open and their hearts gone. It was from this incident that the custom developed of sacrificing people by tearing out their hearts and giving them to the god. Indeed the only food that Huitzilopochtli, the Terror, delighted in, was the fuming heart torn from the breast of a prisoner or a slave.

Onward, ever onward, they trudged. They were now in the valley of Mexico. Chapultepec was soon reached and the tired and footworn wanderers breathed more freely, for they felt they had finally attained their destination. But the Terrible God soon dispelled these dreams of peace. True, they were near their final home, he told them, but they had yet to overcome the resistance of two nations, so he had ordained it, so that their hearts might be strengthened ere they could rest permanently.

Now began the long struggle in the valley. Alternate victory and defeat followed. At one village in the valley peace and tranquillity had settled upon them for so long a time that Huitzilopochtli, fearing that his worshipers would remain there permanently, artfully contrived to bring their false tranquillity to an end. He bade the Mexicans go to the neighboring king of Culhuacan and ask that the king's daughter enter his service. When she came he commanded her to be killed and flayed, and that one of the Mexican nobles dress himself in her skin. The parents of the unfortunate girl were then invited to participate in the ceremonies that followed. When they discovered what had happened they fell upon the Mexicans and drove them into the lagoons surrounding their temporary home. Weeping, the unfortunate Mexicans besought their god to grant them a final peace, for they had no strength to endure any more.

Huitzilopochtli assured them then that the end of their ordeal was approaching and that they would soon find the precise spot where he wished them to build their city.

They had not long to wait for shortly after these events the god appeared in a dream to one of his priests and said:

My son, do you remember how I commanded you to kill Copil, the son of the sorceress who claimed to be my sister; how I ordered you to tear out his heart and throw it away in the canes and brakes of this lagoon? Know now that the heart fell upon a rock and that from it sprang a *nopal* tree. This tree was so large and beautiful that an eagle built his home in it and he maintained himself there eating the best and finest things he could secure. There he still dwells spreading out his large and beautiful wings to receive the warmth of the sun and the freshness of the morning air. Go there to-morrow and you will find him perched on the *nopal* tree and around him you will find a great quantity of green, red, yellow, and white feathers belonging to the birds on which he sustains himself. To this place I have given the name Tenochtitlan.

Tenochtitlan! The journey was over. On the following day all repaired to the temple to render their thanks to the god, and when the pæan of thanks was over the chief priest rose to bless them and to announce what future was in store for the great city:

"Here where the nopal grows we shall have peace and rest and happiness. Here we shall increase in numbers and add prestige to the name of the Mexican people. From this home of ours shall be known the force of our valorous arms and courage; will the world be told of our undaunted hearts by means of which we shall conquer all the nations and countries in the world, subjecting even the remotest provinces and cities, from sea to sea, to our rule. And we shall become the

PRE-AZTEC POLYCHROME VASE

INNER VIEW OF ABOVE

rulers over all these people, over their fields, and their sons and their daughters. Here shall they be compelled to serve and pay tribute to us, for here shall arise a famous city, the queen and ruler over all others, where kings and lords shall be received in court, where all shall congregate and to which the world shall look up as to a supreme court."

Should we be astounded then if from such beginnings and with such a tradition behind them, war and human sacrifice in all their refineries, became like incense to the nostrils of these people? Nor is it unfair to the high degree of excellence the Aztecs attained in the arts of peace, to stress the fact that these former stood in the center of their interest. War and human sacrifice became in their hands a great art and an all-absorbing ritual, and they played with both much as does a skilled artist with a technique he has completely mastered. Thus their ceremonies are full of sham battles, and no ruler could be crowned unless he had first embarked on a war expedition and secured prisoners to be sacrificed to Huitzilopochtli. War became an art and an obsession.

The same held true for human sacrifice. The technique of killing human beings was perfect and the varieties of killing developed, betokened real virtuosity. First, there was the ordinary sacrifice. The victim was stretched on the sacrificial stone while five priests held his arms, legs and head. The sacrificial priest opened his breast with a stone knife and, placing his hand in the wound, tore out the heart, which was then held to the lips of the god or offered directly to the sun. In many instances this sacrifice took place at the top of the temple-pyramid and the body of the victim was thrown down the steps to be carried away and dismembered. Second, there was the sacrifice by decapitation; third, that by flaying; fourth, that by shooting. The captive, in the latter case, was tied to a scaffold and arrows were discharged at him. Finally there was the well-known gladiatorial sacrifice, an unusually dramatic rite. The unfortunate individuals destined for this form of death, were each bound firmly to the center of a circular stone, their arms alone being left free. They were then attacked by four warriors dressed in ocelot and eagle skins. Should the victim, by any chance, succeed in defending himself against the first four warriors a fifth one was selected. In no case was he spared.

Now it goes without saying that no people could practice such rites without their having a far-reaching influence upon their minds and hearts. Theoretically, in fact, we might expect that such customs would make for cruelty and murder-lust in its worst forms. Yet it apparently did nothing of the kind, simply because the vast majority of the victims were prisoners of war or individuals set aside from their fellow-men by religious sanction. The ancient Mexicans, to judge from the descriptions that have come down to us, were kindly and gentle in their treatment of one another despite their attitude toward their enemies. Still one cannot help feeling that terror was in the atmosphere, even though it was unquestionably mitigated by having become partially ritualized. Certainly it is the dominant note in the representations of the deities and in the ceremonies associated with them. If there ever was a pantheon of terror it was that of the Aztecs. A few examples must suffice.

Associated with Tezcatlipoca, a god whose true nature comes out in the epithets applied to him such as "he whose slaves we are," "dreaded enemy," "capricious lord," is the sacrifice of the youth who must impersonate the god for a year before he is killed. Even Quetzalcoatl, one of the more kindly deities of the pantheon, is always represented sitting back to back with the god of death, as if to imply that we must never forget that even the most benign divinity may at any moment deal destruction. With Tlazolteotl, the filth-eater, is connected the shooting-sacrifice and the subtly cruel practice of forcing a female prisoner to go to her death unterrified and with joyful mien. And there is Xipe, the Night-drinker, our lord the flayer, whose delight was to have his victims flayed. Finally we have Mictlantecutli, lord of death, the dread ruler of the netherworld. In one of the famous Aztec documents, the Codex Borgia, we find him depicted as a skeleton, arms and legs painted with colors to symbolize the bones of a newly flayed man. He wears ear-plugs consisting of human heads. He is seated together with the death goddess who is presenting him with a naked human figure, symbolic of human sacrifice. Near him stands a dish filled with blood and smoking hearts. In the center is a skull swallowing a man, pictured as tumbling headlong into its mouth.

The journey to the inhospitable land over which Mictlantecutli presided, the land where, in the words of the ancient Aztec scribe, there is neither "light nor window," may fittingly close our account of this religion of terror. The one redeeming feature of this dreadful journey was that not all Aztecs had to take it. It was reserved only for the souls of those who had died of disease, and for the poorer classes. The first obstacles encountered were two mountains that clashed together and threatened to crush the unwary ghost. Hardly escaped from this peril, the ghost found himself confronted by a huge snake with an enormous and hideous maw and then by a colossal and terror-inspiring crocodile. Eight deserts and eight hills had then to be crossed, and still there was no relief. Here a new affliction assailed the soul, in the shape of a wind consisting of sharp flint knives. Finally the soul arrived at the shores of the river called the Nine-Waters, which had to be crossed on the back of a red-colored dog who must subsequently be killed in a prescribed manner, by thrusting an arrow down its throat.

Adepts in the terrible as the ignorant Spanish conquerors often were, their minds were too dull to have contrived some of the more subtle tortures that fill the annals of Aztec ritual and history. And what perhaps makes the cruelty all the more terrifying and overwhelming, is the fact that it was not individually inspired but represented, on the contrary, the mechanical repetition of a constantly recurring religious drama. This cruelty reached its height in the well-known ceremony in honor of Tezcatlipoca. Who does not know of that strange and creepy ritual in which a youth of unusual beauty and unblemished character spends a whole year impersonating the god, having every wish and whim gratified, only to die at the end of the year at the hands of implacable priests and in obedience to an awesome tradition?

Once every year the priests scanned the faces of the most promising of their captives in order to select from among their number that one who seemed most fitting for the honor of impersonating that unblemished sacrifice the great god Tezcatlipoca demanded. He had to come of noble lineage and possess grace and personal beauty. He who was chosen was immediately placed in the hands of specially selected priests whose duty it was to instruct him in all the arts pertaining to good breeding. This, according to Aztec ideals, meant playing the flute, the art of conversation, the proper manner of saluting those whom he met, a knowledge of flowers and the proper use of straight cane tobacco-pipes.

Wherever he went he was accompanied by eight pages dressed in the livery of the palace. His life was one long series of wish fulfillments. He could go where he wished to by night and day, and eat what he desired no matter how rich it was. But naturally he must do nothing to lose his figure and so, in order to guard against getting too fat, he had at times to live on salt and water.

Wherever he went he was worshiped and adored. For was he not the living image of the god Tezcatlipoca? And thus he wandered from place to place playing on a clay flute. Adorned in the richest and choicest of garments personally furnished him by the king, people streamed from all directions to do him reverence and to kiss the earth he had trod upon. It was indeed a vision of unusual beauty they beheld. His body and face were painted black and he wore his hair long so that it fell down to his waist. On his head rested a garland of flowers and around his body, in the fashion of cross-belts, were tied strings of luxuriant flowers. He wore a necklace of precious stones from which hung pendants of exquisite beauty. His earrings were of gold and his lip ornament consisted of a rare sea-shell. On each arm, above the elbow, were attached bracelets of gold, and strings of gems encased his arms from wrist to elbow. To his feet were tied little bells of gold and around his body, finally, was thrown a mantle made of the richest imaginable material.

All year he walked about clothed in this manner, but twenty days before the fateful festival his garments were changed. Yet though his apparel was much simpler now, it was still rich. New pleasures awaited him. He was married to four young girls who had been specially prepared and educated for this particular purpose and who bore the names of goddesses.

The last two weeks passed rapidly for the doomed man. The four days preceding the great day were given over to banqueting and dancing. All the people, high and low, the king alone excepted, celebrated with the man-god. Each day the dance took place in another ward of the city. Then on one of the last days he was taken to an island lying in the lake of Mexico. Finally the last day approached. Together with his four wives he was placed in a covered canoe generally reserved for the king, and carried across the lake to a little hill. His day of glory was now over: his beautiful companions were taken away from him and, accompanied by eight attendants, he walked to a small temple. In his hands he still carried a number of flutes, all that still remained to him of his year of compulsory happiness and grandeur. Slowly he walked up the temple steps and, as he ascended, he broke a flute on each step. The end was near. As soon as he attained the top, he was seized and immediately sacrificed.

Nowhere else in America do we meet with so poignant a religious drama although we shall often come across ceremonies in which the participants were supposed to impersonate the gods.

For rituals so varied and lengthy and recurring regularly every year, a numerous body of priests and officials was, of course, necessary. But well-organized as the Aztec religion was it could not, for a moment, be compared with that which existed among the Mayas; not so much because Aztec worship was essentially a simplification of the latter, but because, in contradistinction to the Mayas, the priest played a rôle distinctly subsidiary to that of the warrior. Indeed it can be justifiably claimed that the theocratic ideal which dominated the civilizations of Yucatan and Central America, had a tendency to weaken appreciably as it was taken over by the people of the north. It was still fairly strong among the Zapotecs to the south of the Aztecs, but among the Nahuatlan tribes who had preceded the latter in the valley of Mexico it had already lost much of its hold. North of the valley it disappears entirely except in one area, the southwest of the United States, among the Pueblo Indians, where it is clearly a secondary growth.

But if organization of the church is comparatively uninteresting among the Aztecs and their early kindred, that of the state makes up for it.

The Spanish conquerors of Mexico—Cortez among them —have left us vivid descriptions of the wealth and splendor of Montezuma's realm. But their statements are vague on the actual details of social organization and their unfortunate habit of describing whatever they found in America in terms of the absolute monarchies and feudal system that prevailed in their own country, has badly distorted the true state of affairs. Yet enough is clear for us to obtain a tolerably reliable picture.

As might perhaps have been expected, considering its history, Aztec society was a compromise between the democratic institutions the Aztecs brought with them from their northern home and the aristocratic civilizations with which they came into contact in the valley of Mexico. The compromise they evolved was only partly successful and led to contradictions and inconsistencies that have always sorely puzzled historians. The trend toward monarchy and aristocracy had gone so far that most historians have always described Montezuma as a king. It had indeed gone so far that a term which originally was used as an expression of endearment, had become transformed into one of respect, one that could only be used by a commoner when addressing a noble. The same trend of development is visible in the changes which took place in the nature of land tenure and the authority invested in one of the chiefs of the tribe. In other words what had once been a simple agricultural system became complicated and transformed through the development of numerous restrictions, all tending to chain the land workers to the soil and interfere with his freedom of action and the unquestioned ownership of his crops. He who had once been merely the honored and respected military chief of the tribe was thus gradually elevated to a rank closely approximating to that of a king.

Much in this new order of things was manifestly the result of borrowing, but a good deal is surely to be ascribed to the changes wrought in the Aztec social fabric by their slow conquest of a right to a place in the sun, i.e., to a foothold in an unpromising lagoon, and to their imperialistic ambitions which meant the conquests of alien towns and the disposal of alien lands.

At the head of the Aztec state stood the king, or—to be more precise—the Chief-of-Men. He had to be an earnest and sober person, wise, affable and fluent. To these virtues of peace he was to add those of undaunted bravery and careful circumspection. His dress was distinctive. In the pueblo itself he wore his hair bound up behind the occiput and from his bare head towered a bush of green feathers. On the field of battle, however, he wore a long tress or braid of featherwork which hung down from the occiput to the waist or girdle, a type of feather-dress which we all, of course, recognize, for it is practically identical with that of

House Posts, Comox Tribe

DIORITE HEAD OF HUITZILOPOCHTLI'S SISTER

the Dakota warriors of to-day. Where this originated we know. It came from the region from which all things of cultural significance had come, the Mayas. We see individuals dressed in almost identical manner on the bas-reliefs at Palenque.

The powers possessed by the king in civil matters and over the lives of his fellow Aztecs, were comparatively small. Over the fortunes of conquered peoples and over that of the officials delegated by the Aztecs to keep the conquered people in subjection, it was considerable. As a matter of fact the king's power in military matters was fairly great. Yet it was in the ordering of his household that this power was almost absolute, at least it had become so by the time of Montezuma II. Under this Chief-of-Men, the household took on much the appearance of a monarch's court.

Perhaps nothing can so well reproduce the atmosphere which surrounded the whole person of the Aztec king as two speeches that have been preserved, in one of which he is congratulated by a neighboring and friendly ruler on his accession to the throne, and in the other which he himself is purported to have delivered in order to justify certain changes that had been introduced in the managing of his household. Though the phraseology in both cases is in part European, the speeches themselves are unquestionably authentic.

Let us quote *in extenso* the more or less stereotyped speech that the king of Tezcoco is supposed to have delivered on Montezuma's accession to the throne:

A great honor has been bestowed upon all the people of this realm, O illustrious youth, in having you at our head; we have been wise in selecting you immediately and in giving expression to our joy upon your election. Certainly this is true, for now the

Mexican empire is so large and extensive that to rule a world like this, to lift upon one's shoulders so heavy a burden, requires the firmness and force of just your strong and courageous heart, just your sedateness, knowledge and prudence. And for that reason do I say that the omnipotent god loves this city, for he has given us the light to select just the man that the kingdom needs. For who could doubt but that a lord and prince who before his reign had investigated the nine falsehoods of heaven would not, if he were chosen as ruler, show an equally clear appreciation of earthly affairs in order thus to help the people? Who could believe that the great force you have always shown in matters of importance before you undertook the office now bestowed upon you would ever fail you? Who would for a moment doubt that, possessed of such courage, you would ever fail to give succor to the orphan and the widow? Who would not be persuaded that the Mexican empire had reached the culmination of its glory, seeing that the Lord has concentrated in your hands such power, that by a mere glance at you, one can see how you reflect the glory and the greatness of the empire?

Rejoice then, O happy country, that the lord of creation has given you a prince who will be your mainstay in whatever you strive for, a father and a brother in piety and pity. Rejoice then, again, and with good reason, that you have a king who will not spend his time, at the expense of the state, regaling himself and stretching himself on a bed of vices and pleasures, but one who, that he may sleep the more peacefully, keeps his mind alert and remains awake all night, worrying how he can best serve you; one who hardly feels the taste of the most savory titbit, so absorbed is he in his solicitude for the welfare of his people. Remember, then, that I have good reasons for telling you to be happy and breathe freely, O happy kingdom! And you, most generous youth, our mighty lord, since the creator of all things has given you this office, he who in the past has been so kind to you in every way, do you take courage and do not deny those gifts he has given you in this state. May they be yours for many happy years to come!

The second speech gives us an excellent insight into the

viewpoint of an Aztec nobleman. The somewhat strained rhetoric of the speech is quite in consonance with what we know to have been the ideal toward which every Aztec orator strove.

Montezuma is represented as addressing an old man of his court as follows:

"You undoubtedly know, my father, that I have decided that all those who wait upon me shall be knights and the sons of princes and lords. Not only those that help me in my household, but all those who hold any position of importance throughout my kingdom. Indeed I am considerably perturbed at the thought that the previous kings permitted themselves to be served in such matters by people of low birth. But let me justify my opinions.

"You know very well how different is the manner of life of the nobles and the low-born. If the leaders employ people of low birth, especially if kings do so, such men will undoubtedly cause them great embarrassment; for if the king were to send them to accompany his embassies and delegations, the knight, on such occasions, would speak in a courteous and discreet manner, while the person of low birth would disconcert the latter by his vulgar language, and the world might say that we do not know more than the low-born individual. Again, be it remembered that these country folk, no matter how well they have been brought up, always keep the odor of their rusticity about them. Lastly, it is not right nor becoming that the words of kings and princes, which are like jewels and precious stones, should find lodgment in such ignoble receptacles as the mouths of men of low birth. They should always be placed in receptacles worthy of them, like the persons of lords and princes. These people of low birth would only serve to cast odium upon us, for if you sent them to perform actions requiring a noble and a cultured mind they, with their vulgarity and lack of breeding, would but lower and demean our standards. I command you then to deprive those who are of lowly birth of whatever royal office they may possess. Dismiss, in every case, those who come from soil."

We need not break our heads, then, as to whether the Aztec chief had the powers of a king or not. He certainly was surrounded by royal splendor. Indeed he played a two-fold rôle in the Aztec state, first as the glorified and reverenced symbol of a dearly gained unity and secondly as the great war-chief. In his first capacity he was the supreme aristocrat, in his second the arch democrat. This split in his functions remained permanent and effectively prevented Mexico from ever becoming an absolute monarchy, for his hold upon the imagination of the people depended upon his symbolizing Aztec unity, Aztec power, and Aztec imperialism, and these in turn were dependent upon his success in war. Like the noble captive who impersonated the god Tezcatlipoca he must remain unblemished and untarnished, else he too would fall a victim to the gods and be cast down from his high estate. Such indeed was the fate of the last king after he had been defeated by the Spaniards. His people dethroned him and it is even alleged that he was killed by an arrow discharged by one of his Aztec subjects.

Second in importance to the Chief-of-Men was an official with the strange name of Snake-woman. In contradistinction to the office of the Chief-of-Men, however, that of the Snake-woman symbolized peace. When the king embarked on war the latter had to remain home. All our available evidence seems to indicate that the office of the Snake-woman had at one time been even more important than that of the

Chief-of-Men and this would in fact be more in consonance with the normal Indian type of government, wherein the peace chief was the tribal chief and the military chief only of secondary consequence. From the Mayas of Guatemala to the Sioux and Ojibwa of Minnesota and Wisconsin, this allocation of function remained undisturbed. Only here among the Aztecs do we find a break. Not even so venerable and consistent a tradition as this could withstand the glamour which the dazzling success of Aztec arms had thrown over the eyes of her people.

The city of Mexico was divided into four quarters and scattered through these quarters were to be found twenty well-defined groups, probably representing the greatly transformed reminiscence of what had once been clans. Each one of the quarters had a war-chief with a specific title. These titles were very significant. They were "the man of the house of darts," "the cutter of men," "the blood-shedder," and "the chief of the eagle." All these people seem essentially to have been military attendants and the transmitters of the orders and commands of the two head chiefs. What gives the first three added significance, however, was the fact that they appear to have been preparatory stages for the office of the Chief-of-Men, i.e., the king.

Of the numerous other officials the most important was the chief of the twenty "clans," the "speakers" and the collector of the imposts the vanquished towns had to pay, the so-called "gatherer of the crops." The "speakers" are of particular interest, not only because of the function they served but because they are to be met again repeatedly in many places north of the Rio Grande. Briefly it was their duty to submit claims, etc., to the tribal council and to deliver long harangues in justification of the claims. Other "speakers" presented counterclaims and thus they can properly be regarded as the official lawyers for plaintiff and defendant in any action. Such trials, with officials similarly called "speakers," are to be found as far north as the Indians of northern Michigan and clearly represent one of the numerous bonds that connect even such outpost civilizations as the Ojibwa with the great cultures of the south.

Aztec society fell definitely into three classes, the nobles, the common people and the slaves, and the first two divisions were, in turn, subdivided. Among nobles, again, we must carefully distinguish between the members of the rather extensive family of the king and his immediate *entourage*, and those who were the descendants of individuals who had distinguished themselves in war or who held positions of some kind in the far-flung Aztec empire. These nobles could always be distinguished externally from the common people, by the kind of mantles they wore and the military insignia with which these were decorated.

The common people themselves fell into a number of distinct and special groups. First there were the actual tillers of the soil, then the artisans and finally the traders or merchants. The artisans seemed to have been organized into definite guilds, with a common center of worship and numerous rules governing apprenticeship. The gold and silver-workers appear to have occupied a higher position than the others. Next to them came the pottery-workers, the feather, the turquoise mosaic-workers, the cloth-workers and the painters. A native description of the goldsmith's trade has come down to us and gives us an excellent insight into the technique of those who busied themselves with what the Mexicans called "the offal of the Gods." The description follows:—

1. Here is treated the manner of working of the goldsmiths, who make a mold by means of charcoal and wax, applying to it designs and in this manner fuse gold and silver.

2. They commence their work in the following manner: First the master gives them the charcoal, which they grind very fine.

3. And when it is ground they add a little clay, the glutinous earth which they use in their pottery. They mix the charcoal with clay and stir it, and knead it in such manner that the two substances constitute one solid and compact mass.

4. And when they have the mass prepared, they shape it into thin discs which they expose to the sun, and in the same manner they shape still more discs consisting of clay alone, and they expose them to the sun.

5. For two days these objects dry, so that they become very hard.

6. When the charcoal is well dried and very hard, it is cut, then it is carved by means of a little scraper of copper.

7. That which is cut shall resemble the original and must have life, for whatever may be the object that is intended to be manufactured, the form resulting from it must resemble the original and have life.

8. For example, if they wish to manufacture an ornament for the Huastecans, they pierce the partition of the nasal passages, where an arrow is inserted which goes across the face. Then they have the body tattooed, decorated with figures of a serpent by means of obsidian needle-points. They fashion the charcoal paste in this manner, cut it out and cover it with designs.

9. They are very careful to consider what animal they wish to imitate; how its being and its aspect must be represented.

10. If they wish to imitate a turtle, they fashion its form from the charcoal. They make its shell, in which it can move, from the bottom of which its head protrudes and from which its four feet extend and move about.

11. If they desire to give the shape of a bird, the charcoal is cut and carved with its bird plumes, its wings, its tail and its feet.

12. If they wish to make the figure of a fish, they carve out the charcoal in the form of a fish covered with scales, and they mold its fins, its sides and its forked tail.

13. When they desire to make a crab or a lizard, special attention is given to its legs.

14. Whatever, in fact, may be the animal they wish to imitate, it is carved out of charcoal.

15. They manufacture a gold collar studded with precious stones, provided with bells on the lower edge and decorated with reliefs and with designs of flowers.

16. When the charcoal is prepared, it is provided with designs and carved out, they boil the wax and mix it with white copal, through which it becomes very compact.

17. Then they clarify it by filtration, in order that the impurities of the wax, the dirt and the clay which are mixed with it, may be well washed out.

18. When the wax is prepared, they thin it out on a flat stone, and flatten it by means of a cylinder of wood which they roll over it by hand.

19. They thin it out and flatten it on a very smooth stone.

20. When the wax is very thin, like the web of a spider and is not more thick in any one place, they apply it on the charcoal and they cover the charcoal with wax.

21. And they do not do it carelessly, but on the contrary, they carefully cut a small piece nearly corresponding to the dimensions of the object.

22. They coat over the salient parts and cover the hollows, especially where the charcoal has been carved.

23. The wax is then applied to the charcoal by means of a bit of wood.

24. And when all is done in this manner and the wax is put on all parts of the charcoal, they put pulverized charcoal on the surface of the wax.

25. Then they grind the charcoal-powder well, and spread a rather thick layer on the surface of the wax.

26. When this is prepared they put on it another covering; the shell which encompasses the mold and encloses it all over.

27. The making of the shell is the last of the processes intended to give the gold its form.

28. This shell is also made of charcoal, mixed with clay. The

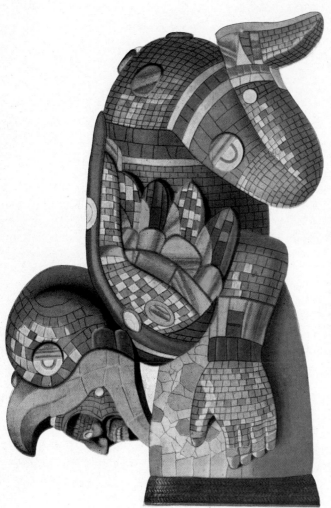

MOSAIC INLAY HANDLE OF AZTEC SACRIFICIAL KNIFE

charcoal, however, is not finely ground, but only roughly crushed.

29. When the mold is enclosed and encompassed by the shell, they let it dry for two more days.

30. Then they put on the spout, which is made of wax also, encompassed by a shell.

31. The latter serves as a drainage canal, by which the melted gold enters.

32. And then finally they place the crucible, which is also made of charcoal and of clay and which is hollow, on the ground.

33. In like manner they set out the mold, with its shell, both made of charcoal.

34. It is there where the gold is melted, in order then to enter the spout, and being conducted by the latter, to flow below and run out.

35. And when it is melted and run into the mold and when, for example, they have manufactured a collar, or one of the various objects mentioned, they polish it by means of a stone.

36. When it is polished, they put it in an alum bath.

37. They grind the alum and soak in it and wash with it the gold jewel which they have cast.

38. They put it a second time in the fire and heat it inside.

39. When it comes out of the fire, they bathe it a second time and smear it with ointment of gold, which is composed of muddy earth mixed with a little salt, by means of which the gold becomes beautiful and very yellow.

40. Thus they rub and polish and make the jewel beautiful, so that it becomes very brilliant, resplendent and radiant.

Important and well-organized as the goldsmiths were their significance fades when compared with that of the merchants known under two characteristic names, "Men who exchange one thing for another" and "Men who take more than they give." The reason for the unusual significance the merchants possessed was really due to certain secondary associations with their trade. In embarking on their distant journeys with the purpose of visiting the marketplaces of other tribes and exchanging their home products for those of other pueblos, a very definite type of group organization was necessary. Such people clearly had to be armed and to have something of the nature of diplomatic attributes. In addition they also had to have carriers to transport their wares and probably a few special warriors to protect them. Such a mercantile enterprise was, thus, like many of its modern prototypes, a war expedition and the merchants brought back with them not only the products of foreign countries but all kinds of miscellaneous information such, for instance, as the strength of the visited pueblos, the easiest mode of attacking them, and everything else that might aid the rapacious imperialistic designs of the Aztec home-land.

The merchant classes, in their turn, had their own stratifications. First there were the merchant princes who dwelt in the aristocratic quarters of the town and who were, to all intents and purposes, equal in rank to the nobles. The nobles naturally resented the position they occupied and jealousies and bickerings were constant between the two. Second in importance were the traders in slaves and lastly, those merchants who visited the lands of the enemy in disguise and who were really spies.

The slaves occupied the lowest position in this extensive social subdivision. But even among the slaves there were grades, the lowest being that of the unfortunate prisoners of war; the next that of persons condemned to slavery for crime and the highest that of children sold into slavery by their parents. These latter could, under certain conditions, be redeemed from slavery, the others never.

No civilization as intricate as this could possibly have been maintained without a well-marked and systematized method of education. It is therefore fortunate that we possess a hieroglyphic record of the whole course of education. This picture tells us exactly what children at the different ages were supposed to do, and even states the amount of food allotted to them. At the age of three, for instance, they were allowed only one-half of a cake of bread for each meal. At four and five the boys are being accustomed to light bodily work, such as carrying small burdens, the girls at this age being instructed in the use of a distaff. The food ration is increased to one cake of bread. At six and seven the boy begins to follow his father to the market-place while the girl begins to spin. The food ration is increased to one and a half cakes of bread and remains so until the age of thirteen. Between thirteen and fifteen the boys are employed in bringing wood from the mountains either by land or in canoes, or in catching fish; the girls spend their time in grinding maize, in cooking and in weaving. At fifteen finally the boys are given two alternatives, either of being delivered to the priests for religious education or being handed over to some instructor for military education.

There were two types of school, those for the common people and those for the nobles. All students were dressed in black and their hair was left uncut. Pupils were under the charge of priests specially delegated for this purpose and the general aim of the education was to instruct the children in those branches most suitable to their future calling and to inculcate religion, good behavior and morals. The main difference between the commoner and the noble was that, whereas the former did the more menial work only, such as sweeping the sanctuary, replenishing the fire in the sacred censers, gathering wood, etc., the latter had in addition to doing all the menial work, to learn literature—mainly heroic lays and sacred hymns—the calendar, writing, the interpretation of hieroglyphs, etc.

The training of girls was limited to the more definite domestic pursuits, keeping the temples clean, spinning, making feather-work, weaving blankets, etc. Particular stress was laid upon teaching them to speak with reverence and to humble themselves in the presence of their elders and to observe, at all times, a modest and bashful demeanor.

Both girls and boys stayed in their schools till they were married and this together with other circumstances connected with their course of instruction, makes it likely that these schools possessed some of the functions of the puberty-fasting lodges found so widely distributed over all North America. In other words we may conceivably be justified in regarding the puberty lodges found among the aborigines of the United States and Canada as representing the last vestige of the elaborate schools of the Aztecs; and the Aztec schools we know were only modifications of the still more elaborate schools of the Mayas.

But let us stop and listen for a moment to hear what an Aztec father taught his child. There we shall find the epitome of all that was high and noble in the outlook of the American Indian, be he a member of the more complicated Aztec and Maya civilizations or a member of the simple and undifferentiated tribes of northern Canada:

Give ear unto me and hearken, O my sons, (says the Mexican parent), because I am your father; and I, though unworthy, am chosen by the gods to rule and govern this city. Thou who are my first-born and the eldest of thy brothers; and thou the second, and thou the third, and thou the last and least—know that I am anxious and concerned, lest some of you should prove worthless in afterlife; lest, peradventure, not one among you should prove worthy to bear my dignities and honors after me. Perhaps it is the will of the gods that the house which I have with so great labor built up, shall fall to the ground and remain a ruin and a dung-hill; that my name shall be no more remembered among men; that after my death no man shall speak well of me. Hear now the words that I shall speak unto you, that you may learn how to be of use in the world, and how to draw near unto the gods that they may show favor to you; for this I say unto you, that those who weep and are grieved; those who sigh, pray and ponder; those who are watchful at night, and wakeful in the morning; those who diligently keep the temples cleanly and in order; those who are reverent and prayerful—all these find favor with the gods; to all such the gods give riches, honor and prosperity, even as they give them to those who are strong in battle.

It is by such deeds the gods know their friends, and to such they give high rank and military distinctions, success in battle, and an honorable place in the hall of justice, making them parents of the sun, that they may give meat and drink not only to the gods of heaven, but also the gods of hell. All such as are thus honored, are revered by all brave men and warriors: all men look on them as their parents, because the gods have shown them favor, and have rendered them fit to hold high offices and dignities and to govern with justice. They are placed near the god of fire, the father of all the gods, whose dwelling is in the water surrounded by turreted walls of flowers, and who is called Ayamictlan and Xiuhtecutli; or they are made lords of the rank of Tlacatecutli or Tlacochtecutli, or they are given some lower post of honor. Perchance they are given some such office as I now hold, not through any merit of my own, but because the gods know not my unworthiness. I am not what I am by my own asking; never did I say, "I wish to be so and so, I desire this or that honor." The gods have done me this honor of their own will, for surely all is theirs, and all that is given comes from their hand; nor shall any one say, "I desire this or that honor," for the gods give as they please and to whom they please, and stand in need of counsel from none.

Hearken, my sons, to another sorrow that afflicts me when I arise at midnight to pray and do penance. Then I ponder many things, and my heart rises and sinks even as one who goes up and down mountains, for I am satisfied with no one of you. Thou, my eldest son, dost not give any sign of improvement. I see in thee nothing manly, thou remainest ever a boy; thy conduct does not become an elder brother. And thou, my second son, and thou, my third, I see in you no discretion or manliness. Peradventure it is because you are second and third that you have become careless. What will become of you in the world? Lo, now, are you not the children of noble parents? Your parents are not tillers of the soil or woodcutters.

What, I say again, will become of you? Do you wish to be nothing but merchants to carry a staff in your hands and a load on your backs? Will you become laborers and work with your hands? Hearken, my sons, and give heed unto my words, and I will point out to you those things which you shall do. See to the proper observance of the dances, and the music, and the singing, for thus will you please both the people and the gods; for with music and singing are favors and riches gained. Endeavor to learn some honorable trade or profession, such as working in feathers or precious metals; for by such means bread can be obtained in time of necessity. Pay attention to every branch of agriculture, for the earth desires not food or drink, but only to bring forth and produce. Your fathers sought to understand these things, for though they were gentlemen and nobles they took care that their estate should be properly cultivated. If you think only of your high rank and are unmindful of these things, how will you support your family? In no part of the world does any one support himself by his gentility only.

But above all study well to provide all those things which are necessary for the sustenance of the body, for these are the very foundation of our being, and rightly are they called *tonacaiutltomio*, that is to say our flesh and bones, because it is by them that we work, live, and are strong. There is no man in the world but what eats, for each one has a stomach and intestines. The greatest lords need food, the most valiant warrior must carry a bag of victuals. By the sustenance of the body life is upheld, by it the world is peopled. See, therefore, my sons, that you be careful to plant maize and maguey, for do we not know that fruit is the delight of children? Truly it cools and quenches the thirst of the little ones. And you, boys, do you not like fruit? But how will you get it if you do not plant and grow it?

Give heed, my sons, to the conclusion of my discourse and let it be written upon your hearts. Many more things could I say, but my task would never be ended. A few more words only will I add that have been handed down to us from our forefathers. Firstly, I counsel you to propitiate the gods, who are invisible and impalpable, giving them your whole soul and body. Look to it that you are not puffed up with pride, that you are neither obstinate nor of a weak, vacillating mind, but take heed to be meek and humble and put your trust in the gods, lest they visit your transgressions upon you, for from them nothing can be hidden. They punish how and whom they please. Secondly, my sons, endeavor to live at peace with your fellowmen. Treat all with deference and respect. If any speak ill of you answer them not again; be kind and affable to all, yet converse not too freely with any; slander no man; be patient, returning good for evil, and the gods will amply avenge your wrongs. Lastly, my children, be not wasteful of your goods nor of your time, for both are precious. At all seasons pray to the gods and take counsel with them; be diligent about those things which are useful.

I have spoken enough; my duty is done. Peradventure you will forget or take no heed of my words. As you will. I have done my duty. Let him profit by my discourse who chooses. . . .

The Aztecs proper were not great artists. The glories customarily associated with them in the valley of Mexico were the work of their predecessors. Even such superficially distinctive Aztec productions as the pottery of the pueblos near Mexico city were not truly Aztec. The center for this pottery lay in Cholula which was an old and sacred city and which merely perpetuated the artistic traditions of the Toltecs. But though the Aztecs were neither original nor even great artists they were skillful enough to keep something of the old tradition in architecture and sculpture, while in certain special branches like mosaic-work they apparently achieved something of unusual distinction. How much gold and silver-work still survived from the great civilizations that had preceded the Aztec and how much they, themselves, still manufactured, can be seen from the description of the loot the Spaniards captured. Rarely has there been such booty. Take, for instance, the partial inventory that was sent to Charles V:

1. A cast of silver weighing twenty-one and a half quintal when it was placed in the melting pot.

2. A round mirror like the sun; another with the head of a lion, all of gold.

3. A large necklace like a gorget of gold.

4. A large disc of gold with a monster of the figure of a man.

5. Two gold flutes.

6. Three rosettes of gold like artichokes; a rosette of gold with six petals and six gold beads.

7. A piece of chalchihuite set in gold and in it a little tree.

8. A turtle of gold set in chalchihuite.

9. A shield of gold with a banneret and three rods fastened on the back.

10. A head of gold with a face of greenstone; a head of greenstone set in gold, with ears of snakes; a head of greenstone set in gold with plumes of gold hanging down.

11. A death's-head of gold.

12. A head of greenstone set in gold, with gold flowers; sixteen heads of monsters, all of gold, differing one from the other.

13. A piece of gold with five hearts and a round green-stone; another long one set in gold.

14. Five butterflies, three of gold and stone.

15. Eight spindles with their whorls and a spinner which carries a spinner, all of gold.

16. Nine gold spoons.

17. Three gold tigers.

18. Six lip-ornaments of gold; lip-ornaments of amber adorned with gold.

19. A lizard of gold with little chain of gold.

In another inventory we find among other things the following:

1. A large shield with some moons of stone, mosaic work and much gold.

2. A shield of the image of a man in gold whose breasts have been cut open for sacrifice, a gush of blood emanating from these sacrificial cuts; some scalloped shells of silver.

3. A golden hat.

4. An eagle of gold.

In all the manifestations of culture that we have so far been discussing the Aztecs were found to be either borrowers or compromisers. In one respect only were they great and original, as colonizers and empire builders. For the genius they here displayed there is no parallel in the history of aboriginal North America. After they had once secured a footing in the inhospitable lagoons of Mexico, town after town succumbed to their attacks and by the time the Spaniards arrived, they had humbled kingdom after kingdom and their empire stretched from the valley of Mexico to the Isthmus of Tehuantepec, and from sea to sea. From being in vassalage to a neighboring chief they developed into the most cruel and obdurate of all tyrants, exacting tributes of all kinds from far and near.

From the towns of the Pacific coast there came tributes of cotton garments, four thousand bundles of fine feathers, two hundred sacks of cocoa, forty tiger skins and one hundred and sixty birds of different species. From the Zapotecs in the south, came forty pieces of gold of a specified size and twenty sacks of cochineal. From the towns of the Gulf of Mexico they received cocoa, gold, twenty-four thousand bundles of exquisite feathers of various colors, six necklaces, two of the finest emeralds and four of commoner description, twenty earrings of amber set in gold, a hundred pots of liquid amber and sixteen thousand loads of Indian rubber. From the far south came likewise six hundred measures of honey, forty large jars of ochre for paint, one hundred and sixty copper shields, forty round plates of gold of fixed dimensions, ten small measures of fine turquoise and one load of smaller turquoise. Other conquered towns paid their tributes in building material, in reeds, in stones, etc., while still others furnished various articles for the king's household. The poorer people paid their tributes in the form of snakes, scorpions and other obnoxious creatures, even in lice.

The remarkable thing about this far-flung empire was the fact that it had developed from nothing to its apogee in two hundred years. The instrument by which it achieved this greatness was the warrior, and we cannot more fittingly close this chapter than by describing what war meant to the Aztec.

Valor, success on the warpath, this was the highest of all earthly honors, inculcated from earliest childhood by parent and priest. Their wars were almost in the nature of religious crusades. Even the king could not receive his crown until he had embarked on a war expedition and taken ample prisoners to be sacrificed at the feast given in honor of his coronation.

When a boy of fifteen had returned from his first war exploit bringing with him a prisoner he had captured with the aid of others, the father would turn on him almost brutally and say, "My child, the sun and the earth have washed and renewed thy faith because thou didst dare to attempt the capture of an enemy in company with others. Lo, now it were better to abandon thee to the mercies of the enemy than thou should again take a prisoner with the aid of others because, should it so happen, they will place another tuft over thine other ear and thou wilt appear like a girl. Truly it were better thou shouldst die than that this shouldst happen to thee."

Thus spurred on the youth naturally would not rest until he had successfully gained all the honors that were attainable. If he took as many as three prisoners he was entitled to command over others; the capture of four prisoners made him a captain and he had the privilege of wearing long lip-ornaments, leather-earrings, and gaudy tassels. Five prisoners elevated him to the rank of an "eagle who guides" and he could wear a head plume with silver threads and specially decorated mantles. And so we see him in the picture-writings, first carrying the *impedimenta* of the chief priest as he goes into the field to embolden the warriors and to enforce orders. Then we see the devices on the shield, the manner of body painting, the armor, the headdresses and the various ornaments warriors were permitted to wear according to the number of captives each had taken.

Three, possibly more, distinctive military societies existed and entrance into them was open to practically all warriors. The first military order was named Princes, the second,

Eagles, and the third, Tigers. The members of the first were distinguished by having their hair tied on the crown of their head with a red thong and worked into as many braids as the deeds of valor performed by the wearer. The Eagles on the other hand wore a kind of costume in the form of an eagle's head, and the Tigers wore a particular kind of armor spotted like the skin of the animal whose name they bore.

The Aztec warriors must then have presented a magnificent sight as they marched into battle, encased in their armor and with their decorated shields and gorgeous war costumes. There one could see headdresses made of the rich feathers of the *quetzal* bird, corselettes of green feathers worked with gold thread, helmets of silver set in gold bands, the *tocivitl,* a garment reaching to the knees made of yellow macaw feathers embroidered with gold and crowned by a golden cast plumed with *quetzal* feathers.

As soon as war was declared spies were immediately sent forward to reconnoiter and to investigate the nature of the land to be attacked as well as the apparent resources of the enemy. Then after the proper religious rites had been performed, everything was put in readiness for the march. The priests with their idols started a day in advance and the others followed. Perfect order was maintained *en route.* When near the enemy's country the chiefs traced out the camping ground each military division was to occupy. Before the battle commenced the chief addressed the troops telling them of the honor that would fall to all those who emerged victorious and counseling them to place their trust in the great god Huitzilopochtli.

In the fighting itself no special tactics were observed. A number of men were always kept in reserve to replace the wounded or exhausted. The archers, the slingers, and javelin-throwers would begin their actions at a distance and then gradually creep nearer until they came to close quarters with the enemy where they used their swords and spears. Sometimes their retreat was feigned in order to draw the enemy into a previously prepared ambuscade. The main object of course was not to slay the enemy but to capture him alive.

Such was the army upon which the greatness of the Aztec empire rested. Specialized and well-organized as it was, however, it did not essentially differ from the great tribal war and hunting expeditions that form so integral a part of the life of most of the Indians north of the Rio Grande. Detail upon detail of the warrior's ideal, of his war customs and war costumes, we shall find again among the tribes of the United States especially in the Plains. But the inner cohesion was gone and the terrible and relentless purpose for which this machine had been forged, the subjugation of other peoples and the obtaining of suitable sacrifices to be offered to the great god of war, Huitzilopochtli, this fortunately was lost. One gory custom still persisted, the cutting out of the heart of the enemy. This attenuated remembrance of the Aztec sacrifice to Huitzilopochtli survived among not a few tribes as far north as Canada.

And so we behold the Mayan splendor shine with a fainter and utterly transformed luster. Everything has suffered some sea-change. Art has lost its originality, the primary function of the hieroglyphics is gone and they have degenerated into a puerile rebus utterly inadequate for indicating dates with any precision—the culture-heritage has become more and more attenuated. But be this as it may, the compromise civilization of the Aztecs was still so complex, economically, socially and artistically, that everything north of it seems mean in comparison. Then, too, be it remembered, Aztec culture has more than a specific significance for us, for it preserved many a trait and ceremony, many a thought and ideal that unquestionably belonged to the Mayas but which through lack of information we are no longer able to discover there. We must, therefore, after allowing for inevitable distortions and transformations, think of the Aztec as a generalized Maya civilization, and if we encounter startling resemblances between the Aztecs and the aborigines of the United States, these must not be attributed to any direct influence exerted by the Aztecs but to the fact that these people, too, have preserved some reminiscence of all those multiple cultural impulses that at different times radiated from Guatemala and Yucatan.

From now on we shall see the heritage disintegrate more and more, lose form and texture and whatever cohesion it still possessed. The prehistoric pueblos of northern Mexico and the southwest of the United States still retained the formal structure and they may conceivably have possessed some of the ancient spirit that had animated the golden past. But among the modern pueblos of the southwest only the bare shell is left. The constituent elements that once filled this mold are, it is true, still to be felt in the atmosphere but each one has become an entity in itself and entered into new combinations. Everywhere in the United States thereafter we shall instinctively feel and possibly even at times detect these old elements, flying around hither and thither, utterly divorced from their original matrix and uniting eclectically with anything that happens to come along.

CHAPTER IV

THE CHILDREN OF THE SUN: THE ANCIENT PERUVIANS

On Sunday, June the twenty-sixth, 1541, the little town of Lima was rife with rumors of conspiracy and impending disaster. The civil wars that were to afflict Peru for many years to come, had but lately broken out and jealousies, hatreds, and a spirit of revenge for real and fancied wrongs were rampant among the Spanish conquerors. Francisco Pizarro, the conqueror of the Incas, had ample cause for expecting just retribution at the hands of his enemies, but he disdained to entertain even the shadow of a fear. Surrounded by a party of friends he sat at his dinner and was much annoyed at what he took to be unnecessary noise in the courtyard. Only when the servant rushed in to announce that a company of Spaniards had broken into the building shouting, "Long live the King! Death to the tyrant!" did he realize how serious was the nature of the tumult outside. Hastily buckling on his armor he prepared to defend himself. The combat was of but short duration. While grappling with one opponent he received a wound in the throat and as he sank to the floor the conspirators plunged a sword into his body. "Jesu," he exclaimed, as he traced a cross with his finger on the bloody floor and bent down to kiss it.

Thus ended the career of one of the worst hoodlums in history. He had spent his life in a search for gold and for power. Both he had enjoyed, but in attaining them he had disorganized and destroyed one of the most interesting experiments in civilization, the fascinating culture of the Children of the Sun, the Incas of Peru.

Of the difficulties which that experiment in government had had to surmount only those can properly judge who have traversed Peru. Uninhabitable deserts alternate with almost equally uninhabitable mountain plateaus. Any attempt to build up a unified government had to make allowance for the limitations imposed by the natural configuration of the country. To add to these obstacles there was, in addition, a heterogeneous population with peoples in all stages of cultural advancement, from the highly cultured descendants of the older civilizations which the Incas themselves had only partially assimilated, to the crude and wild tribes who swarmed in the east. Little wonder then that the old soldier Cieza de Leon insisted that "in this land of Peru there are three desert ranges where men can nowise exist. One of these comprises the forests of the Andes, full of dense wildernesses, where men cannot live nor ever have lived. The second is the mountainous region extending the whole length of the Cordillera of the Andes which is intensely cold and whose summits are covered with eternal snow, so that in no way can people live in this region. The third comprises the sandy deserts in which there is nothing to be seen but sand hills and the fierce sun which dries them up."

Alternating with these deserts there were thickly populated sections. The ravines and dales of the Andes repeatedly open out into deep valleys so closed in that the cold winds do not disturb them unduly. Such valleys were exceedingly fertile and the villagers living there sturdy and healthy. But let us again follow Cieza. "Wherever there are groves of trees the land is free from sand and very fertile and abundant. In ancient times these valleys were very populous and to-day there are still Indians living there although not as many as in former days. As it never rains they do not roof their houses as is the custom in the mountains but build large houses of adobe, with pleasant terraced roofs of matting to shade them from the sun. To prepare their fields for sowing they lead channels from the rivers to irrigate the valleys and the channels are made so well and with so much regularity that all the land is irrigated without any waste. This system of irrigation makes the valleys very green and cheerful. At all times they raise good harvests of maize and whatever else they sow. Thus although I have described Peru as being formed of three desert ridges yet from them, by the will of God, there descend valleys and rivers without which no man can live. And this is the reason why the natives were so easily conquered, for if they rebelled they would all perish of cold and hunger."

But though all will agree that they could easily be conquered both by natives as well as by the White invaders, the conditions so vividly described by Cieza militated even more strongly against any attempt at centralization. And yet it was just this centralization that the Children of the Sun actually achieved.

Children of the Sun, the rulers of aboriginal Peru, had been from time immemorial. The culture Pizarro encountered was, however, like that of the Aztecs built upon the ruins of a preceding civilization and the most precious of all the heritages which it had received, had just been this assumption that the creator Sun-god ruled supreme, creator and vivifier of all things, and that the king was his incarnation on earth. The earlier people called him Pachacamac, the Incas called him Uiracocha, and to him they intoned a glorious hymn:

O Uiracocha! lord of the universe,
Whether thou art male
Whether thou art female;
Lord of reproduction
Whatsoever thou may be.
O lord of divination,
Where art thou?
Thou mayest be above,
Thou mayest be below,
Or perhaps around
Thy splendid throne and scepter.
O, hear me!
From the sky above,
In which thou mayest be;
From the sea beneath,
In which thou mayest be;
Creator of the world,
Maker of all men;
Lord of all lords,
My eyes fail me,
For longing to see thee,
For the sole desire to know thee.
Might I behold thee,
Might I know thee,
Might I consider thee,
Might I understand thee!
O look down upon me,
For thou knowest me.
The sun—the moon—
The day—the night—
Spring—winter,
Are not ordained in vain
By thee,
O Uiracocha!

> They all arrive
> At their destined ends,
> Whithersoever thou pleasest.
> The royal scepter
> Thou holdest.
> O hear me!
> O choose me!
> Let it not be
> That I should tire,
> That I should die.

And so it came to pass that the most renowned of all Peruvian temples was that at Cuzco erected to the sun-god. So enriched had it become at the hands of successive sovereigns that the Incas themselves called it "The place of gold." Sarmiento, one of our most trustworthy early sources and the person who had seen it in all its pristine splendor, claimed that there were but two edifices in Spain that could vie with it in workmanship. Its interior was even more magnificent. On the western wall was pictured Uiracocha himself, with a human countenance looking forth from amidst innumerable rays of light extending in all directions.

The Spanish chroniclers took delight in describing it and Prescott has rendered it into dignified English prose. "The figure of Uiracocha was engraved on a massive plate of gold of enormous dimensions thickly powdered with emeralds and precious stones. It was so situated in front of the great eastern portal that the rays of the morning sun fell directly upon it at its rising, lighting up the whole apartment with an effulgence that seemed more than natural and which was reflected back from the golden ornaments with which the walls and ceiling were everywhere encrusted. Gold, 'the tears wept by the Sun,' as the Peruvians called it, was everywhere and every part of the interior of the temple glowed with burnished plates and studs of precious metal. The cornices which surrounded the walls of the sanctuary were of the same costly material and a broad belt or frieze of gold, led into the stone-work, encompassed the whole exterior of the edifice."

The worship of the sun had so entered into the very marrow of their life that the Incas ascribed to it all that was beautiful and useful in the world, and whenever in their rapacious imperialistic enterprises, the Incas stopped to justify the tyrannical impositions they forced upon the conquered peoples, it was on the basis of their being the Children of the Sun, who had come with a new dispensation for mankind. Garcilasso de la Vega who himself belonged to the royal line has left us the Inca *credo:*

"Know," a kinsman once told him, "that in ancient times all this region was covered with forests and thickets and the people lived like brute beasts without religion nor government, nor towns, nor houses; without cultivating the land nor covering their bodies, for they knew how to weave neither cotton nor wool to make garments. . . . Our father, the Sun, seeing the human race in this poor condition, had compassion upon them and from heaven sent down to earth a son and a daughter to instruct them, so that they might adopt them as their god; and also to give them precepts and laws by which to live as reasonable and civilized men, as well as to teach them to dwell in houses and towns, to cultivate maize and other crops, to breed flocks and to use the fruits of the earth as rational beings do, instead of existing like beasts. With these commands and attentions our father, the Sun, placed his two children in the lake of Titicaca saying to them that they might go where they pleased and that at every place that they stopped in order to eat or sleep, they were to thrust into the ground a scepter of gold which was half a yard long and two fingers in thickness. This staff he gave them as a sign and a token that in the place where, by one blow on the earth it should sink down and disappear, it was the desire of our father, the Sun they should remain and establish their court. Finally he said to them: 'When you have reduced these people to our service, you shall maintain them in habits of reason and justice by the practice of piety, clemency and meekness, assuming in all things the office of a pious father toward his beloved and tender children. For thus you will form a likeness and a reflection of me. I do good to the whole world, giving light that men may see and do their business, making them warm when they are cold, cherishing their pastures and crops, brightening their fruits and increasing their flocks, watering their land with dew and bringing fine weather and proper season. I take care to go around the earth each day that I may see what is necessary in the world and act as sustainer and benefactor. I desire that you shall imitate this example as I have sent you, my children, to the earth solely for instruction and benefit of those men who live like beasts. And from this time I constitute and name you as kings and lords over all the tribes, so that you may instruct them in rational works and government.' "

And what was the nature of the government for which this suspiciously modern justification was advanced? It was the most remarkable theocratic socialistic state of which we have any record outside of ancient Egypt. The Incas, unlike the Aztecs, not only succeeded in conquering the alien peoples but they went further—they deprived them of all independence, broke their spirit, and incorporated them completely into the new state. This the Aztecs, for instance, were able to do in the case of only one town and then only a short time before the conquest.

At the head of the state stood the divine ruler who bore the title of the Only Inca. He was placed at an immeasurable distance above his subjects. But while formally this government was a pure despotism there seems to be no reason for believing that the Inca possessed the arbitrary power which we are accustomed to associate with European and Asiatic despots. Being at the same time both civil, religious and military head of the state and with a divine lineage, his power seemed unlimited and all authority to be completely centralized in his hands. The early chroniclers in fact claimed that he raised armies and often commanded them in person, imposed taxes, made laws, appointed the judges who executed them, that he was, in short, the source from which all power and emolument flowed.

His dress and his court were in consonance with his divine claim.

The only manner, for example, by which the Inca could communicate with his people was by means of state progresses through the kingdom.

When the Incas visited the provinces of their empire in time of peace, they traveled in great majesty, seated in rich litters fitted with loose poles of excellent wood, long and covered with gold and silver-work. Over the litter there were two high arches of gold set with precious stones, and long mantles fell around all sides of the litter so as to cover it completely. If the Inca did not wish to be seen, the mantles remained down, but they were raised when he got in or came out. In order that he might see the road, and have fresh air, holes were made in the curtains. The mantles and curtains were covered with rich ornamentation. On some were embroidered the sun and the moon, on others great curving serpents and what appeared to be sticks passing across them. These were borne as insignia or arms. The litters were raised on the shoulders of the greatest and most important lords of the kingdom, and he who was employed most frequently on this duty, was held to be most honored and in highest favor.

Around the litter marched the king's guard with the archers and halberdiers, and in front went five thousand slingers, while in the rear there were lancers with their captains. On the flanks of the road, and on the road itself, there were faithful runners who kept a lookout and announced the approach of the lord. So many people came out to see him pass, that the hillsides were covered and they all blessed their sovereign, raising a great cry and shouting their accustomed saying: "Very great and powerful lord, son of the Sun, thou only art Lord! All the world in truth hears thee." Besides this, so adds the chronicler, they said other things in a loud voice and went little short of worshiping the Inca as a god.

Along the whole road Indians went in front, cleaning it in such a way that neither weed nor loose stone could be seen and that all was smooth and clean. The Inca traveled as far as he chose each day, generally about four leagues. He stopped at certain places where he could examine into the state of the country; hearing cheerfully those who came with complaints, punishing those who had been unjust, and doing justice to those who had suffered. . .

So insistent was the feeling that the sovereign was raised far above every one—nobleman or commoner—that he was compelled to marry into his immediate family, his official wife always being his half-sister.

Yet despite external appearances to the contrary the power of the Inca was not absolute. Like most true bureaucracies the state was governed by its officials and in virtue of the well-organized and skillfully adjusted hierarchy of departments. What gave the sovereign his extensive influence and power was the fact that all the important officers in the realm, particularly all the high positions in the church, were in the hands of his immediate family over whom he naturally exercised considerable control. He did not, as some maintained, appoint them to these positions however. These positions were their prerogatives.

Though theoretically the sovereign was at the head of the church, his powers were always delegated to specially selected individuals. The high priest was generally his own brother and an individual second only in dignity to the Inca. He in turn filled all the subordinate positions under him. Since the chief priests of all the temples had likewise to belong to the royal family, it is evident that in all ultimate matters pertaining to ritual and religion, the sovereign and his immediate family ruled supreme. The power of the priests, however, was greatly circumscribed and narrow in its scope. It was confined entirely to matters connected with ritual. The control of the church, therefore, gave the royal family little political power, however important it may have been in adding to its prestige and to the reverence in which it was held.

Inca society was based on a rigorous and clear-cut caste system consisting of nobles and commoners between whom marriage was prohibited. The nobles fell into two very distinct subdivisions, the members of the royal family and the deposed chiefs of conquered nations with all their descendants. The extreme centralization which was one of the astounding and marvelous features of Inca government, was due to the fortunate circumstances that all positions of importance, the command of the armies, of distant garrisons and the control over the provinces, were bestowed upon members of the royal family and that wherever possible they were required to live at the court.

To the nobles of the second class only minor posts were assigned. Their authority was local and confined to the districts in which they and their ancestors had been raised,

WOODEN CUPS FROM CUZCO

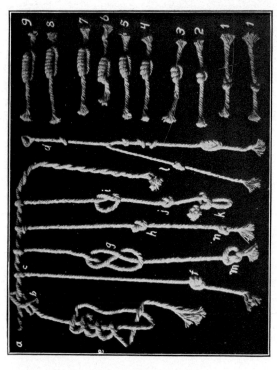

QUIPU AND METHOD OF TYING KNOTS

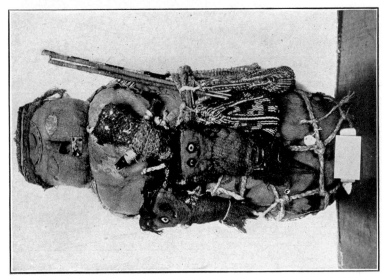

PERUVIAN MUMMY

a very wise arrangement, indeed, for in this way whatever local autonomy the central government permitted, was in the hands of those who knew most about it and whose authority and decisions would be most acceptable to the conquered peoples. To keep their hold even on these minor officials they were from time to time required to visit the capital.

For purposes of administration an old fourfold division of the tribe was utilized. The whole kingdom was divided into four provinces just as was the city of Cuzco, and four main roads radiated from the capital of the whole kingdom to the capital of each of the four provinces. Over each province ruled a governor who belonged to the immediate household of the sovereign. These provinces were further subdivided into four sections, each having a population of ten thousand and over whom presided a sub-governor, also taken from the nobility. Finally there was a still more minute subdivision of the people into population units of one thousand, five hundred, one hundred, and fifty, respectively, with a graded hierarchy of officials presiding over them. Assuredly bureaucracy would go no further.

In the division of the land the Incas exhibited the same genius for organization. The whole kingdom was divided into three parts, the revenues of the first going to defray the expenses of the very costly ritual of the Sun and its enormous officialdom, those of the second to the maintenance of the royal family, i.e., the whole caste of the nobility, and those of the third being used for the people. The land assigned to the people was broken up into small allotments, its size dependent upon the needs of each individual family. Every Peruvian had to marry at a prescribed age and he was at marriage provided with a dwelling and a piece of land sufficient for his own maintenance and that of his wife. As children were born to him the land allotment was increased, the amount for a son being double that for a daughter. In order to carry out such a regulation efficiently a redistribution of the soil was made every year and a tenant's possessions were increased or diminished according to the size of his family.

The land itself was of course cultivated wholly by the people and the soil was tilled in a definitely prescribed rotation; for example, that belonging to the Sun, in other words, to the church, coming first; that belonging to the old, the sick, widows, orphans, and soldiers engaged in actual service coming second; that belonging to the individual tenant third; and that belonging to the Incas last.

Similar regulations prevailed in all the other industries in the empire, such as the taking care of the flocks of llamas, the manufacture of cloth, the working of the mines, the execution of the great public works, etc. The care and breeding of the flocks of llamas, for instance, was attended to with the greatest minuteness. Those in charge of these flocks lived a life of considerably greater freedom than that which prevailed in the more temperate parts of the variegated Inca empire. One of the earliest Spanish chroniclers has left us an excellent description of many of the details connected with this matter.

"With regard to the flocks," writes Ondegardo, "they made many rules, some of which were so conducive to their preservation that it would be well if they were still observed. It may be said that in a great part of the kingdom, the people are maintained by the flocks. They flourish in the coldest regions, and there also the Indians are settled, as in all parts of the Collao, and on the sides towards Arequipa and the coast, as well as throughout *Carancas, Aullagas, Quilluas* and *Collahuas.* All those districts, if it were not for the flocks, might be looked upon as uninhabitable; for though they yield various crops it is a usual thing for three out of five years to be without harvests, and there is no other kind of produce. But, by reason of the flocks, they are richer and can dress better than those who live in fertile districts. They are very healthy, and their villages are more populous than those in the warm lands, and the latter are even more frequently without their own products than those who possess flocks. The flocks are sent down with wool, and return laden with maize."

After the llamas were sheared, the wool was deposited in public magazines and then distributed to each family according to his wants. The spinning and the weaving now began. Both the quantity and quality of the fabric manufactured, was determined upon at the capital and the work was then apportioned among the different provinces. As it was quite important to see that all the multifarious details connected with the manufacture of the different articles were entrusted to the most competent hands, special officers were appointed to superintend all operations. These officials entered the various households to see that each family employed the materials furnished for its own use in the manner that was intended, so that no one should be unprovided with the necessary apparel.

To carry out carefully supervised undertakings of this kind, wherein each individual had a prescribed place and prescribed work to perform, exact statistics of population were necessary and these were obtained by keeping a register of all the births and deaths throughout the country. A general survey of the country was likewise made, in order to gain a correct idea of the character of the soil, its fertility and the nature of its product. Only thus could the central government be in a position to determine the amount of requisitions so that the work could be apportioned among the respective provinces best qualified to execute it.

The records were kept by means of the famous *quipus*, that strange system of cords and knots that so astonished the early Spanish chroniclers. In a *quipu* there is always a main cord from which branch-cords hang down like a fringe. These branch-cords are so fastened as to form groups which generally contain an equal number of cords in each group. To the main cords are frequently attached subsidiary cords and from the latter, in turn, still others are suspended. Knots appear only on the branch- and subsidiary-cords. There are many kinds, the main ones being respectively the overhand knot, the knot formed by passing the cord, two, three, four, five or more times through the loop of the overhand knot, the long knots, and the "Flemish" knot. These knots all had definite numerical values depending upon the type of knot and upon its position. The "Flemish" knot is used for the number one, ten, and one hundred, the long knots for ten or one hundred, and the overhand knot for ten, one hundred, one thousand and ten thousand. In one of those *quipus* described the knots in the lowest row were used to express units, in the next tens, in the next hundreds, and in the next thousands. Often the cords were of different colors.

It has generally been assumed that the *quipus* were used only for ordinary counting but recently a well-known scholar has insisted that a certain amount of evidence exists tending to show that they may also have been used for certain calendrical purposes, such as determining the solar year, the time of the synodic revolutions of the planet Venus, just as among the Mayas, and possibly even for calculating the time of the synodic revolution of the planet Mercury.

Ondegardo, the remarkably able Spanish lawyer to whom we are indebted for much of our information on the social organization of the Incas, states that nothing was left to chance. The task of apportioning the labor, for instance, was assigned to the local authorities and great care was taken that it should be done in such a manner that while the most competent hands were selected, no labor should fall disproportionately on any particular individual.

Not a detail was neglected. Every person had to work to the best of his ability at the thing he could do most efficiently. Most Peruvians of the lower class were husbandmen but those whose work was of such a kind that they could not be expected to till the soil at the same time, miners, mechanics and artisans, for instance, were exempted.

But if every one had to work no one, on the other hand, was overworked. No one was required to give more than a stipulated portion of his time to the public service. His place was then taken by another. Nor did any one have to worry about this public service interfering with his ordinary pursuits or the welfare of his family. Just as those engaged in public undertakings were maintained at the state's expense so were their families.

Like the Roman, the Inca empire was held together by good roads, good aqueducts, good bridges and advantageously placed fortresses. Nothing impressed the Spanish conquerors more than the Inca public roads. The most famous and the one that must have presented the greatest difficulties in its construction was that which extended from Quito to Cuzco and from Cuzco to Chile. We know from a vivid description of this great highway given by the Spanish viceroy what these roads were like.

From the time of the Inca Uiracocha's reign, there were built, every half-league, small houses well roofed with wood and straw. Among the mountains they were constructed against the rocks. The roads were lined with these small houses at regular intervals. The Incas ordered that in each house there should be two Indians with provisions, stationed there by the neighboring villages. They were not permanently to be left there, but were relieved by others from time to time. The system of government was so efficient that it was only necessary to give the order to be certain that these men would always be at their designated stations.

Each province took charge of the posts within its boundaries, including those which were on the coast deserts or in the region of the snow. When it was necessary to give notice to the rulers in Cuzco, or in any other part, of any event that had taken place or which was connected with their service, the men at the posts set out from Quito or Tomebamba, or from Chile or Caranqui, or from whatever other part of the empire, whether along the coast or in the mountains and they ran with great speed, without stopping, each one covering over a half a league, for the Indians who were stationed at the posts were chosen from among the most active and swiftest of all their countrymen. When one approached the next post he would call out to the men who were in it and say: "Start at once and go to the next post with the news that such and such has happened." And thus news was relayed to the Inca or the governor of a province. When the other runner heard what was shouted at him, he started with the utmost speed, while the runner who arrived went into the house to rest, and to eat and drink of what was always kept in store there.

So well was this running performed, that in a short time people at distances of 300, 500, and even 800 leagues knew what had passed or what was needed or required.

One of these roads passed over the grand plateau, and the other along the lowlands on the borders of the ocean. The former, from the character of the country, was much the more difficult achievement. It was conducted over pathless sierras buried in snow; galleries had to be cut for leagues through the living rock; rivers to be crossed by means of bridges that swung suspended in the air; precipices to be scaled by stairways hewn out of the native bed; ravines of portentous depth to be filled up with solid masonry; in short, all the difficulties that beset a wild and mountainous region and which might appal the most courageous engineer of modern times were encountered and successfully overcome. The length of the road, of which scattered fragments only remain, is variously estimated from fifteen hundred to two thousand miles, and stone pillars, in the manner of European milestones, were erected at stated intervals of somewhat more than a league, all along the route. Its breadth scarcely exceeded twenty feet. It was built of heavy flags of freestone, and in some parts, at least, covered with a bituminous cement, which time has made harder than the stone itself.

The other great road lay through the level country between the Andes and the ocean. It was constructed in a different manner, as demanded by the nature of the ground, which was for the most part low, and in large part sandy. The causeway was raised on a high embankment of earth, and defended on either side by a parapet or wall of clay;

and trees and odoriferous shrubs were planted along the margin in order to regale the sense of the traveler with their perfumes, and refresh him by their shades. In the strips of sandy waste which occasionally intervened, where the light and volatile soil was incapable of sustaining a road, huge piles were driven into the ground, to indicate the route to the traveler.

All along these highways, inns, or *tambos*, as they were called, were erected, at the distance of ten or twelve miles from each other, for the accommodation, more particularly, of the Inca and his suite, and those who journeyed on the public business. There were, in fact, few other travelers in Peru. Some of these buildings were on an extensive scale, consisting of a fortress, barracks, and other military works, surrounded by a parapet of stone, and covering a large tract of ground. These were evidently destined for the accommodation of the imperial armies, when on their march across the country. The care of the great roads was committed to the districts through which they passed, and a large number of hands was constantly employed to keep them in repair. This was the more easily done in a country where the mode of traveling was altogether on foot.

The suspension bridges were often extraordinarily audacious. They were made of the tough fibers of the maguey or of osier. The osiers were then woven into cables of the thickness of a man's body and stretched across the water, being conducted through rings or holes cut in buttresses of stone raised on the opposite banks of the river and there bound securely to heavy pieces of timber. A number of these enormous cables bound together formed a bridge which, covered with planks, well secured and defended by a railing of osier afforded a safe passage for a traveler. . . .

Over such roads and bridges the Peruvians traveled incessantly and transported material of all kinds, and it was over the fairly well-preserved remnants of these ancient roads that a modern explorer suddenly came upon the ruins of a most magnificent fortress-city, Machu Picchu. We shall let the explorer, Dr. Bingham, himself tell us of the approach to the great ruins:

"Leaving the ancient fortress Ollantaytambo and continuing on down the valley over a newly constructed government trail we found ourselves in a wonderful canyon. . . . Not only did it have snow-capped peaks, great granite precipices and a dense tropical jungle: it had also many reminders of the architectural achievements of a bygone race. Wherever the encroaching precipices permitted it the land between the retaining walls and the river was terraced. With painstaking care the ancient inhabitants rescued every available strip of arable land from the river. . . . On a precipitous and well-nigh impregnable cliff, walls of stones carefully fitted together had been placed in the weak spots so that the defenders of the valley, standing on top of the cliff, might shower rocks on an attacking force without any danger of their enemies being able to scale the cliff.

"The road following in large part an ancient footpath, is sometimes cut out at the side of sheer precipices and at others obliged to run on frail brackets propped against the side of overhanging cliffs. . . . We had a hard climb first through the jungles and later up a very stiff, almost precipitous slope. Apart from a hut in the vicinity and a few stone-faced terraces, there seemed to be little in the way of ruin. . . . But after we had rested a while we finally went on to the top of the ridge."

Then when the party had about given up all hope they suddenly found themselves in the midst of a tropical forest, and beneath the shades of the trees they could make out a maze of ancient walls and the ruins of buildings made of blocks of granite, some fitted together in the most refined style of Inca architecture. They had found Machu Picchu, a veritable city in the clouds.

What significance did this most inaccessible of cities have? Essentially it was a refuge-place, impregnable and invulnerable from every point of view. Yet it may also have had a far more romantic past. It may have been the cradle of the Inca empire, for according to an old Inca tradition that cradle was to be sought in one of the most inaccessible canyons of the Andes at a place called "The Abode of Windows." Now windows were found to be one of the distinctive features of Machu Picchu architecture. Is not Machu Picchu then simply another name for the sacred Abode of Windows? It would be futile to attempt to solve that riddle now, but certain it is that the architecture found there is clearly Incan although containing many traits that are different from the Incan style at Cuzco and other typical sites. Surely, however, the Incas must have passed through here before their great empire had been forged, possibly at a time when even they could little have dreamt how great and distinctive was to be their achievement. . . .

Such in broad outlines were the main features of Inca polity. To complete the picture it is only necessary to describe the manner in which, after the reduction of an enemy, his country was incorporated into the empire of the conqueror. The first step was a religious one. The worship of the sun was introduced and temples which would take care of the numerous priesthood were erected. It was the duty of the priests to expound the new faith to the conquered people. The second step was also a religious one. The images of the gods of the conquered were removed to Cuzco and placed in temples where they could be worshiped by everybody as inferior deities. Then the census of the people and an economic survey of the country was taken. The land was divided according to certain principles well recognized throughout the whole kingdom. Whatever changes were introduced were always of such a nature that the estates remained in the hands of their former proprietors. On the whole the ancient customs and laws of the conquered people were left intact.

In the case of the common people of a conquered country, a far more obnoxious system of assimilation was adopted, particularly where there was the least suspicion of disaffection. Thousands would be transported to some distant quarter of the kingdom where they were complete strangers and where mutual jealousies and hatreds would effectually check mutiny or rebellion. These conquered colonists played a great rôle in the Inca society. There were three classes of them. The first was employed in agriculture and industry and had more particularly to take care of the flocks belonging to the Inca and the Sun, as agriculturists, as cloth-spinners, as silversmiths, sculptors, idol-makers, quarrymen, and laborers. The second class was used in the various garrisons scattered throughout the kingdom. The third class were the colonists, and due care was taken to select them properly and not to impose upon them unnecessary burdens. They were always settled in valleys that seemed fertile and which had previously been uninhabited. The rulers were careful that the individual colonists selected from among the conquered population were always settled in climates similar to their own. The new land would be divided among these new settlers and flocks and provisions given them until such time as they would be in a position to reap their own harvests. Finally, to make their lot as light as possible, no tributes were exacted of them for a stated number of years.

As a last measure, in order to take no chances that their plans for assimilation should go astray, the Incas removed all the deposed rulers and their relatives to Cuzco where they were compelled to learn the language of the capital and the customs of their new lords, in addition to basking in the sunshine of the splendors and privileges of the royal court itself. Indeed the official language was systematically imposed upon the conquered people and with this object in view all towns and villages in the conquered country were provided with teachers.

Yet remarkable as was the type of social organization evolved by the Incas we know that its claim to originality was unjustified and simply represented the arrogance of the *parvenu* conqueror. In all forms of art, for instance, the Incas were borrowers and at best only imperfect imitators. Their artistic achievement pales before that of their great predecessors, before those civilizations which stretched from the Isthmus of Panama to northern Chile.

Perhaps the two most remarkable features of architecture and sculpture are the monolithic gateway and the rows of enormous monoliths found at Tiahuanaco, at the southern end of Lake Titicaca, and the monolith associated with the aboriginal fortress of Chavin de Huantar, far to the north of Tiahuanaco. The sculptural friezes figured on the Tiahuanaco monoliths have no counterpart in America. One figure is of particular interest, a human form represented with shortened legs, his head surrounded with rays ending in puma-heads and circles. The fringes of his shirt and sleeve are decorated with the same puma-head motif. On his chest he carries an animal-like ornament

FIGURE ON THE GREAT STONE GATEWAY AT TIAHUANACO

curved into a semilunar shape and in each hand rests a staff the end of which is carved to represent the head of a condor.

The well-known authority on Peruvian archæology, Joyce, has well described the great monoliths: "The great monoliths in their present condition, standing some sixteen feet apart, bear some resemblance to the stone circles of

Europe, but the most recent excavations have proved that they were connected by a wall built with stone blocks without mortar and that the enclosure was entered by a staircase of large monolithic steps in the center of the eastern side. Within the enclosure is found a rectangular depression, to which the stairway gives immediate access and opposite the stairway, to the east of the great enclosure, is a smaller square enclosure built in the same manner but with grotesque heads sculptured in relief on the supporting columns of the wall. Immediately west of the great enclosure is a third, intermediate in size between the other two and furnished with a double wall; and at the northwest corner is a small building with three cell-like compartments and two lesser enclosures are furnished with stone-lined drains. . . . Within the northwest corner of the great enclosure is the famous monolithic gateway which is the most remarkable ruin in America."

In sculpture, in the working of gold, of copper, and of bronze, in the molding of pottery, in the manufacture of fabrics and textiles, the glory had departed before the Incas came upon the scene. What, in the following pages, we shall say about the art of Peru applies, therefore, far more to the civilizations antecedent to that of the Inca than to the Inca.

The use of copper was very extensive. Objects of all descriptions were made of it, more particularly implements of everyday use. Bronze was produced by the conscious mixture of various quantities of tin. But in skillfulness of workmanship and beauty of design, even the best copper and bronze objects looked miserable enough compared to those wrought of gold and silver. Within recent years many of such gold objects have been found in tombs. One tomb contained forty pounds of gold, another two hundred and still another four hundred. They had all conceivable shapes—discs, earrings, bracelets, bells, crowns, shields, pan-pipes, flageolets, circular rings, semiglobular vessels and vases of different sizes. One remarkable find has been described by the well-known French scholar, Paul Rivet:

"Lying on the floor of the tomb rested a skeleton. Over it was found a great quantity of gold and silver plates alternating so regularly that they must unquestionably have been once attached to a cloak that had been thrown over the body. The fringes of this cloak, too, must have been formed of small pieces of gold. At the entrance was discovered a great bundle of chonta-wood—sticks, chased and covered with lamellæ of gold and silver. To cover the opening completely these were placed vertically, four circular plates of gold and silver alternating, two of gold and two of silver, and varying from forty to fifty centimeters in diameter. Behind the skeleton lay a veritable treasure—needles, hatchets, pan-pipes and figurines, all of gold. Most wonderful of all was a feather whose shaft was wrought of gold and whose plumage of silver."

In another tomb was found a highly decorated golden breastplate. Its face was embossed and it was more than one-half of an inch high. The rim was flat and a small circularly raised plate and wire attached the mask to three hollow rings.

The Spanish conquerors were too busy melting the golden objects they obtained into bullion and they were too obsessed with calculating their values according to avaricious European standards to leave us any detailed description of their beauty and workmanship. A few details however we know. The historian Oviedo saw several beautifully-wrought vases

richly chased, of very fine gold and measuring twelve inches
in height and thirty around. Others tell us of goblets, ewers,
salvers, ornaments and utensils for the temples and the royal
palaces, tiles and plates for the decoration of the public
buildings as well as imitations of plants and animals. There
was a magnificent representation of an ear of maize in which
a golden ear was sheathed in broad leaves of silver from
which was suspended a rich tassel of threads of silver.
Some claim—and it may very well be true—to have seen
a fountain which sent up a sparkling jet of gold, while birds
and animals, wrought out of the same material, were represented as playing in the waters at its base.

Yet it is in pottery and the manufacture of textiles that
the ancient peoples of Peru achieved their greatest distinction and with which we generally associate them. The wares
can be arranged in terms of their relative antiquity and
show characteristic differences of style from period to period.
The style denominated the Tiahuanaco is distinguished by
the more conventional type of its painted decoration and
the greater variety of colors employed. Closely allied to
this Tiahuanaco style is that distinguished by the colors in
which the vases were painted, namely red, white, and black.
Then came the period of black pottery, characterized by its
superior technique but undeniably inferior in artistic inspiration. Finally came the Inca period.

Each style had a marked tendency to prefer certain subjects over others, but taking ancient Peruvian pottery as a
whole it can be said that rarely, if ever, has it been excelled
by that of any other people, the Greeks and the Chinese
included, in artistry of workmanship and variety and originality of design. It contained, in addition, a complete
description of ancient Peruvian civilization. Every plant,

Pre-Incan Tapestry

Poncho from Pachacamac

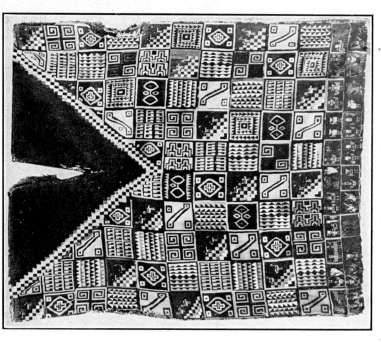

Poncho from Titicaca

NASCA POTS

every animal, every type of dress, every type of house, scenery, the various methods of livelihood, details connected with the ceremonials, gods, even diseases—all are represented either in the round or painted.

To us the most interesting examples are naturally those portraying scenes in Peruvian life. On one vase we have the representation of a sacrifice. We recognize the priest, his two aides and the victim. To the right we see the figure of a personage crouching. On another pot we see a slave with his body mutilated and blind, playing upon a tambourine while his captors dance to the music of a syrinx. On still

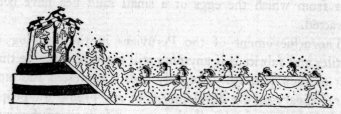

PAINTING ON POTTERY DEPICTING THE PAYING OF HOMAGE
TO THE INCA

another we have depicted people paying homage to the Inca. The Inca is represented in a house built on terraces. Two runners are ascending the terraces followed by a man who is probably the chief of some conquered tribe. Another man is being carried in an ordinary sedan-chair and must be inferior to him, while the still lesser rank of a third chief is indicated by the fact that he has a rope around his neck. On a fourth vase we have the detailed representation of a hunting-scene. We see the deer driven into a net where they are being killed with clubs and heavy darts. Finally, to give an example of the variety of the subjects selected, we have a vessel on which are to be seen rushes and their roots, with fish swimming among the rushes and birds flying above them.

The same tremendous variety of subject-matter is to be seen in the shapes of the vases themselves. Most remarkable are the portrait vases. Their number is legion. They give us an unusual insight into the physiognomies of the people, from the Inca and the nobles to the poorest commoner and slave. No phase of life is unrepresented. We even get glimpses into aboriginal surgery and disease such as representations of an amputated foot with a cap being placed over the stump, and a man examining the sole of his foot from which the eggs of a small sand flea have been extracted.

The achievement of the Peruvians in the weaving of textiles and fabrics is if anything still more remarkable than that of their pottery. Not only does it represent the most extraordinary textile development of any prehistoric people but in harmony of color, the beauty and fastness of the dyes, and the perfection of the spinning and weaving, these fabrics belong in a class all by themselves, even when compared to those of European or Asiatic peoples. The loom does not seem to have been known in earlier times. The warp was arranged in a frame and the weft was put in by hand, by means of wooden needles, each wound with thread of a different color. The main outlines of the design then ran parallel with the warp and weft and the design was built up in patches of color. The methods of decoration employed were various. Patterns were either introduced by means of embroidery after manufacture or painted on the cloth. Sometimes, on the other hand, the cloth itself was dipped into the dye, certain portions of it being tied tightly so that the dye could not penetrate. Sometimes, finally, garments were made up of a patchwork of variously dyed pieces which form symmetrical patterns in reciprocal colors.

The subjects selected for representation in textiles were far more limited in scope than was the case in pottery. In the main geometrical and animal motifs were used but scenes of daily life were not infrequent.

One Inca custom still remains to be mentioned, the widespread prevalence of mummification. The Incas apparently regarded life after death in the same vivid fashion as did the ancient Egyptians. Not only did the dead need food but they needed all the garments, textiles, arms, implements and even domestic pets. All these were placed in their graves or rather tombs. The nobles and more important individuals naturally wanted their favorite wives and a body of retainers as well, and to grant them this favor these individuals were accordingly interred with them. The body of the deceased was generally preserved by some process or other. The internal organs were removed and the body arranged in a squatting position, wrapped in a garment of fine cotton enveloped first in many wrappings of cloth and then in a tightly-fitting mat secured by a net. The mummies of the Inca sovereigns were preserved in the Sun temples at Cuzco seated around the walls on golden chairs near the image of the Sun. Though secretly removed at the time of the conquest they were afterwards discovered. "The bodies were so perfect," says Garcilasso, "that they wanted neither hair, eyebrows, nor eyelashes. They were in the clothes such as they had worn when alive, with the crowns on their heads, but without any other sign of royalty. They were seated with their arms crossed over their breasts, the right one over the left and the eyes cast down as if they were looking on the ground."

Such was the culture of the Incas. As in the case of the Aztecs much of their civilization they had inherited from their predecessors and, often enough, far from its being an improvement it represented a definite and marked deterioration. Yet so great was the glamour attached to the name of Inca that it has only been in recent years that scholars have definitely disproved the Inca claim to most of the achievements formerly credited to them. We have now an imposing series of cultural stages through which ancient Peruvian history seems to have passed. What is even more significant is the fact that we can now trace the mutual influences that the Maya and Peruvian civilizations exerted upon one another. While it would be wrong to contend that the great civilizations of the Pacific coast of South America owed their origin to influences from Mexico yet it is quite clear that in their earliest phases they were so influenced, and that this influence seems to have been much stronger and more persistent in Ecuador than south of it.

Yet running through all these periods there was one constant thread, the worship of the Sun, and one insistent claim, that the Incas were the Children of the Sun. And so the prayer that was offered up during the great August ceremonies at Cuzco by the high priest of the Sun was at one and the same time the prayer of the conquered and the conqueror, of the slaves and of the noblemen, and could proudly point to an antiquity of more than a thousand years:

O Creator! O conquering Uiracocha, ever present Uiracocha!
Thou who art in the ends of the earth without equal!
Thou who gavest life and valor to man saying
Let this be a man;
And to woman, saying

Let this be a woman!
Thou who madest them and gave them being!
Thou who art in the high heavens
And among the clouds of the tempest,
Grant this with long life
And accept this sacrifice,
O Creator!

CHAPTER V

WHEN during the Mexican War General Winfield Scott landed at Vera Cruz and marched on Mexico City, he traversed the same route that Cortez had taken more than three hundred years before. Cortez had come by boat from Cuba. From Tabasco, not far from the present little port of Puerto Mexico, he proceeded along the coast to the site of Vera Cruz, a town which he himself subsequently founded. Nor had he been the first to march along these aboriginal trails and roads. As early as 100 B.C., indeed, centuries earlier, they had resounded to the tramp of invading hosts from Yucatan, Guatemala and Chiapas, for it was along these roads that the Mayas had come.

The Mayas had always been a restless race. In their homeland in Guatemala and Yucatan town after town had been abandoned. Though we may be certain that no one cause could have been the determining one yet it seems likely that if we could but pierce the thick clouds of darkness that shroud early Maya history, of one thing we would be certain—that unfriendly barbarians were pressing upon them from all sides, attacking whenever possible and slowly but surely absorbing them. No highly integrated culture has ever been able to resist those two deadly foes—barbarians and the jungle. Least of all the Mayas, for highly integrated as their civilization was along the lines of art and specialized knowledge, it possessed two fundamental defects, lack of political cohesion and unity, and an unfortunate centralization of all knowledge in the hands of a priestly caste.

But if the jungle and the barbarians did finally bring Maya culture to an abrupt halt they could not utterly destroy it. The jungle, after all, could at times be evaded and the barbarian was bound to be less of a barbarian after he had felt the invigorating warmth of a high culture. And then too, high cultures have their own methods of attacking their hereditary enemies. When direct frontal attacks are unavailing a slow persistent penetration can be resorted to. Long and tenacious defense is in itself a form of offense. When finally then the odds became too great and Maya culture definitely succumbed, not a little of its heritage had become incorporated into the life of the barbarian hordes.

To understand how the Maya conquered Mexico and the United States, we must therefore try to discover how they evaded the jungle, how they gradually acted as a leaven to the surrounding barbarians and how, at times, a kind fate allowed even a frontal attack to be successful.

Once they could gain the coast of the Gulf of Mexico they were comparatively safe. It is therefore not surprising that their first efforts should have been to reach that narrow neck of land which we call the Isthmus of Tehuantepec. That isthmus could be approached in two ways, either by plunging through tropical and mountainous regions like Chiapas or making directly for the Gulf. To reach the Gulf directly was much easier. It is not surprising therefore that we encounter, as far to the northwest as the northern part of the state of Vera Cruz, a Maya language, the Huaxtecan. But of the Maya culture, as we know it from Yucatan and Guatemala, much had already been lost, unless indeed we are to suppose that the Huaxtecans represent an early and archaic phase of Maya culture. The former interpretation is far more likely, for there is a definite and gradual loss of feature upon feature of Maya culture as we proceed from northern Yucatan, through Tabasco to Vera Cruz. Indeed not very far south of the Huaxtecans themselves there had once flourished a civilization—that of the Totonacans—which had had far-reaching resemblances to that of the Maya. The language of these Totonacans was either a much modified Maya or one that had incorporated into itself many Maya words.

As far as northern Vera Cruz, therefore, the frontal attack, it can be said, had been largely successful. Whether this was due to the absence of an enemy or to the ineffectuality of their resistance we do not know. What we do know is that the Mayas were apparently able to settle down here, found towns, maintain their language, and preserve the less fragile elements of their old cultural heritage. The hieroglyphs, the sumptuous cities with their civic centers, gorgeous temples and monoliths, these were gone forever. But the cultivation of maize and all that this implied, the old religion, the old legends, and the old social structure, these were still intact.

Yet here in northern Vera Cruz the trail stops quite abruptly. What had happened? Had the pressure of the barbarians become too great or had the barbarians absorbed them?

Most historians prefer not to guess and they leave the question unanswered. Perhaps that is the wiser. But we suspect that these good people have been somewhat led astray into seeking for the continuance of these early Maya influences in the region to the north of Vera Cruz, that, in fact, they have been what might be called land-obsessed. For now that the region between northern Vera Cruz and Galveston has been surveyed and mapped, who indeed would dream of pushing through it? To-day in order to reach Galveston and New Orleans from Tampico or Vera Cruz we take a boat. So apparently did the ancient inhabitants of Vera Cruz. And indeed it is on the lower Mississippi that the trail which petered out so abruptly in northern Vera Cruz is to be found again. Here along the great river and along its eastern shore and, still farther, to the Atlantic itself, there once flourished all that still remained intact of Maya culture north of the Rio Grande. We call the people who once lived there the Mound-Builders. True enough the culture that these Mound-Builders possessed had markedly deteriorated even from the Huaxtecan level. But the wonder is that so much still survived. Maize was still the dominant interest, pyramidal structures were still numerous; the gods were somewhat emasculated but essentially still the same and the social organization was fundamentally still intact.

And so the first main invasion of the United States came from the sea and ascended the majestic Father of Waters. But if we insist so strongly upon the all-pervading influence of the invasion from Mexico, this does not mean that the Mound-Builders had not achieved anything before this foreign impact. Yet it is not for a moment to be compared with their achievement after this impact.

But let us now return to those Mayas who took the overland route in their endeavors, so we may surmise, to reach the Atlantic coast. Here the invasions must have begun early and have been frequent. Certainly the earliest of them must have been made in large force, for though not strong enough to carry many phases of their culture along with it. This particular stage of their northward progress brought them to the state of Oaxaca, in southern Mexico. Whether the fundamental traits of the civilizations found there, those of the Mixtecs and the Zapotecs, are of Maya origin, is somewhat problematical, but that they became encrusted with Maya elements, is manifest.

The civilization of these peoples was almost as markedly theocratic as was that of the Maya. We know something about the head-priest and the priestly caste. The Mixtecs, for instance, had a high-priest whose power was equal to that of the king. Indeed the office was always held by some member of the royal family and was hereditary. A rigorous novitiate was exacted from all priests, including the understudy of the high-priest and throughout this period absolute chastity was imposed. The ordinary priests might, after a period of four years marry, but whoever wished to, could continue this monastic life indefinitely. It was from the ranks of the latter that those were chosen who filled the higher offices around the king. Even the heir to the throne was compelled to undergo such a novitiate.

The chief priest and the king were both embalmed after death and their bodies deposited in the sacred grottoes, of which there existed many in the Mixtec country. Their mummies were placed on stone benches hewn out of the rock. Such a mausoleum also contained, in separate apartments, statues of the protecting deity of the king and priest.

Among the Zapotecs a king was at one and the same time both high-priest and sovereign. So great was the veneration in which he was held, states an early authority, that he was never allowed to touch the ground. If people incidentally encountered his cortège they threw themselves prostrate upon the ground. It would mean death to see his shadow. Even the great nobles entered his presence with eyes lowered and uncovered head.

There were two orders of priests, a higher to which apparently only the members of the nobility belonged, and an inferior order. Of the latter there were many varieties. Perhaps the most important of the minor priests were those charged with interpreting the auguries concerned with divination. Of the latter there were many kinds, divination by fire, by water, by the flight of birds, by examining the entrails of sacrificed animals, etc. Certain priests lived lives of complete abstinence or spent them in meditation and seclusion, dwelling in rough huts and drawing blood from themselves, to be offered to their special deities.

Both the Mixtec and Zapotec country was divided into subdivisions ruled over by sub-chiefs directly subordinated to the king, and paying tribute to him. Land was inherited in the male line and was inalienable. Serfs worked the land and were apparently kept under strict surveillance by special officials. A specially privileged class, here as everywhere else in Central America and Mexico, were the merchants. Their position seems to have been an unusual one and in certain districts they were apparently allowed to marry into a rank above their own.

The Zapotecs had a fairly clear-cut idea of a supreme deity who seems to have been known by a large variety of names. Among the more important deities were the primal pair of gods, "The maker of all beasts" and "The maker of men and fishes," the deity of the earth, a vague god connected with the most sacred shrines and called by the Zapotec "Heart of the kingdom"; the rain god; the god of harvest; the god of the merchants and of wealth; the god of poverty; of lust; of dreams; of the underworld, etc. There is no indication of sun-worship. In addition there were, of course, numerous personal guardian deities represented in the form of idols, as well as special deities presiding over the special days of the year and over the cardinal points. These last were very important and we shall describe them briefly.

The Zapotecs divided their ritual year of two hundred and sixty days into four periods of sixty-five days, periods which had definite reference to the four cardinal points. The names which they give to the four deities presiding over these periods and directions meant "the god" and "the rain god." In one of the old codices they are represented as follows. The first, the east, is a figure wearing as a helmet-mask an alligator's head; he is a good and fruitful deity. The second, the north, has as his mask, a death's-head; he signifies drought and death. The third, the west, wears the head of an unknown animal. The fourth figure, the south, wears the vulture's head. There is a fifth figure representing the center. His colors are those of the gods of the night-heaven and twilight and the symbols accompanying him refer to war.

The calendar system and the glyphs are regarded by some as derived from the Mayas. They bring up many difficult problems. The former are simpler than the Maya. Does this mean deterioration or did the Maya perfect a simpler system which they had borrowed from the Zapotecs? The latter assumption seems more probable. Only the ritual calendar was known. As we have pointed out it was divided into four periods of sixty-five days. These were again divided into five groups of thirteen days. As among

the Mayas there were twenty day signs, and a recent inves-
tigation of them has led an eminent scholar to the conclusion
that the Zapotec names associated with them formed the
connecting link for apparently irreconcilable differences in
the Aztec and Maya designations. The only conclusion to
be drawn is that the Zapotec calendar represented the transi-
tion between that of the Maya and the Aztec. This same
transitional phase is indicated by the glyphs. The numerals still appear in the Maya notation but the glyphs themselves are quite distinct.

But interesting as this Zapotec civilization was, for us its
importance lies in the rôle it was destined to play in the history of aboriginal America. The Zapotecs and Mixtecs were
to be the intermediaries between the Mayas and all those
tribes that lay to the north and west of Oaxaca; their culture was to form the main ingredient in the next stage of
the cultural advance to the north. This stage is represented
by the so-called Toltecs.

The Toltec represent the most interesting transformation
of the merged Maya-Zapotec culture. Three distinct waves
of civilization converged here in the state of Vera Cruz.
The first, the archaic, by which we mean the early basic cultural substratum, brought agriculture, pottery, the loom and
weaving; the second, representing the Maya invasion proper,
carried hieroglyphs almost to the area occupied by the Toto-
nacs. The third and most important came from the Zapotecs
and Mixtecs. Its center seems to have been Oaxaca. From
there it must have spread at an early date, first to Tehuacan
and Cholula, in the state of Pueblo, and to the Guerrero-
Oaxaca frontier, then secondly, to western Vera Cruz. Thus
it converged on the Valley of Mexico from all sides.
Finally, pushing further north and west it was to have a

very important subcenter in Michoacan and to overrun Zacatecas, Durango and western Jalisco. In greatly transformed form, but still essentially intact, it was finally to reach Sinaloa and Sonora. From there it was to make a triumphant entry into the southwest of the United States and survive, to a marked extent, in the highest culture attained north of the Rio Grande—that of the Pueblo Indians.

Throughout this extensive region the archæological remains show everywhere obvious indebtedness to Toltec art. We find pyramids, sculpture, pottery and decorative details, all going back to the great inspiration that came from the south. The workmanship, of course, is everywhere markedly inferior. In the temples vaulted ceilings are no longer to be found and in construction adobe bricks with concrete facings take the place of rubble and cut stone.

Let us pause for a brief moment to mention the more important of the Toltec remains, those at Cholula, San Juan Teotihuacan, Xochicalco and Tula.

Cholula, near Pueblo, had a series of mounds on which temples had once stood. It was a sacred city identified with the culture-hero Quetzalcoatl and is famous for its wonderful representation of the serpent. Its polychrome pottery-ware is among the finest known from ancient Mexico.

San Juan Teotihuacan, near Mexico City has, as we have seen, three great pyramids rising in four sloping terraces, and a road lined with smaller ones. Some large sculptures have also been found there but the most distinctive features of the site, only recently discovered, are the sculptured stones on the three sides of the temple erected on the so-called "pyramid of the Sun." The colors are still preserved and the heads of the plumed serpents and the obsidian butterflies still retain in part their inset eyes of obsidian. Very characteristic of this site are likewise the pottery figurines and dolls with movable arms and legs.

Xochicalco, near Cuernavaca, is a mound with courts, terraces and pyramids. One of the temples still standing is decorated with great plumed serpents, seated human figures and hieroglyphs.

Tula, fifty miles north of Mexico City, has numerous sculptures and great sculptured columns with feathered serpents and gigantic figures. These columns are crowned by true capitals. Architecturally it is closest to some of the structures at Chichen Itza in Yucatan. . . .

This Toltec civilization was to become so important and vital that it, in its turn, was to spread to Oaxaca, leaving its impress at Mitla and it was even to influence the old motherland of culture in Chiapas and Yucatan. It seems to have differed in one essential respect from the earlier Maya invasions. We may reasonably assume that the carriers of the earlier Maya cultural invasions had been either Maya or at least people who had a large admixture of Maya blood. It was otherwise with the Toltec. They were almost certainly not Maya in blood and culture and probably represented barbarians who had come from the north and had adopted a sedentary mode of life under the influence of the Mayas. We may even go further and surmise that these barbarians may have been the first outposts of the Nahuas, the early kindred of the Aztecs, the peoples who were destined to conquer all of Tlaxcala and the valley of Mexico.

Thus was the torch of Maya civilization passed on from

tribe to tribe, and thus were Mexico and the United States thoroughly conquered. Along the Gulf of Mexico to Vera Cruz and then by sea to the mouth of the Mississippi; overland through Chiapas, Oaxaca, the valley of Mexico, Michoacan, Jalisco, Sinaloa, Sonora to Arizona, New Mexico, Colorado and Utah—over all this tremendous area the conquest extended. A whole economic system migrated to the United States. Strange things were to happen. Tribes of marauding barbarians, akin to the lowly Comanche and Ute, were to feel the impact of the Toltec culture, and moving southward to become the famous Nahuas and Aztecs of history. After the year 600 A.D. this crisscrossing was never to cease.

For the United States two cultural areas were to emerge out of these major and minor invasions, one to the east of the Mississippi based on the early Maya influx and, in a sense, more truly a direct descendant of the Mayas, and another in the southwest of the United States based predominantly on the Toltec influx and thus only indirectly a direct descendant of the Maya, although earlier influences unquestionably reached them too. The two slogans for aboriginal United States were henceforth to be Cliff-Dweller and Mound-Builder. Under the banner of Cliff-Dweller and Mound-Builder aboriginal America was to become civilized; the ties with the great fountain head of all aboriginal American culture were to become looser and fainter and finally fade away completely in the woodlands of Canada. From that time onward eclecticism was to become the watchword.

POTS IN SHAPE OF CORN AND GOURDS

NASCA POT REPRESENTING CON-
VENTIONALIZED MUMMY CARRY-
ING COCA LEAVES

PACHACAMAC POTTERY DEPICTING MAN EXTRACTING SAND FLEAS FROM
HIS FOOT

POT IN SHAPE OF SANDAL

POT DEPICTING MAN CARRYING JAR

CHAPTER VI

THE CONQUESTS OF THE SUN-GOD

THE historian Montesinos narrates that when the great pre-Inca ruler of Peru, Huira Cocha, was rebuilding Quito, he heard of a warlike people who lived on the other side of the mountain range which runs from Santa Maria to the Straits of Magellan. As soon as he heard of them he desired to subject them to his rule. But in order to first learn something about them he sent six leaders with an ample number of soldiers to enter that country. This they did, and soon they found themselves among forest peoples living along the shores of mighty rivers. These natives were practically naked. The Peruvian forces could make but little headway against them and their comparatively small force was soon lost. Eventually they made their way back to Cuzco and told the great sovereign what they had witnessed. He made no further attempt to conquer them. Yet though these simple barbarians were externally to remain unaffected by that remarkable civilization which Huira Cocha symbolized, they had even at that early date felt some of its invigorating rays and in the years that were to come many a trait of Peruvian culture, pre-Inca and Inca, was to filter through the thickly forested sierras and rivers.

Not long after Huira Cocha had made this preliminary survey of the above simple people he embarked upon another imperialistic enterprise. With a powerful army he moved against the Guayaquil, living along the coast. The chroniclers say that "he went with an easy mind, although the way was very rough, because in the sacrifices which he had ordered to be held before the journey had been begun, he had had very good auguries and replies. At least so the priests who knew how to interpret the entrails of sacrificial animals had declared. He went by way of the villages of Calacoli and Pululagua and the traces of the roads which he then built are to be seen to-day and cause wonder."

On this eventful journey he had many physical obstacles to overcome. At one place he had to build a bridge of osier cables. However, when these rather large cables had been constructed, much to his dismay, he found that the river was so broad, so deep and had such strong currents, that his labor had all been of no avail. Seeing that it would be impossible to build a sufficiently strong bridge he had *balsas* constructed and in these his men went out to engage with the enemy as soon as they had become fairly expert in their management. The battle lasted many days, sometimes favoring one side and sometimes another, depending entirely upon how the river currents behaved. Finally Huira Cocha ordered his captains to attack the enemy from all sides. Possibly even that would not have availed the Incas had it not been for dissensions among the enemy which led the principal chief to send messengers to Huira Cocha and to offer him his allegiance and that of his district. When the other chiefs noticed this they went off to their villages and thus enabled the Incas to conquer. The Inca chief could then disembark without hindrance on the opposite shore where the city of Guayaquil now stands. He granted many favors to the chief who had surrendered and to his district and, by their aid, he was eventually able to conquer all the people who lived in the territory of Guayaquil.

In such manner did the pre-Inca and the Inca rulers extend their civilization on all sides. For the history of aboriginal America the conquests of the Incas, however, pale somewhat in comparison with the influence and the conquests of their predecessors. In the short period associated with Inca domination, at best but four hundred years, the Incas were in fact almost exclusively occupied in extending their sway over their predecessors and had really little time left for anything else. To extend their sway over their predecessors was indeed a task of sufficient magnitude and it had barely been accomplished when the Spaniards arrived. Whatever civilization came to the inhabitants of South America west of the Andes and along the Amazon and its tributaries, these people owe not to the Inca but to the pre-Incan civilization. Only in a few cases, even, did the Inca conquer the conquered.

That these pre-Inca cultures of Peru, Ecuador and Bolivia were very old, we know from numerous indications. Even Maya influences, for instance, go back possibly as far as 100 B.C. By the years 200 to 500 A.D. these pre-Inca civilizations, both the mountain and the coastal, had attained full maturity and were spreading north and south and across the Andes to the valley of the Amazon and its tributaries, as well as down the eastern slopes of the great mountains into the inhospitable Gran Chaco of Argentine.

As in Mexico and North America we must think of the diffusion of Peruvian culture in terms of successive invasions. But the cardinal difference between the history of aboriginal culture in South America as compared with that in North America lies in the fact that here in South America the early invasions were of a far less definite and dramatic kind. It would be quite wrong to imagine armed hosts from Peru marching across the land to transplant their civilization among the Brazilian barbarians. Rather must we imagine a continuous diffusion of traits, a process similar to what has taken place among the Eskimo of Alaska who were in contact with the highly-specialized Indians of the northwest coast of North America.

It must have been at a very early period in their history that the Peruvian civilizations had passed on agriculture and pottery to the simple peoples of Brazil like the Aruak, Caribs and Tupi-Guarani. Yet the jungle and the older barbarian possessors of the land did not allow the higher Peruvian culture elements to remain long intact. They soon became contaminated, disunited and dispersed.

Though typical Peruvian myths and the typical Peruvian head-hunting customs were to be found in eastern Brazil, for instance, these were after all but distant echoes of that grand old civilization hidden away in the mountain recesses and fastnesses of Bolivia and Peru. Their presence in no way bespoke any attempt at new cultural integrations such as we shall see was the case in North America. Agriculture and pottery, two traits that have always traveled together in America, these even the simplest peoples of eastern South America were never to lose. But they were never to elaborate them to any appreciable extent, and agriculture was never to have those multitudinous cultural by-products, generally associated with them in North America, such as elaborate ceremonials and rituals and complex political and governmental units. In fact it can be said that in spite of the presence of agriculture, the autochthonous inhabitants of Brazil never really became sedentary. Despite the continuous and persistent pressure from the other side of the Andes these barbarians always tended to relapse into their ancient ways.

But we must make two exceptions. One portion of the Aruak people was subjected to the double influence of the Mayas and the pre-Inca Peruvians. These Aruak, called Taino, were destined to overrun the West Indies, particularly the larger islands and to establish there a fairly high civilization, distinguished for its achievement in wood-carving, stone work, pottery and an elaborate social organization. In their turn these Taino were to exercise not a little influence on the Indians of the southeastern part of the United States.

The other exception refers to the unusual development of pottery found along the eastern part of the Amazon. Here and in scattered districts to the south, we find a very superior quality of ware. The characteristic trait of the urns and vases found is that they generally were made in human shape and were not infrequently covered with molded ornaments. How to explain their presence so far from Peru and Bolivia is difficult. Possibly they are the last vestiges of somewhat extensive invasions of which all other traces have disappeared.

But if the older civilizations of Peru were to exercise only comparatively little influence on the major part of South America east of the Andes and then only through a process of slow infiltration, they were to completely submerge the region along the Pacific slope as far north as the Isthmus of Panama and as far south as Chile. This could only have been done by a real conquest.

It is perfectly clear that the oldest culture in Peru is that which at one time existed along the coast. It is there that the great city of Pachacamac with its famous temple stood.

There were, in fact, two temples: The older one standing on an artificial terraced plateau of about four hundred square yards and being surrounded by a large enclosure. Outside the entrance there was a double colonnade and a group of small buildings. Throughout this whole area we find numerous terraces and terraced pyramids. South of Pachacamac lay another center, Nasca, famous for its pottery and north of Pachacamac lay still a third, Trujillo, also known for its remarkably finished ware.

These local cultures spread along the coast to the north and eventually gave rise to greatly transformed centers in Ecuador, Colombia, and among the Chiriqui of the Isthmus of Panama. Not long after the conquest of the coast had begun expeditions must have made their way into the mountains as well, for we find the Tiahuanaco culture at Lake Titicaca suddenly becoming saturated with numerous features of this coastal civilization. After that time, it is true, the mountain culture was to become fairly independent and develop parallel with that of the coast. We should not be surprised then if we discover its irradiations as far north as Ecuador and Colombia. Our picture is still further complicated by influences that came from Guatemala.

Fundamentally, however, the great civilizations of the Chibcha in Colombia and of the Cauca in Ecuador were built on the basis of the culture that had come to them from the coast of Peru. Like the Aztecs they seem to have preserved many old features which the early coastal civilization had apparently lost. It may, in fact, be claimed that if we have a right to consider the essential features of Colombian culture as replicas of what had once prevailed along the Peruvian coast, the strongly monarchial tendencies of the

Incas were more than foreshadowed by these remote ancestral cousins of theirs.

The early Spanish chroniclers have left us a good picture of Colombian society, notably of that of the Chibcha. At the head of the state stood the king with unlimited powers who seems to have had both civil and military powers concentrated in his hands. Like the Inca the appointment of the priests was one of his prerogatives. As at the Inca court and at that of the last Aztec ruler, no commoner dared look him in the face. In his presence people had either to turn aside or assume a stooping attitude and no messenger ever appeared before him without carrying a gift of some kind. If not claiming to be of divine descent the ruler of the Chibcha nevertheless surrounded himself with all the appurtenances of a divine king. His throne was made of gold and studded with emeralds. When he traveled his litter hung with golden plates and officials preceded him clearing the path of obstacles, spreading textiles and scattering flowers before him. His headdress was of gold, and a golden crescent ornamented his brow. Even his nose- and ear-ornaments were of the same material.

Never was a monarch surrounded with so much gold and yet never did a monarch have to submit to so severe and so humiliating a probation as that which awaited the heir to the Chibcha throne. For at least five years he had to retire from the world and live secluded in a temple. Only at night was he permitted to leave it. Frequent scourgings alternated with vigorous fasts. Constrained by oath he had to confess to any breach of the regulations by which he was hedged about on all sides. Penance followed penance, and so the mortification of the flesh continued month after month and year after year. Then when the great day of freedom approached his nose and ears were pierced so that he could wear the ornaments to which his exalted rank entitled him. It was then that he made an offering of gold animal-figures to the gods.

But he was to be amply repaid for his trying ordeal. The state ceremonies connected with his installation awaited him. Perhaps nothing more fairylike has ever taken place. Even if we allow for imaginations fired by stories of El Dorado, the spectacle this installation presented must have had many of the qualities of a romantic wish-fulfillment. The whole population participated in it. All repaired to the sacred lake of Guatabita dressed in their finest apparel. Everywhere shone ornaments of gold and gorgeous feathers. On the banks of the sacred lake innumerable sacrificial fires were kindled and the air was laden with a thick and seductive incense. The new ruler approached. Naked, his body was anointed with adhesive earth and then covered with powdered gold dust. But this was only the beginning. A romantic journey still lay before him. With four minor chiefs he embarked upon a raft ornamented with gold. A mound of gold and emeralds was piled at his feet. Then amidst the acclaim of the assembled people and to the sound of whistles, the raft slowly floated toward the middle of the lake. As soon as it arrived there, the new sovereign plunged into its waters and washed off the gold dust. Subsequently the gold and the emeralds that had been piled on the raft were thrown into the sacred waters.

The religion of the Chibcha shows very clearly how the Inca preserved the older faith. These Chibcha were the original Children of the Sun. To the Sun, at the wonderful temple southeast of Bogota, offerings were made of gold, emeralds, and incense. But the main sacrifice was that of little children who had been purchased in infancy from the distant provinces. According to the religious beliefs of the Chibcha these children were to act as intermediaries between penitents and the offended deity. The most profound veneration was paid to these children. Their feet were not even permitted to touch the ground. They spent their short lives as singers in the temple. Then when they had reached the age of puberty they were sacrificed and the victims' blood and heart were offered to the sun, amidst the accompaniment of music and song. Human sacrifice was indeed something of a Chibcha specialty much as it was among the Aztec.

The civilization of ancient Ecuador was quite similar to that of Colombia but on a somewhat lower level except possibly for its achievements in stone sculpture and goldsmithing.

North of the Chibcha we find the original coast culture petering out markedly. There it had to compete with influences coming from Mexico. As a result the civilizations of this area show very clearly the composite nature of their origin.

In this manner did the ancient Peruvian pre-Inca civilizations conquer the coast and the mountain plateaus from Nasca and Lake Titicaca as far north as the Isthmus of Panama. As we have seen in the case of Mexico so here, too, we behold certain sub-cultures acting as intermediary between the basic civilization and the rest of South America. The rôle that the Zapotec of Oaxaca had played in the dissemination of Maya culture the Chibcha of Colombia were to play in the diffusion of early Peruvian civilization, and what the Mound-Builders were to be for the region east of the Mississippi, the northwestern Aruaks were to be for Brazil and the West Indies.

But we must now turn our attention to the sweep of the earlier Peruvian culture toward the south and the southwest, across the Andes and down its western slopes. Immediately to the south, and along the coast, we find a peculiar and interesting situation. Pottery and agriculture are found, as well as a number of copper objects, but these are all associated with elements belonging to a comparatively simple people. Everything, in fact, indicates that we are here on the margin of Peruvian influence. Yet strangely enough, beyond this comparatively simple culture we come to a people with a comparatively high development, the Araucanians. Surprising as was the achievement of this warlike and unusually intelligent race, it increases still further when we realize that it had all been accomplished in a very short period of time.

Unlike the rest of South America the civilization attained by the Araucanians was almost exclusively the work of the Inca. The Inca conquest must indeed have been very complete for we find extensive stone-habitations, terrace-cultivation, chambers with monolithic pillars, woven cloths, and the llama, the last indicating that these people were pastoral as well as agricultural. In the short time between their adoption of Inca culture and the conquests of Peru by the Spaniards, the Araucanians succeeded in spreading some traits of the late Inca culture among the wilder tribes to the east and they thus became of considerable importance for the history of the southern portion of aboriginal South America. In the southwest, across the Andes, we meet with a much older culture. Here as in Ecuador and Colombia, the Peruvian influences go back to the pre-Inca civilizations, probably to a modified phase of the Tiahuanaco culture of Lake Titicaca. This civilization, called the Calchaqui, once prevailed in the northwest portion of the present Argentine. The sun was the great deity and masked dancers were common. Agriculture was extensively practiced. Copper was common but gold, though found, was rare. The most characteristic feature of the region was its magnificent polychrome pottery with its elaborate painted decorations. Everything pointed to a very complex culture much older than that of the Inca.

From the Calchaqui certain elements were diffused among the wild tribes of the Gran Chaco and thus over a large part of Argentine, Paraguay, Araguay, and southern Brazil. To all intents and purposes, however, Peruvian influences stopped with the Calchaqui just as further north they stopped at the western slope of the Andes. Beyond the Andes, we cannot too often insist, in Brazil, Bolivia, the Guianas and Argentine, dwelt barbarians—the northern Aruaks alone excepted—to whom but faint gleams of the El Dorado ever came.

CHAPTER VII

THE EPIC OF THE WANDERERS

FEW things in the history of America have quite the pathos of the well-remembered words with which the ill-fated Montezuma greeted Cortez when he received him at Mexico City. "I have been perturbed for many days now," he told him, "ever since I cast my eyes toward that unknown land from which you have just come, the land of clouds, the country of the mists. For this my ancestors told me long ago, that some day you would come to visit your own home again, and that some day you would return and sit once more upon your ancient throne."

It was a glorious and wonderful land to which Montezuma had reference. Under the shadow of a curved mountain blue waters spread out on all sides. There white roses bloomed and white bulrushes revealed the shining sands of a shore delectable to behold. The rarest foods were so common that people despised them. All plants matured quickly and grew to enormous size. When the cotton matured it took on the most resplendent colors— glowing red, delicate pale-rose, yellow, green, orange, violet-blue and deep gray. Gold and silver and the rarest of green-colored gems lay around unnoticed for they had no value. And all this splendor had vanished long before the remote ancestors of the Aztec Montezuma had come to Mexico-Tenochtitlan! All this had vanished when the great lord Quetzalcoatl had departed.

Generations before Quetzalcoatl had come from Yucatan by way of Cholula. His appearance was strange indeed. His skin was white. He had a broad brow, great eyes, long black hair and a large round beard. Never would mankind forget what he had taught them—to be chaste and to be moderate in all things; to offer no sacrifice of blood of man or animals, but to delight only in offerings of bread, roses and other flowers, of perfumes and sweet odors and to indulge in no war or violence.

Yet wonderful as was this happy land its glory was destined to come to an end. Three sorcerers, gods in disguise, among them Tezcatlipoca and Huitzilopochtli, came to dethrone him. To Tezcatlipoca was delegated the task of deceiving the gentle god-king. So the former transformed himself into a hoary-headed man and went to the house of Quetzalcoatl, saying to the servants there, "I wish to see and speak to your master." Then the servants said, "Go away, old man, thou canst not see our king, for he is sick, thou wilt annoy him and cause him heaviness." But Tezcatlipoca insisted, "I must see him."

Then the servants bade the sorcerer to wait, and they went in, and told Quetzalcoatl how an old man insisted that he must see the king and would not be denied. And Quetzalcoatl answered, "Let him come in. Behold, for many days I have waited for his coming." So Tezcatlipoca entered, and he said to the sick god-king, "How art thou?" adding further that he had a medicine for him to drink. Then Quetzalcoatl answered, "Thou art welcome, old man. Behold, many days I have waited for thee." And the old sorcerer spoke again, "How is thy body, and how art thou in health?" "I am exceedingly sick," said Quetzalcoatl, "all my body is in pain. I cannot move my hands nor my feet." Then answered Tezcatlipoca, "Behold this medicine that I have; it is good and wholesome and intoxicating. If thou wilt drink it, thou shalt be intoxicated and healed and eased at heart, and thou shalt not have in mind the toils and fatigues of death and of thy departure." "Where," cried Quetzalcoatl, "have I to go?" "To Tullantlapallan," replied Tezcatlipoca, "where there is another old man waiting for thee. He and thou shall talk together, and on thy return thence thou shalt be as a youth, yea, as a boy."

And Quetzalcoatl hearing these words, his heart was moved, while the old sorcerer insisting more and more, said, "Sir, drink this medicine." But the king did not wish to drink it. The sorcerer, however, insisted, "Drink, my lord, or thou wilt be sorry for it hereafter. At least, rub a little on thy brow and taste a sip."

So Quetzalcoatl tried and tasted it and drank, saying, "What is this? It seems to be a thing very good and savory. Already I feel myself healed and quit of mine infirmity; already I am well." Then the old sorcerer said again, "Drink once more, my lord, since it is good, so thou shall be the more perfectly healed." And Quetzalcoatl drank again and he made himself drunk. He began to weep sadly. His heart was eased and he moved to depart, for he could not rid himself of the thought that he must go. This had, in fact, been the snare and deceit of Tezcatlipoca. And the medicine that Quetzalcoatl drank was the white wine of the country, made from the magueys that are called *teumetl*.

And so Quetzalcoatl started on his long journey. But Tezcatlipoca, not content with his success, decided to destroy the people over whom the gentle Quetzalcoatl was the spiritual ruler. So one day, disguised as a mendicant, he stood in the market-place upon which the palace of King Vemac looked down and the king's daughter seeing him, fell in love with him and sickened. Only when the mendicant was brought into her presence and became her husband did she recover. But the king's subjects were very much vexed at this marriage. "What," they said, "of all the people could not a worthier person have been found to be our sovereign's son-in-law than this foreign mendicant?" Then the king desiring to rid himself of his distasteful son-in-law told his subjects to take him along on a war expedition, desert him and let him die. But the cunning stranger contrived otherwise and returned triumphant so that the king had to acknowledge his valor.

Then came the final deceit and catastrophe. Tezcatlipoca adorned himself with the rich feathers called *tocivitl*, and commanded the Toltecs to gather together for a festival, first sending a crier to the top of the mountain called Tzatzitepec, to call in the strangers and the people afar off that they might dance and feast. A numberless multitude gathered at Tula. When they were all gathered, Tezcatlipoca led them out, young men and girls, to a place called Texcalapa, where he himself began and led the dancing, playing on a drum. He sang, too, singing each verse to the dancers, who sang it after him though they knew not the song beforehand.

Then a marvelous and terrible thing was seen. From sunset till midnight the beat of the countless feet grew faster and faster; the tap, tap, tap of the drum closed up and poured into a continual roll; the monotonous song rose higher, wilder, till it burst into a roar. The multitude became a mob, the revel a riot; the people

began to press upon and hustle each other; the riot became
a panic. There was a fearful gorge or ravine there, with
a river rushing through it called the Texcaltlauhco. A
stone bridge led over the river. Tezcatlipoca broke down
this bridge as the people fled. Grim spectator of this fearful revel, he saw them tread and crush each other down
under foot, and fall over into the abyss. Those that fell
were turned into rocks and stones. As for them that escaped, they did not see nor think that it was Tezcatlipoca
and his sorceries who had wrought this great destruction;
they were blinded by the witchcraft of the god and were out
of their senses like drunken men.

During all this time Quetzalcoatl continued on his journey southward. At Cholula he remained twenty years and
then passed away by the road he had come, taking with him
four of the principal and the most virtuous youths of the
city. He traveled for one hundred and fifty leagues and
he came to the sea in a distant province of the south. Here
he took leave of his companions and instructed them to tell
their fellow-citizens that a day would come in which white
men would land upon their coasts, and that they would
come by way of the sea from the direction in which the sun
rises. . . .

It was this prophecy that Montezuma had reference to
in his simple and reverential welcome to Cortez.

But what does this legend signify? Is it simply one
more variant of the version of the Golden Age with which
mankind has deluded itself in all lands, or is it merely another example of that frequent and inextricable mixture of
truth and fiction found so universally in the annals of all
nations? Scholars were long in doubt. For some time
most of them were inclined to dismiss the whole matter as

POTS REPRESENTING MUSICIANS

POTS REPRESENTING PERSONIFIED CORN

POT REPRESENTING PERSONIFIED BAT

ACOMA MASKED DANCER IMPERSONATING
A DEER

ACOMA MASKED DANCER (*Drawn by a Native*)

a puerile wish-fulfillment. But now we know better.
This legend is what so many legends have turned out to
be, a symbolical disguise for a real happening. In a fore-
shortened and mythological dress it portrays the coming of
that Toltec culture of which we spoke in a preceding chapter. Here we have a picture of that culture as seen through
the idealized and distorted vision of the descendants of those
barbarians who, coming from the north, finally overwhelmed and destroyed it. Not individual gods and
heroes are here involved but nations and cultural movements.

What is to be marveled at is not that so much has been
distorted as that the general outline of the actual occur-
rences have been so well remembered. It is a fact that the
Toltec culture came from the south; it is a fact that it was
eventually overwhelmed and that it spread secondarily over
the south again, and it is a fact that Cholula was both an
early and a late Toltec center.

Thus the legend of Quetzalcoatl is the precipitate of a
great cultural movement. Tezcatlipoca and Huitzilopochtli are the symbols of the barbarian northerners. Well
could the subjects of the last Toltec king Vemac complain
that it was demeaning for him to marry his daughter to the
northern god Tezcatlipoca disguised as a mendicant. Their
complaint is but a symbolical description of the first infiltration of the barbarians, just as the presence of Tezcatlipoca on a war expedition symbolizes the still greater influence these barbarians were acquiring, and the destruction in
the gorge the final annihilation of the Toltecs.

We must not therefore look askance at the occurrence of
legends concerning the great human hero who has come
from a distant clime to bring all the elements of culture to

a people, for many historical facts may very well be imbedded in these myths. Indeed we shall see that the epic of Quetzalcoatl has analogues in Oaxaca, Yucatan, Guatemala, in Venezuela, Colombia and Peru; and that where this specific type of epic stops, there the full force of Maya and Peruvian influence stopped. Beyond lie the peoples that have only secondarily been influenced by these basic civilizations and this fact, too, is faintly reëchoed in the epics of these people and in the rôle and significance possessed by the divine heroes who are credited with having founded their culture. Legend thus shall lead us by the hand to corroborate what archæology and ethnology have taught and to give us at times glimpses of cultural movements about which archæology and ethnology are unfortunately silent.

In Oaxaca, among the Zapotec and Mixtec, two peoples who were the most important centers from which spread the Maya and the Toltec cultures, we find a figure strangely like that of Quetzalcoatl. He, too, had come to the land by sea, from the southwest, and he, too, had taught gentle doctrines of reform. He, too, was persecuted and driven away. But the doctrines and the culture he implanted in Oaxaca took firm root and the priest-king who ruled in Oaxaca when the Aztecs conquered it, claimed to be directly descended from the long-bearded stranger. Just as in the case of Quetzalcoatl this legend reflects an historical fact fairly accurately. The higher culture—it was the Maya— did come to Oaxaca from without and the peoples of Oaxaca did succeed in developing very special traits that were at variance with that of the Maya.

As we proceed further south to the Chibcha and to Yucatan we find in the legends about Votan, Kukulcan and

Zamna, the same traits—heroes who have come from some distant place to introduce the higher elements of culture. Votan manifestly symbolizes the rather late invasion of Chiapas by the Mayas and the founding of the city of Palenque, and Kukulcan symbolizes the spread of Maya culture northward to Chichen Itza.

The legends of the culture-founder in South America are quite similar. In Colombia we find the figure of Mochica. Like Quetzalcoatl and his Mexican analogues, he belonged to a race distinct from that of the Chibcha. He brought the Chibcha all the culture they ever possessed. He introduced the cult of the sun and placed the land under two rulers. But he, too, had an enemy, his beautiful wife. All the wiles she possessed, and she had many, she employed in trying to undo all the good her husband had wrought. Finally he had to drive her away and she became the moon. But when his work was done he, too, had to leave. Far from the scene of his labors, in a beautiful valley, he spent thousands of years in the practice of asceticism.

And thus we finally come to Peru and to Uiracocha. Our old friend Cieza de Leon has left us an excellent description of the Peruvian account of the coming of Uiracocha:

Things being in this state, the sun, shining very brightly, came forth from the island of Titicaca, in the great lake at the Callao, at which every one rejoiced. Presently afterwards, they say, that there came from a southern direction a white man of great stature, who, by his aspect and presence, called forth great veneration and obedience. The man who thus appeared had great power, insomuch that he could change plains into mountains, and great hills into valleys, and make water flow out of stones. As soon as such power was beheld, the people called him the Maker-of-created-things, the Prince-of-all-things, Father-of-the-Sun. For they say that he performed other wonders, giving life to men and animals, so that by his hand great benefits were conferred on the people. And such was the story that the Indians who told it to me say that they heard from their ancestors, who in like manner heard it in the old songs which they received from very ancient times. They say that this man went on towards the north, working these marvels along the way of the mountains; and that he never more returned so as to be seen.

In many places he gave orders to men how they should live, and he spoke lovingly to them and with much gentleness, admonishing them that they should do good, and no evil or injury to one another, and that they should be loving and charitable to all. In most parts he is generally called *Ticiviracocha*, but in the province of the Callao they call him *Tuapaca*, and in other places *Arnauan*. In many parts they built temples in which they put blocks of stone in likeness of him, and offered up sacrifices before them. It is held that the great blocks at Tiahuanaco date from that time. Although, from the fame of what formerly had passed, they relate the things I have stated touching Ticiviracocha, they know nothing more of him, nor whether he would ever return to any part of this kingdom.

Besides this, they say that, a long time having passed, they again saw another man resembling the first, whose name they do not mention. But they received it from their forefathers as very certain that wherever this personage came and there were sick, he healed them, and where there were blind he gave them sight by only uttering words. Through acts so good and useful he was much beloved by all. In this fashion, working great things by his words, he arrived at the province of the Canas, in which, near to a village which has the name of Cacha, and in which the Captain Bartolome de Terrazas holds an *encomienda*, the people rose against him, threatening to stone him. They saw him upon his knees, with his hands raised to heaven, as if invoking the divine favor to liberate him from the danger that threatened him.

The Indians further state that presently there appeared a great fire in the heaven, which they thought to be surrounding them. Full of fear and trembling, they came to him whom they had wanted to kill, and with loud clamor besought him to be pleased to forgive them. For they knew that this punishment threatened them because of the sin they had committed in wishing to stone the stranger. Presently they saw that when he ordered the fire to cease, it was extinguished, so that they were themselves witnesses of what had come to pass; and the stones were consumed and burnt up in such wise as that large blocks could be lifted in the hand, as if they were of cork. On this subject they go on to say, that, leaving the place where these things happened, the man arrived on the sea-coast, where, holding his mantle, he went in amongst the waves and was never more seen. And as he went, so they gave him the name of *Uiracocha,* which means "the foam of the sea." . . .

After we leave the great civilizations a semihuman culture-founder who is at the same time a wanderer is rarely found in the mythology of the other tribes of North and South America. In fact, he appears only once and then exactly where we might have expected to find him, in the region of the lower Mississippi. Of the various migration-myths none is more interesting than that recorded by the old French historian Du Pratz, which he claims to have heard from the guardian of the temple. Mixture of fact and fable as it is, it clearly records certain historical events still vaguely remembered and belongs to the same general category as the stories mentioned above and those we shall mention below:

Before we came into this land we lived there under the Sun. We lived in a beautiful country where the earth is always good. It is there that our Suns remained because the ancients of the country were unable to force us out with all their warriors. They came, indeed, as far as the mountains, after having reduced under their power the villages of our people which were in the plains. But our warriors always repulsed them at the entrance of the mountains and they were never able to penetrate there.

Our entire nation extended along the great water where this

great river loses itself. Some of our Suns went up this river to find a place where they might conceal themselves far from the ancients of the country, because after having been a long time good friends they had become ill disposed and so numerous that we were no longer able to defend ourselves against them. All those who dwelt in the plains could not avoid submitting, and those who had retired into the mountains remained alone under obedience to the great Sun. The ancients of the country wished, indeed, to force those of our people whom they had subjugated to join them in order to make war on us, but they preferred to die rather than attack their brothers and especially the Suns.

But those who had ascended along the west side of the great river, having discovered this land which we inhabit, now crossed the river on a raft of dry canes. They found the country such as they desired, suitable for concealing themselves from the ancients of the country, and even easy to defend against them if they ever undertook to attack us there. On their return they reported this to the great Sun and the other Suns who governed the villages.

The great Sun immediately had those informed who remained in the plains and defended themselves still against the ancients of the country, and ordered them to go into this new land and build there a temple and to carry there the eternal fire in order to preserve it. There came hither a great number, with their wives and their children. The oldest and the Suns, relatives of the great Sun, remained with those who kept with the great Sun and in the mountains. They remained there a still longer time, as well as those who lived on the shores of the great water.

A large part of our nation being then established here, lived a long time in peace and in abundance during many generations. On the other hand, those who had remained under the Sun, or very near, for it was very warm there, did not hasten to come and join us, because the ancients of the country made themselves hated by all men—as much by our nation as by their own. Here is how the ancient word says that that happened.

The ancients of the country were all brothers—that is to say, they all came out of the same country—but each large village on which many others depended had its head master, and each head master commanded those whom he had brought with him into this land. There was then nothing done among them that all had not consented to. But one of these head masters raised himself above the others and treated them as slaves. Thus the ancients of the country no longer agreed among themselves. They even warred against one another. Some of them united with those of our nation who had remained, and all together they sustained themselves well enough.

This was not the only reason which retained our Suns in that country. It was hard for them to leave such a good land, and besides their assistance was necessary to our other brothers who were established there like ourselves and who lived along the shore of the great water on the side toward the east. These extended so far that they went beyond the Sun, since there were some of them from whom the Sun heard sometimes only at the end of five or six years, and there were yet others so far away from us, whether along the coast or in the island, that for many years they had not been heard of at all.

It was only after many generations that these Suns came to join us in this country, where the fine air and the peace which we enjoyed, had multiplied us into a number as great as the leaves on the trees. These Suns came alone with their slaves, because our other brothers did not wish to follow them. . . .

Apart from these tribes all the peoples north of the Rio Grande have completely forgotten that their culture came to them from the south. And this is natural enough, for culture has come to them through the descendants of the descendants of those who first brought it and, in many cases, it has reached them not as the result of an invasion in force but by slow infiltrations. Some faint recollections we cannot help feeling are to be found exactly in those regions where we might have expected them—in the southwest and the southeast. There we come across long migration-tales in which we hear of abodes that have been abandoned and of a glorious paradise-like bliss which all once enjoyed. But of a stranger coming to teach them new ways and to bring civilization, of that they know nothing. All is lost in an impenetrable mythological gloom. Even the last faint echoes finally die out completely and not only do the semi-barbarians and the barbarians of the north feel no connection with the rest of mankind, but they arrogantly and chauvin-istically announce that the deities have created them and their culture out of nothing.

Yet here where one trail peters out completely, another can be said to be faintly if inconsistently visible. Every-where throughout North and South America we encounter a fascinating myth about two brothers who are deities and Children of the Sun. The world becomes filled with the renown of their great deeds. As we follow them from tribe to tribe, their identity and their significance changes. Offhand we are inclined naturally enough to ascribe no im-portance to these changes. But when we study them more carefully a startling fact seems to emerge, namely, that all these transformations are of a progressive kind.

As we proceed north from Yucatan the two divine brothers lose more and more of their attributes, become more and more functionless and finally, among the Ojibwa of Canada their story has degenerated into a pleasing fairy story for children, old and young. A similar fate befalls these heroes as we leave the Peruvian and Colombian high-lands and wander eastward across the Andes. The pro-gressive deterioration of the hero and the myth associated with him seems to follow closely in the wake of the dif-fusion of culture from the Mayas and Peruvians.

Let us begin with the Mayas. The two brothers are deities, the children of parents who afterwards become the sun and the moon. Their father is defeated by the people of Xibalba, the Maya hell, and subsequently beheaded. The children are magically conceived and after discovering the identity of their parent, proceed to Xibalba to avenge his death. After this has been accomplished and the father restored to life, he and his adherents become the sun, the moon and the stars, respectively. One interesting detail must still be mentioned, the enmity of the heroes and of their half-brother, for though it is of slight significance here, it looms very large in some of the other versions of the legend.

Among the Aztecs the situation is somewhat confused owing partly to the poor versions that have come down to us and partly to the complicated history of the Aztec cosmological myths. The attributes and adventures belonging properly to only two brothers are here connected with a number of brothers, all of them well-known gods, Tezcatlipoca, Quetzalcoatl, and Huitzilopochtli. They were all associated with the sun; they are all gods and they are all at enmity with one another.

In the southwest of the United States, among the Hopi, we meet both the two brothers again. They are diminutive in size and are born of the sun and the foam-cap. One is slightly older and wiser than the other. The younger brother is rash, quick, and sure of action.

Though the figures have undergone great transformations it seems clear that we are here dealing with the two brothers of the Maya story and with the Quetzalcoatl and Tezcatlipoca of the Aztecs. Like so many other details connected with the culture of the Indians of the United States the Hopi version is closer to the Maya than it is to the Aztec. As in the Maya version the adventures of the two children of the Sun take place in the dark caverns of the world. But the heroes in the Hopi version have not entered these caverns willingly or in search of adventure. They have always dwelt there and their task is no longer to obtain revenge for the decapitation of their parent but to deliver mankind from the gloom in which it has been enveloped. Slowly and only after many trials do they succeed in leading mankind from one world to another and so emerge into the light of the sun. When they reach the surface of the earth they are compelled to battle with people of an earlier emergence. The rather romantic but intuitive American ethnologist, Cushing, has recorded a beautiful version of the Hopi myth:

When the world was new, men and the creatures lived not and things were not on the top of the earth, but below. All was black darkness as well above as below. There were four worlds, this world, the top of the earth, and three cave-worlds, one below the other. No one of the cave worlds was large enough to contain all living creatures and men, for they increased in the lowest first cave-world so as to overfill it. They were poor and knew not whither to turn in the black darkness, and when they moved, they jostled one another. The place was filled with the filth and dung of those who dwelt in it. No man could turn to spit but he spat on another, or cast slime from his nose but it fell upon another. The people filled the place with their complainings and exclamations of disgust.

It was said by the masters, "Being thus it is not well," and, "How can it be made better?" and, "Let it be tried and seen!" Two boys, the older brother and the younger, said, "Yes, let it be tried and seen and it shall be well; by our wills shall it be well." So said "The Two" to the masters and to the priest-chiefs of the dwellers in the cave-world. "The Two" pierced the roofs of the caves and descended to the dark abode of men and beings. They then planted one after the other all the plants which grew, hoping that one of them would grow up to the opening through which they had descended, yet have the strength to bear the weight of men and the beings; and that by climbing it they might deliver themselves into the second cave-world. At last, after many, many trials, the cane was found so tall that its top grew through and so strong that men could climb on it to the top. It was jointed that it might be like a ladder readily ascended, and ever since then the cane has grown in joints as we see it to-day along the Colorado.

Up this cane many men and creatures climbed to the second cave-world. When a part of the number had climbed out, fearing that the second cave-world—which was so dark that they could not see how large it was,—would prove too small, they shook the cane ladder so that those who were coming up, fell back. Then they pulled the ladder quite out, preventing the others from ascending. It is said that those who were left, ultimately came out. They are our brothers to the westward.

After a long time the second cave-world became filled with men and the beings, as had been the first. Wrangling and complainings were heard as in the beginning. Again the cane was placed under the roof, and thus once more men and the creatures found deliverance. Yet those who were slow to climb out were shaken back or left, as had been a part of the number in the first cave-world. Though larger, the third cave-world was as dark as were the others. Fire was found by "The Two" with which torches were set ablaze, and by the light of these men built their huts and kivas or traveled from place to place.

Times of evil came while the creatures and men dwelt in this third world. Women became crazed. They neglected all things for the dance. They even forgot their babes. Wives became mixed with wives so that husbands knew not their own from others. Then there was no day, but one night. Throughout this night women danced in the kivas, ceasing only to sleep. Whereupon fathers became mothers to the neglected little ones. When these little ones cried of hunger, the fathers carried them to the kivas where the women were dancing. The mothers, hearing their cries, came and suckled them. Then, again forgetting them, left them to be cared for by the fathers, to rejoin the dance.

These troubles caused men to long for light and to seek again deliverance. They ascended to the fourth world which was this world. But when they came out, they found it as dark as it had been below, for the earth was closed in by the sky, as had been the cave-worlds by their roofs. Men went abroad and did their doings only by the light of torches and fires. They found the tracks of only one being, of the single ruler of the unpeopled world, the tracks of Corpse Demon or Death. They fled eastward and the people sought to follow them, but the world was damp and men knew not what to do in the darkness; for waters seemed to surround them everywhere and the tracks to lead out into the waters.

There were with men,—who came forth with other creatures from the cave-worlds,—five beings, Spider, Vulture, Swallow, Coyote and Locust. The people and these beings consulted together, that they might make light. Many, many attempts were made, but without success. It was decided that Spider should first try. She spun a mantle of pure white cotton. It gave some light, but still not enough. She is therefore our grandmother. So the people procured and prepared a very white deerskin which had nowhere been pierced. Of this they formed a shield-case, which they painted with turquoise paint. Lo, it shed forth such brilliant light when they had done, that it illuminated the whole world. In its light the cotton mantle-light faded. So they sent the shield-light to the east where it became the sun, and the mantle-light they sent to the west where it became the moon.

Now down in the cave-world Coyote had stolen a jar which was very heavy, so heavy that Coyote was weary of carrying it. He therefore decided to leave it, but was curious to see what it contained. So now that it was light he opened it, whereupon many shining fragments and sparks flew out and upward, singeing his face in their passage. Hence the coyote has a black face to this day. These became the stars.

By these lights it was found that the world was indeed very small and surrounded on every side by waters which made it damp. The people appealed to Vulture who spread his wings and fanned the waters, that they flowed away to the east and west until mountains began to appear. Across these "The Two" cut channels through which the waters rushed away, wearing their courses deeper and deeper, thus forming the great canyons and valleys of the world. The waters have kept on flowing for ages, until the world has grown and is still growing drier and drier. Now that it was light and land appeared, the people easily followed the tracks of Death whither they led toward the eastward. Hence Death is our greatest father and master, for we followed his tracks from the exit of the cave-worlds; and he was the only being that awaited us on the great world of waters where now is this world. Although all the waters had flowed away, all the earth was damp and soft, hence it is that we may see to this day, between this place toward the westward and the place whence we came out, the tracks of men and of many strange creatures. For the earth has since changed to stone and all the tracks are preserved as when they were first made.

Thus did the Mayan gods become transformed as the memory of Maya culture faded more and more from the mind of man.

And so the legend passed from tribe to tribe, remembered more accurately in one place and less accurately in another. Before finally disappearing completely we find a remarkable version of it in that small isolated area of northern Wisconsin where so many faint echoes of the ancient glory have been preserved—among the Winnebago of Green Bay.

Just as the Winnebago were almost absorbed by barbarians so, too, did this last reflection of a cultural heritage that had come down originally from the Maya through the Mound-Builders and their tainted descendants, finally lose all semblance to its prototype as it spread over the forests and lakes of Canada.

CHAPTER VIII

THE MOUND-BUILDERS

Not far from the present site of St. Louis, but in the State of Illinois, there stands a remarkable structure. Situated in the midst of a group of about sixty artificial mounds, and rising to a height of a hundred feet, is to be found the most extensive of all mounds north of the Rio Grande—Cahokia. Four terraces lead to the top, and it embraces an area of twelve acres. Though everything else about it may be doubtful, one thing is clear, that it must have taken many years to construct, and that it presupposes a very extensive sedentary population.

American scholars are still at loggerheads as to the identity of the people who built this and the other numerous mounds scattered so lavishly over the eastern half of the United States. Three generations ago it was the consensus of opinion that they had been built by a wonderful people who had preceded the Indians, and who had come from outside the United States. But then about fifty years ago, a strong reaction set in against this view, and against ascribing to outsiders the erection of any of the prehistoric structures found within the confines of the United States. This, coupled with an increased knowledge of the Indians, led most authorities to insist that all these mounds and enclosures had been the work of the ancestors of the Indians still dwelling approximately in the vicinity of these prehistoric works. Indeed, what seemed adequate evidence was advanced to show that within recent times even, travelers and explorers had encountered Indians who were still capable of building mounds of various descriptions.

Thus did the pendulum swing to the opposite extreme. The skill required for the construction of most of the mounds, and the culture that must have been connected with them, was minimized in order to obviate the hated prospect of assuming an invasion from without. But alas! as the mounds yield up more and more of their treasures it becomes increasingly clear that their builders belong to a civilization far superior to anything known to-day in the United States, or to anything that was encountered when the Europeans first came to this country. Nowhere else do we find pottery of so wonderful a workmanship and of so remarkable a variety; nowhere else do we find a copper industry even remotely comparable.

But though we are now certain that the civilization of these Mound-Builders represents the greatest cultural achievement north of Mexico, this realization, far from simplifying our problems, seems to have increased them. As mound after mound is opened and explored, we find a hopeless potpourri. Objects requiring the greatest dexterity of workmanship exist side by side with the simplest utensils imaginable, and mixed with them are artifacts that we can justifiably associate with the culture of certain living tribes. Confusion upon confusion! Northern elements mingle with southern, eastern with western. It would be vain to seek for order here. Only one explanation seems possible, that we are in the midst of the débris of an ancient and superior culture that has been more obliterated in one place and less in another, transformed in one area and specialized in another.

We find the same confusion but upon a much higher plane, of course, in the valley of Mexico and the surrounding regions. There we know that an archaic was succeeded by the so-called Toltec culture, and that this Toltec culture was slowly adopted, remodeled and attenuated by the barbarians who converged upon the valley of Mexico from all sides. Let us see whether a similar explanation will not hold for the valley of the Mississippi and the adjacent Gulf regions.

All along the lower regions of the Mississippi Valley, from Louisiana northward, through Arkansas and Tennessee, the ground is literally covered with earthworks of various types, the most important of which are pyramidal mounds and enclosures. Their distribution is exceedingly suggestive. The pyramidal mounds are rarely found in Ohio, Indiana and northern Illinois, and the enclosures, although having a much wider distribution, are typical of this northern area. In other words, where the pyramidal mounds stop, the enclosures increase. But that is only one part of the story. Where the pyramidal mounds stop, smaller mounds, either conical or in the shape of animals, greatly increase in quantity. Wisconsin is practically covered with them. Now what does this all mean? Are we here in the presence of an insoluble problem? We do not think so. Let us glance at these pyramidal mounds for a moment.

Their typical form is that of the truncated and quadrangular pyramid. Some are not high, and to all intents and purposes present to-day at least the appearance of earthen platforms. Others have terraces extending outward from one or from two sides, while still others have a roadway leading up to the level surface, and one that is often graded. Usually this graded pathway is placed at right angles on one side. Occasionally the main pyramidal structure is surmounted by a small conical tumulus. As a general rule all these pyramidal mounds show indications of having once possessed edifices of some kind. Their resemblance to the pyramidal foundations of the sacred precincts of the Maya, Toltec and Aztec, is patent, and it needs no stretch of the imagination to picture their level tops as having once been covered with temples.

We are undoubtedly in the presence of some mute testimony to the main invasion of the United States by the Maya; some reminiscence of the trail that stopped in the northern part of the state of Vera Cruz, to be resumed again under altered conditions, along the valley of the lower Mississippi. Clearly a struggle must have taken place. This struggle would seem to have been of a twofold nature, an actual attempt by the invaders who had presumably already mixed to a considerable extent with the people, to conquer the tribes they encountered; and repeated and desperate attempts on the part of these invaders to keep their heritage intact, by surrounding themselves with fortifications or retiring to inaccessible regions. The contest, we may surmise, was an unequal one, and the original owners of the soil soon hemmed the invaders in on all sides. Even in that area where the pyramidal mounds are most abundant and where we must assume that the invaders had had their greatest success, we already see them defending themselves behind enclosures and fortifications. As we proceed north these enclosures and fortifications increase in size and number. Scholars have often wondered why in the north these earthworks are found in rather out-of-the-way and inaccessible places. But that is exactly where we would expect to find the remnants of an ancient and hard-pressed culture to take refuge.

But we need not depend upon the evidence of the mounds alone for our hypothesis that this region was a veritable melting-pot of peoples. As was pointed out in the previous chapter, the whole valley of the Mississippi, from New Orleans upward, swarmed with tribes speaking diverse languages, and originally coming from all parts of the United States.

To the simple aboriginal peoples of the United States the Mound-Builders must have been as idealized a nation as were the Toltecs to the invading Aztecs and their earlier kinsmen. It is safe to assume that the aboriginal possessors of the land were attracted to the settlements of the Mound-Builders, and that they came from all directions but always with hostile intent. The damage they eventually inflicted was irreparable in many ways. Fortunately, however, either they did not always come in sufficiently large numbers to destroy the settlements of the Mound-Builders immediately, or the Mound-Builders had succeeded in digging themselves too deeply into the valley to be dislodged easily. The history of the Aztecs was in large measure repeated here and the barbarians, in the course of their destructive attacks on the invaders, themselves became civilized. They adopted agriculture and a sedentary mode of life, and took over even some of the more complicated religious and social customs of the people they were slowly but surely exterminating. The more elaborate techniques of the highly civilized invaders were, however, gone forever. The art of constructing elaborate mounds was completely lost. With it went the skill and artistry required for the manufacture of the pottery that had been the glory of these people. Copper work of an elaborate kind also became a lost art although, like pottery, some form of it survived, if in a rather rudimentary fashion.

It is interesting to see the hold that copper kept upon the imaginations of the simpler people who had overwhelmed the Mound-Builders. In distant northern Michigan, even to-day, legends are filled with references to it. But it is no longer an ordinary object; it has become sacred. To obtain it, a magical process must be resorted to, so the priests declare, involving the sacrifice of a young virgin. Among the Ojibwa of northern Michigan, only specially-qualified medicine-men know how to procure it. They must call to their aid the mysterious sea-serpents that infest the waters of Lake Michigan. Going down to the shore, they throw tobacco into the water and utter their prayer of allurement to the dread sea-gods. A young girl is then placed naked upon the shore. Soon the sea-serpents appear and making immediately for the human sacrifice, decapitate the poor victim. Then the medicine-men approach, and with specially prepared knives made of red cedar, cut off a small portion of the so-called "horns" of the animal god. These "horns," it is claimed, are really made of congealed copper, and as the piece cut off by the priests falls on the sand, it assumes a liquid form. Only when it has congealed again does it become copper. And this is all that the Ojibwa of northern Michigan and Wisconsin and Minnesota still remember of copper! And yet they are almost at the very source of most of the copper deposits of the United States —Isle Royale and the Calumet peninsula.

But let us retrace our steps and beginning with Wisconsin, make our way south, keeping close to the Mississippi and its affluents. Here in Wisconsin we find the northernmost outposts of the Mound-Builders. In the southern part of the state we encounter a large earthwork and numerous small mounds. This earthwork, misnamed Aztalan, extends around three sides of an irregular parallelogram with the west branch of the Rock River forming a fourth side. The space enclosed is seventeen and two-thirds acres. The total length of the wall is twenty-seven hundred and fifty feet, it is about twenty-two feet wide, and from one to five feet high. It clearly belongs to the great series of enclosures which mark the northern advance of the Mound-Builders, and has become of unusual significance because of the recent discovery within its ruins of a worked object that unquestionably came from Mexico.

But the most peculiar feature of Wisconsin archæology are the effigy mounds, earthworks of various sizes definitely intended to represent specific animals. Some of them were undoubtedly made by the ancestors of the Indians living in Wisconsin to-day. Others, probably the vast majority, were constructed by outsiders, who had come from the south, and were clearly a direct offshoot of the Mound-Builders of Ohio and Illinois. In one of the effigy mounds recently excavated two distinct cultures were brought to light, both quite distinct from the later culture found on the sites in the immediate vicinity. The people who constructed these mounds practiced cremation and erected altars for this purpose, just as did the Mound-Builders to the south. And like the latter they had several types of sacrifice—sacrificial earths, property sacrifice, animal sacrifice, and possibly human sacrifice. Of all these traits we have just mentioned, only one persisted for a long time, the custom of constructing the effigy mounds. That, too, degenerated until it lost

all of its original significance and became secondarily identified with the clan animal.

That the majority of the Wisconsin effigy mounds are the
work of the Mound-Builders there seems to be little question. Indeed, it seems very likely that this northern van-
guard of the Mound-Builders reached southern Wisconsin
in considerable force. The effigy mounds found almost
everywhere seem to indicate that they still had enough vigor
to specialize in the cultural goods they had inherited from
their remote ancestors, for effigy mounds are essentially a
Wisconsin specialization.

As we leave Wisconsin and proceed to southern Illinois
the earthworks, mounds, the finds in the graves, everything
becomes more striking. In Union County, for instance, two
copper plates were discovered, one showing dancing figures
definitely reminiscent of the Maya, and another a bird
similar to the one found in Georgia. We are here within
the radius of the true Mound-Builder culture. Its center
lay somewhat to the south and the southeast, toward Tennessee and Georgia. It is in Georgia, in fact, that we find
what is probably the most remarkable series of mounds
within the United States, those at Etowah.

Situated in the midst of a fertile valley, the Etowah
mounds occupy a central position in an area of some fifty
acres. On the south and the east they are bounded by the
Etowah River, on the north and west by a large, artificial
ditch. Within the enclosure formed by the moat and the
river are seven mounds, three of them very large in size.
The central mound rises about sixty-five feet above the level
of the valley, and is quadrangular in outline with a diameter
of two hundred and twenty-five feet. As seen to-day,
shorn of vegetation, its outlines stand out sharply. Its

ascent was accomplished through the intervention of terraces rising one above the other. These terraces are sixty-five feet in width, and extend from the mound toward the southeast. Near the eastern angle, a pathway leads to the top.

The copper objects found within them are perhaps more interesting than the mounds themselves. One copper plate represents a human figure with wings about seventeen inches long and eight inches wide; another a human figure without wings, a third, a bird, and a fourth, some kind of a badge. Upon examining the human figures, we are at once struck by their resemblance to objects found both in Mexico proper and in Central America. Nor can we assume that the tie binding these Mound-Builders with ancient Mexico was a purely accidental one, for beautifully worked copper plates of identical character extend into Ohio, and even into northern Illinois. In addition, engraved shells with similar representations have been found in Georgia, Tennessee and Arkansas. Here at Etowah were discovered a few crude, gold objects, and further north, in Ohio, we find copper pendants plated with thin sheet-gold, a technique specifically Mexican. And since we are speaking of gold, it might be well to point out that the most interesting gold objects found in the United States come from Florida, and that they, too, are definitely reminiscent of Central America and Mexico.

Who, in the face of these facts, can any longer deny to the Mound-Builders their right to being considered the torch-bearers of culture for the eastern half of the United States, and thus indirectly for practically all of aboriginal America, with the exception, of course, of the Pueblo region, and the northwest coast? And who can deny their direct relation to the great civilizations of Mexico? As we have pointed out before, their first contact with these ancient Mexican civilizations clearly goes back far beyond the times of the Aztecs, far beyond the times of the Toltecs. It is to be sought in the very first migrations from Mexico along the shores of the Gulf of Mexico and across its waters.

We must bear this in mind if we wish properly to understand the specialized nature of certain features of the Mound-Builder culture. The earliest Maya influences reached them at a time when Maya culture itself had not as yet become definitely specialized and fixed in every direction. Particularly was this true of pottery, and it is consequently in pottery that we find the greatest variety and apparently the most marked originality. The types of pottery were infinite. We find bowls, pot-shaped vessels, wide-mouthed bottles, jars and high-necked bottles. All these could, in turn, be modified in a thousand different ways depending upon the fanciful features given to the rim, neck or body. In size, the bowls vary from little toy vessels an inch in diameter and depth, to fully twenty inches across the top and from six to twelve inches in diameter. Most remarkable are the fanciful shapes given to many of these bowls. Every species of animals is practically represented. The same variety is apparent in connection with the carved tobacco-pipes.

Such were the styles introduced by the Mound-Builders. Their pottery was destined to but a brief existence and it has nowhere survived among living Indian tribes. The carved tobacco-pipes, on the other hand, spread over the whole of the United States and retained quite a hold even on the comparatively simple Algonquian tribes who swarmed over this area in later years.

Within the last few years new light has come to us concerning the probable descendants of these Mound-Builders. In Louisiana there has been discovered a type of pottery which possesses definite affinities with that used by one of the subdivisions of the Caddoan tribes, within historical times, so that here, at last, we can fairly properly claim that the continuity of certain phases of the Mound-Builder culture has persisted without interruption. Bearing in mind the complexity and individuality of the ritualistc organization of most of the Caddoan tribes, we are justified in asserting that here, too, we are dealing with something more than the mere reflection of the old Mound-Builder culture.

CHAPTER IX

THE SACRED FIRE

EVERYWHERE throughout the region inhabited by the Mound-Builders excavations have disclosed altars and crematories. It was at first supposed that the presence of so many altars and crematories might betoken the existence of frequent human sacrifices. But this assumption is rather far-fetched. It is far more likely that we are here dealing with fireplaces, probably belonging to the precincts of ancient temples. In the absence of direct evidence let us turn for information to the peoples who unquestionably inhabited this region for a long time and whose descendants are known to us as members of the great Siouan and Mushkogean stocks—the Kansa and the Quapaw; the Natchez, the Creek and the Cherokee. Can these tribes throw any light upon our problem? Let us see.

When the French first explored Louisiana they became acquainted with a tribe called the Natchez. Nothing of their culture survives to-day but some of the earlier travelers were very good observers and they have left us excellent descriptions of their customs and manners. This holds particularly for the French historian Du Pratz.

Now the Natchez were famous for a number of things, particularly for their sun-worship and their temple. Du Pratz inquired about both and this is the story the guardian of the temple told him:

"A very great number of years ago there appeared among

us a man and his wife who had descended from the sun. We did not believe that he was the son of the Sun or that the Sun had a wife by whom he begot children, but when both of these were seen they were still so brilliant that it was not difficult to believe that they had come from the Sun.

"After delivering a long speech in which the man told them how they were to arrange their life he informed them that he had brought with him a temple in which was to be preserved eternally a fire, which he would have the Sun send down to them. The wood with which this fire was to be fed must be a pure wood without bark, and eight wise men were to be chosen from among the tribe to guard and tend this sacred fire day and night." . . .

To this sacred fire no sacrifices, libations or offerings were made and yet, so Du Pratz assures us, their entire cult consisted in maintaining the eternal fire. It was their belief, in fact, that the great Sun watches with particular attention over the chief of the guardians of the temple.

Much further to the east we find the same reverence for the sacred fire. Among the Cherokee it was definitely connected with mound-building. A mound was built up with earth and on top of it was placed a circle of stones. A fire was then kindled in the center of this circle. An open place was left in the center and a hollow cedar-trunk was let down which fitted around the fire and protected it from the earth. The whole mound was then finished off smoothly and the town-house built upon it. One individual called the fire-keeper always stayed in the town-house to feed and tend the fire. Before the most famous of the Cherokee dances, the Green Corn Dance, took place, it was the custom to have all the fires in the village extinguished and have the people get new fire from the town-house. This new fire was called "the honored and sacred fire."

Surely we have here an excellent clue to the meaning of the numerous crematories and burnt-remains so characteristic of the ancient mounds. And if this has persisted to the present-day Cherokee, we may reasonably assume that many of the integral elements of the Mound-Builders' civilization have also come down, however greatly transformed and re-interpreted they may have become in the process.

It would be hopeless to seek for one unified culture in this region. The only single thing that seems constant, is this worship of the sacred fire, a trait that has clearly been diffused wherever the southern Sioux and the kindred of the Cherokee, the Iroquoian peoples, wandered, and wherever their influence extended. To the Winnebago, in northern Wisconsin, the fire was still addressed as "our grandfather who stands at all times in the center of the dwelling." Even in northern Michigan, among such a comparatively simple tribe as the Algonquian Ottawa, there were two permanent officials whose sole duty it was to tend to the fire.

Apart from the sacred fire, however, and apart from the ever-present maize, no single unified civilization existed here any more than did a single language or race. Yet two subtypes of culture do seem to emerge and it is these that we shall try to characterize briefly, for they are bound to throw considerable light on the nature of the later cultures that developed out of the débris of the Mound-Builder civilization, and may even give us some suggestions as to the different ways in which Maya influences had come to the Mississippi.

These more or less typical subcultures are very well represented by two specific tribes, on the one hand by the Creek and their kindred and, on the other, by the Natchez and the tribes immediately adjacent.

The economic basis of the life of both was maize. Like fire the worship of maize permeated every element of their life. Their main ceremony was grouped around it. Essentially this consisted of eating in common and in a religious manner, new maize which had been sown for this specific purpose. It was a solemn feast. When the maize was to be planted, a new plot of earth was chosen that had not been cultivated within the memory of man. This plot was first freed of all the trees and brushwood growing upon it. Everything connected with the working of the field and with the culture of the maize had, among the Natchez, to be done by warriors. The smallest operations were not regarded as unworthy of them. For any one but a warrior to have touched the maize would have been regarded as profanation. So sacred and revered was it that it was believed that any person who so profaned the field, would never be able to leave it but would perish miserably. As soon as the stalks approached maturity, the warriors went to the place where the maize was to be eaten and where a kind of granary had been erected. Du Pratz has left us a remarkable description of this feast.

As soon as everything was disposed and prepared for the harvest and the maize was ripe, the warriors went to gather it. In fact the entire nation prepared itself to participate in the great feast. At daybreak everybody was already astir. The old men as well as the women and children all left at sunrise. Each one brought the utensils necessary for preparing the grain, and, as soon as they arrived, they collected the wood to make a fire at the proper time. The old warriors prepared the litter on which the Great Sun, such was the title of the chief, was to be brought. This litter was composed of four red bars which cross each other at the four corners of the seat which has a depth of about one and a half feet. The entire seat was garnished inside with common deerskins. Those which hung outside were painted with designs according to each man's individual taste.

Those who prepared this conveyance were the foremost and the oldest warriors of the nation. The litter itself was placed on the shoulders of eight men, and no others were allowed to take it out of the village. Thus only sixteen men remained there, for all the others had departed shortly after sunrise with the war-chief. These men the leader dispersed a hundred paces apart, placing eight in each relay. For this purpose he only chose the strongest and most vigorous warriors. The others waited at the open space with him to receive the Great Sun. After these dispositions had been made and the warrior's post had been painted and placed in the middle of the space with considerable ceremony, the Great Sun came forth from his cabin adorned with the ornaments which indicated his dignity. He seated himself in the litter and then the eight oldest warriors placed him on the shoulders of those who had been designated to carry him.

Scarcely had those in the open space perceived him than the whole nation, which was breathlessly awaiting him, filled the air with cries of joy. Soon he arrived at the side of the cabin which had been prepared for him. Before descending he made a circuit of the square and when he approached the sacred maize, saluted it three times reverently.

All the warriors whom he had left behind followed him

at their leisure but without stopping, and there remained in the cabins only the old men and old women who were no longer able to walk, and the sick. The guardians of the eternal fire did not leave the temple. Their wives carried them some of the dishes prepared of sacred maize.

The Great Sun then allowed his warriors to rest awhile so that they might have time for the making of the new fire, which was produced by rubbing two pieces of wood against each other. Any other method of producing it would be profane. During this interval the Great Sun himself remained with the other Suns each of whom wore a similar diadem. Only the great war-chief was distinguished from the other Suns by his costume. He had a large white feather fastened to his hair, at the end of which was a red tuft which carried a tassel of the same color. This feather extended above the others in his diadem by about two inches.

When the great war-chief felt that all the warriors were ready, he went with four that had previously been chosen, to distribute the maize for the women. With them he presented himself before the "throne" and addressing the Great Sun said: "Speak, we await your word."

Then the chief arose and leaving his cabin, bowed toward the four quarters of the world, commencing with the south. As soon as the chief and the warriors had gone to the granary, he raised his arms and hands to heaven, whither he also directed his looks and said: "Give them the maize," and then seated himself again. The great war-chief thanked him and went on. Then all the others did the same. The women and the young people kept a profound silence and prepared their baskets to go after the maize. They went to the granary as soon as the thanks of the people had been given.

During the time of the thanksgiving, each of the four warriors with their great chief ascended a ladder, quickly took the coverings off the granary, throwing the pieces aside, and gave maize to the female Suns and afterward to all the women who presented themselves. As soon as they had received it these ran and fled as if they had stolen it. Those who had remained in the cabins placed themselves in front of the others and acted as though they wished to snatch them away. They emptied it on skins and husked it quickly. Scarcely had they enough of it to make one crushing than they put it into their mortars to shell it. The pot with boiling water was on the fire. They threw this meal into it and hastened to cook it. As soon as it was cooked they awaited the word to eat it for they would never touch any of it before this order had been given.

This whole operation was gone through with so much eagerness that one might have received the impression that they had not eaten for many days. The servants of the Great Sun, although very numerous, did not have their food prepared as soon as the others. In the midst of all these movements those warriors who were then at leisure amused themselves by singing war songs.

When all was cooked, the speaker announced to the grand-master of the ceremonies that the provisions were ready. The food was brought to the great chief in two plates. He rose as he received them, and going out, presented it to the four quarters of the world. Then he sent some to the great war-chief, saying in a loud voice: "Eat." Then every one ate.

The repast lasted a rather long time, because the warriors ate first, then the boys of all ages, except those who were nursing, and, finally the women and the children.

As fast as the warriors finished their meal they went outside and remained standing in front of their cabins. As soon as there were enough of them they formed two responsive choirs along the two sides of the open space and sang war songs. This lasted only half an hour and was ended the instant that the great war-chief went and struck a blow on the post. This signal opened the scene for speeches. The great chief began immediately. He related his exploits and the number of enemies he had killed. He finished in a raised tone of voice, which those who were acquainted with the deeds he had mentioned, answered with a great shout in order to certify to its truth. All the warriors, in turn, according to the degrees of estimation in which they were held, did the same as their chief. Finally the young men had permission to go and strike the post and say, not what they had done, for they had never been to war, but what they proposed to do. All this was meant to be a kind of training for them. For as it was an honor for them to speak well in public, so it also was a disgrace for them to acquit themselves poorly. The warriors applauded by cheering them. The desire of meriting public approbation in the present, and of acquiring in the future the same glory that warriors enjoy, excited the youths to lively emulation.

Night finally came. Then the open space was surrounded with more than two hundred torches made of dried canes, which were continually renewed. They were of the size of a small child and bound in five places. In the great light which they shed the men danced ordinarily until day. In the middle of a vacant space, proportioned to the number who were going to dance, a man seated himself on the earth with a native drum consisting of a pot, in which there was

ACOMA DEITY CALLED RAINBOW BROTHER (*Drawn by a Native*)

BLACKFOOT WARRIORS

UTE INDIANS DANCING IN TAOS PUEBLO

a little water, and which was covered with a deerskin stretched extremely tight. He held this drum in one hand and beat time with the other. Around him the women arranged themselves in a circle at some distance from each other, carrying in their hands very thin disks of feathers which they turned while dancing from left to right. The men enclosed the women with another circle which they formed at some distance from them. Each one had his rattle with which to beat time. The rattle was a gourd pierced at the two ends, through which a stick was passed, of which the longest end served as a handle, and in which some little stones or dry beans had been placed. The women turned from right to left and all kept time with remarkable accuracy. The circles contracted and enlarged according to necessity.

On the next day, no one appeared in the open space until the Great Sun came out of his house in the morning. He walked some moments alone with the great war-chief, and had his drum beaten against the post. Immediately the warriors hastened out of their cabins and formed two groups which were distinguished by the color of the plumes with which their heads were adorned. One group had white feathers and took the side of the Great Sun; the other red feathers and took the side of the great war-chief.

Then the game of the *pelote* was played. The two chiefs threw the ball back and forth for some time, from one to the other. The two groups were always on their guard, for at the moment when one least thought of it the Great Sun might throw it in the very thick of the warriors. This ball must never fall or be carried. It would then be snatched forcibly from the one who so seized it, and no one would then help him.

This ball game had two goals, the cabin of the Great Sun and that of the great war-chief. Ordinarily the game lasted two hours. When the ball touched one of the cabins, that side gained the goal, and the game was at an end. The winning side received from the chief of the opposite side a present of considerable value as well as the right to wear as a mark of victory, certain plumes until the following year or until the next time that they played ball. After the game the warriors danced the war-dance to the sound of the drum. Then all went to bathe.

The other days were like the preceding, and the feasts lasted as long as there was maize to eat, for none was brought back to the village; and even when there was no more to be distributed all the cabins were visited to know how much still remained in each family. Where too large a quantity was found, a tassel of maize was suspended at the door and those who did not have enough were informed by this means the place where they might find more.

When all was finished, the Great Sun had the drum beaten and orders given that he be taken back to the village. The warriors were again arranged in relays and took him back in the same way that they had brought him out. As soon as he had arrived at his home, he sent them out on a great hunt. . . .

Thus did the great feast of grain, or maize, terminate. We have described it at such great length because it epitomizes so well much of what we shall find among the tribes to the north of the Natchez; and because it shows so clearly the inextricable mixture of complex and simple traits that characterizes so many of the civilizations of the Indians north of the Rio Grande. It is the old story over again.

the compromise-civilization that results when barbarians try to assimilate higher cultures.

Many of the elements common to the Natchez and the Creek, it is reasonable to assume, go back to the first major Maya invasion, to the same invasion that must have brought the builders of the mounds. It is quite suggestive that the culture elements which these two tribes have in common, disappear as soon as we leave the area where maize and the sacred fire play the dominant rôle. Yet although the tribes to the north and the east of the Cherokee and Creek did not preserve the early Maya tradition so well in this respect, they adhered very tenaciously to other aspects of it, particularly to the social organization.

But let us now turn to the Creek again. All Creek towns were divided into two divisions, the White or Peace towns, wherein no blood could be shed, and which were governed by a civil official, and the Red towns, where blood could be shed and which were governed by military officials. Only among certain of the Gulf tribes did such a peculiar classification of towns exist. The general idea must, however, have been fairly well disseminated and it is found among not a few of the tribes to the northwest, where it became secondarily associated with a fundamental trait of society, the dual organization described in the prologue of this book.

The characteristic feature in the laying-out of the town was the public square-ground which was sacred and generally situated in the heart of the town itself. Around this square, facing the four points of the compass, were grouped four lodges, one for the head-chief and the leaders of the ceremonies, one for the warrior-chief, one for the warriors and one for the women, children and strangers. In the middle of the open space burnt the sacred fire.

Naturally the first thing that comes to the mind of any one who is at all acquainted with the ethnology of the ancient Maya, is that here in the town-square we have the last faint reminiscence of some of the features distinctive of that great culture such as, for instance, the civic center and the sacred four gods of the cardinal points. And is not this fourfold organization also typical of the cities of the Toltec and their cultural heirs, the Aztecs? It is not too far-fetched to make such a claim. In other words, then, what had once been the typical and fundamental division of the town into four quarters has here deteriorated into a fairly meaningless fourfold grouping around the public-square; and what had once been a glorious and magnificent civic center with wonderful stone-temples and public buildings has become a simple dancing-place with rude and crude wooden structures ranged around it.

Just as the civic center of the Mayas and the fourfold subdivision of the Aztec and their kindred became a focus of dissemination so, too, was this true for the town-square of the Creek and their kindred. Among all the Siouan and Iroquoian and among many of the Algonquian tribes to the north and northwest, the general layout of the village and the position of the two important lodges as well as that of the head-chief and the war-chief, can be said to represent modifications of this town-square.

The chief of each town acted solely as a civic head and he was its representative in all public matters, external and internal. Essentially he was the symbol of group unity. He was always chosen from a certain clan and his tenure of office was for life. Next in rank was the warrior-chief selected from among three warriors who had themselves been chosen at large from among the various clans. To-

gether with the chief they formed the chief's council. One
of the main functions of these warriors was to act as police
and execute sentences. The only other officials of importance
were two men selected because of their recognized ability
and knowledge of the ceremonies, and whose main duty was
to procure leaders for the various dances if they did not
care to dance themselves.

Like practically all the tribes of the southeast, the Creek
and their kindred were organized on a clan basis, with
descent in the female line. And since descent was traced
back to some totem-animal itself, a man was forbidden to
kill or eat it.

But the most interesting feature of Creek life was the
annual harvest-ceremony called the "busk," meaning "act
of fasting," from the fact that no maize could be partaken
until it was over. As in the case of the Natchez, the matur-
ing of the maize was the basic element in this ceremony.
The harvest-ceremony in fact represents a whole series of
rites and dances performed in a certain order at a certain
time of the year. They thus fall into the same category
as do the extensive series of ceremonies associated with
specific periods of the year among the Mayas, Aztecs, and
Pueblo. Among the tribes to the north and northwest of
the Gulf all these ceremonies are still to be found, but always
as disassociated elements assuming not infrequently new
forms and often possessed of considerable vitality, although
generally persisting as generalized rituals. Many of them
have lost most of their significance and new interpretations
have been given to not a few.

The Creek rites began when the maize crop was about
ready for harvesting. First the top layer of soil from the
square-ground was cleared off and heaped into a pile. This

was henceforth treated as sacred soil and as symbolizing the earth. Then the lodges around the public square were put into order and their roofs repaired.

On the first day two pleasure dances were performed, one called the Crazy Dance and the other the Drunken Dance. Both must at one time have had a religious function but that has long since been forgotten. Then two roots regarded as sacred and as possessing the virtue of purifying the blood, were brought to the square, to the accompaniment of singing and whooping. These roots were to play a considerable rôle on the following days for drinks were to be brewed of them and the dancers to get lustily inebriated.

The second was the really important day. Every person steeped his medicine in his own pot and then, after a considerable amount of dancing, each one of the occupants of the four lodges solemnly drank the concoction. It was really an emetic and was taken in order to superinduce vomiting. It was supposed to serve as a propitiatory purification to the maize deity.

Of the dances that then took place the Feather Dance was the most important. Wands about six feet long with white heron feathers attached to them, were brought from the chief's lodge. Carrying these wands, the participants in the ceremony danced around the square for some time. Then whooping and rushing to the various lodges, they raised their wands high in the air and stuck them in the ground.

When the ceremony of the emetic was finished the town-chief cleared away the pile of ashes that still remained in the center of the square from previous fires and kindled a new fire with fresh wood. Sparks from this new fire were then, with great solemnity, carried by the women to their own hearths. This rekindling of the new fire possessed for the Creek a deeply religious significance. A new year had begun which was to be symbolized in numerous ways. All personal differences that might lead to disputes were effaced and a new season of friendship and peace begun. Even damaged property was put out of the way.

Toward evening the festivities for this day were terminated by what had originally been a ritualistic racket-ball game but which had long since lost all of its older significance. In this widespread game the two goals were about a hundred and fifty yards apart. Each player had two sticks with a netted scoop at the end with which to catch the ball. Three groups of players were ranged on each side, one guarding the goal, the other holding the center of the ground and the third halfway between them. The ball was thrown up in the center and the players tried to throw it with their sticks through the opposite goal. Twenty goals won the game.

After the ball game all the men proceeded to the nearest place for water. There they plunged in, washed off their paint and prepared themselves for the solemn sunset meal of maize.

Thus ended the second and most important day of the annual ceremonies. Here we see maize and fire still reigning supreme, almost as supreme as they had done among the Mayas and Aztecs. The ceremony as practiced when the French and Spaniards first came to this region was clearly of composite origin. The worship of maize, like so many other things among the Gulf peoples, represents the great Maya invasion that brought the Mound-Builders, but the fire renewal and the ball game seem to belong to the later Toltec inroad. Both influences were, however, stronger among the

Natchez. The influence these early invaders exerted upon the Creek and their kindred does not seem to have been as marked in the domain of social organization as it was in so many other matters.

In this respect the Natchez were quite different. Their social organization has the most marked affinities with that of the ancient Mexicans, a fact which it is very important to bear in mind when tracing the spread of civilization from the Gulf northward. Those tribes that were to come under the more immediate influence of the Creek and their kindred, were to have a social organization which was definitely democratic and which contained no suggestion of castes; those on the other hand who were to come under the influence of the Natchez and their kindred, were to develop a more aristocratic type of government with a fairly well-marked division into classes.

To understand what the nature of this aristocratic type of government was we must again turn to that most fascinating of all tribes of this area, the Natchez. Their system of government has been admirably described by Du Pratz. We can here only give a brief account.

The Natchez had two castes, the nobility and the people. The people were called by the strange name of Stinkards. The Stinkards had a language entirely different from that of the nobility, to whom they were submissive to the last degree. The nobility were divided into Suns, Nobles and Honored Men. The Suns received this name from the fact that they were believed to be descended from a man and a woman who had come from the sun.

Since the Natchez had a clan system and since descent was reckoned in the female line, the nobility had to intermarry with the much despised Stinkards. The children of

PAGE FROM THE DRESDEN CODEX DEPICTING THE END OF
THE WORLD

such marriages were still called Suns, but the males enjoyed this privilege only during their lives, for their children belonged to the group of Nobles, and the male children of these Nobles were only Honored Men. These Honored Men, however, could, by warlike exploits, raise themselves again to the rank of Nobles, but their children again became Honored Men, and the children of these Honored Men were lost among the people and kept in the ranks of Stinkards. The son of a female Sun was a Sun like his mother, but his son was only a Noble; his grandson an Honored Man; and his great-grandson a Stinkard. It thus not infrequently happened that a Sun could live to see his posterity lost among the common people.

Since descent was reckoned in the female line, daughters transmitted their title of nobility in perpetuity. In spite of this fact, however, women played no particularly great rôle in the government of the state nor could they ever be chiefs.

The chief of the Suns was called the Great Sun and he wore as an emblem indicative of his position a feather-crown, strangely reminiscent of the crown worn by the Aztec kings and the headdress of the Sioux. This crown was composed of a cap and a diadem surrounded by large feathers. The cap was made of a netting which held the diadem in place. It was made of black threads, whereas the diadem itself was red and embellished with little beads. The feathers which surmounted the diadem were white. Those in front were often eight inches long and those behind four inches. These feathers were arranged in a curved line and at the end of each there was a tuft of hair, while above it there was a little hairy tassel only an inch and a half long and dyed a very beautiful red.

The essential traits of this system can be summarized as follows:

Nobility
{
Suns = Children of Sun mothers and Stinkard fathers.

Nobles = Children of Noble mothers and Stinkard fathers.

Honored People = Children of Honored women and Stinkard fathers, or, of Noble fathers and Stinkard mothers.
}

Stinkards = Children of Stinkard mothers and Honored Men, or, of Stinkard fathers and Stinkard mothers.

We have here clearly a remarkable survival of what has all the earmarks of the old Aztec caste system. Yet we are not, for one moment, of course, to imagine that the Aztecs themselves introduced it. There is not the slightest justification for such an assumption. The Natchez simply obtained it from the same source as did the Aztecs and their Nahuatl predecessors—from the Toltec.

This caste system was adopted by all those people with whom the Natchez came into direct contact, particularly by some of the Caddoan tribes that once lived in southern Texas, and by the southern Siouan. As it extended north it became more and more simplified, the Suns and Nobles being definitely and irresistibly pushed to one side by the Honored People. Even among the Aztecs the possibility of such a displacement was already foreshadowed. Among the Natchez this process had gone one step farther.

As we have just indicated, this caste system gradually degenerated and became transformed in diverse ways as it passed from tribe to tribe. All the privileges and insignia that had once clustered around the nobility became associated with new political divisions and with various societies and ceremonies. Among such Siouan tribes as the Osage this disintegration was, externally at least, already complete. But many of the associations, privileges and prerogatives of the former nobility still persisted in a remarkable manner among certain societies and rituals of the various Siouan tribes scattered over the middle west. Who would not immediately think of the castes of the Natchez and of the ancient Aztecs in perusing recent accounts of the Omaha and the Osage Indians, particularly the account of the "Rite of the Chiefs" among the latter?

Far to the north among the Plains Indians these societies were to disintegrate still further merging finally with other rites and giving rise to those curious military societies that played so important a rôle there and which we shall describe in a subsequent chapter.

Of the numerous customs of the Natchez that were to spread northward we can only touch on one more, that connected with warfare.

The Natchez were preëminently warriors. To be a successful warrior was their greatest ideal, as we might very well have expected from the descendants of alien invaders who had so definitely imprinted their culture upon the original inhabitants of the land, and who still symbolized the terrific resistance they must have once encountered in a very remarkable ritual of which Du Pratz has left us an excellent account:

Anciently a great Sun having suddenly heard of a great tumult in his village, went out quickly to quiet it and fell into the hands of a hostile nation which had come to surprise them. But the warriors having immediately run to his assistance, took him back and put their enemies to flight.

In order to recall this honorable deed of their history, all the warriors separate themselves into two bodies distinguished by the color of their plumes. The one party has white plumes; the other, which represents the enemy, has red ones. The two bands place themselves in ambush near the cabin of the great chief. They advance a short distance making many movements and contortions and uttering great cries.

The great Sun then comes out of his cabin in all his apparel, but rubbing his eyes as if he had just awakened. The enemies throw themselves upon him and endeavor to carry him away, when the other warriors rush up and take him out of their hands. This action takes place without any accident on either side and without quarrels, but not without noise. The cries of the enemies are cries of death while attacking; those of the nation attacked are cries of fear and terror. There are some heard which seem to be intended to encourage them. But the enemy continues the cries of death so long as the great Sun is in their hands. The nation running against the enemies approaches them. Both make many movements which denote the stratagems of war, which last half an hour. During this time the great Sun defends himself with a war-club of the ancient pattern, made entirely of wood. He knocks down a great number of the enemy without, however, touching them. The mere motion of the blow throws them down, and in fact the blow approaches so near their heads that one would say that he really struck them.

I was surprised to see playing such a magnificent rôle with so much activity and address this venerable old man, the great Sun, whose glances shot terror into the hearts of his enemies, to which they bore witness by their different cries, which although without any articulation, are distinct and have their signification.

Finally the nation attacked comes and joins with the enemies. These latter tremble on seeing the fury painted in the eyes and the gestures of those arriving. These cries change. Those who represent the Natchez knock down a great number of them (the enemy), who get up again after the Natchez have passed beyond them. Finally the enemy flee and are pursued as far as a wood, which is represented by a thicket of canes, which is always left for the young people.

The Natchez then bring back their prince, and satisfied with such a complete victory, and at having rescued the great Sun from such great danger, utter cries of joy, with which the air reverberates and which the echoes of the neighboring woods repeat in their turn. The entire nation which sees his return indicates its satisfaction by redoubled cries of joy mingled with love, which appear genuine. The old men, the women, and the children, who are merely spectators along the edge of the open space, endeavor to imitate the warriors by their cries of joy. In a word, the general happiness is so lively and so natural that it offers an interesting spectacle, and I avow sincerely that I have taken as much pleasure in this mimic warfare as in any comic piece I have ever seen presented at the theater. It is certainly true that a battle of this kind fixes the attention of the spectator extremely, because it is only a pantomime, and, besides the gestures, it is necessary to know how to distinguish the different cries.

The great Sun, having been led back to his cabin, rests there and recovers from the violent movements he has gone through with, which are such that an actor of thirty would have difficulty in sustaining them for such a long time. Nevertheless, this prince was more than ninety years old. While he rests the warriors who had represented the enemies reënter among the people by groups, and pretending to be ignorant whether their sovereign is wounded or not, because they do not see him appear, utter sighs so plaintive that they draw pity from strangers. This entire spectacle is very amusing, and not being entirely satisfied with what the chief of the guardians of the temple told me about them I wished to see these feasts with my own eyes, and I have seen them more than once.

Scarcely has the great Sun rested half an hour when he comes without his crown. Then the cries of joy and respectful salutation are heard from all sides, but they cease as soon as they see him take the road to the temple. He stops in the middle of the open space opposite the temple, before which he makes a kind of obeisance. Bowing very low, and without bending his knees he takes up a little earth which he throws on his head, and then turns successively toward the four quarters of the earth, doing the same thing in each direction. Then, without changing his position, he looks fixedly at the temple, which he has to the south of him, and extends his arms horizontally (or in a cross) and remains without more movement than that of a statue. He remains in this attitude about half an hour. Then the grand-master of ceremonies comes to relieve him and do the same thing. This one is himself relieved at the end of a similar period of time by the great war-chief, who remains there equally long.

During the prayer which the prince makes a profound silence is preserved, and when he has reëntered his cabin, plaintive cries begin again and cease only when the two chiefs have completed their ceremony, because then the great chief comes out of his cabin, dressed with ornaments which proclaim his dignity, which are the crown of feather diadem. A necklace of large pearls and feathers hangs from the diadem. They bring his throne which is a large stool with four feet made from one piece of wood. As soon as the sovereign appears on his throne cries of happiness are heard and last until the end of the feast. This throne is covered with a beautiful skin, well painted and ornamented with different designs. He seats himself on his throne, and the warriors cover his shoulders with a beautiful bison robe and his feet with many peltries. The women make him presents of different kinds, uttering meanwhile loud cries of joy, and the last who brings them terminates the feast.

All these ceremonies outside being finished, the Suns conduct the sovereign back into his cabin. If there are strangers, he has invited them to eat. One can rest by taking a walk until evening if he wishes to see the dance which takes place on every feast day in the cabin of the great Sun. . . .

Warriors were divided into three classes—the true war-riors so-called, the ordinary warriors and the apprenticed warriors. When war had been decided upon a war-feast was prepared. To this feast all the warriors repaired. They were painted from head to foot. Their clothing was of the scantiest, a belt and a breech-clout. From the belt hung suspended their most important weapon, the war-club. In one hand they held a buckler made of two round pieces of buffalo skin bound together and having the diameter of one and a half feet.

But let us again recapitulate Du Pratz:

The war-feast took place in a plain, the grass of which had been cut over a number of times. Each person repaired thither armed. The war-calumet was planted in the middle of the assembly at the end of a pole from seven to eight feet high. Dishes were ranged in a circle of twelve to fifteen feet in diameter. There was thus enough space left between them whenever the number of warriors was large. This diameter was sometimes twenty feet. An important rôle was played by certain dishes. These were not made of clay, but of hollowed wood.

In the middle stood the largest one in which lay a great dog roasted whole. This dish was placed at the foot of the calumet. The others were arranged by threes in a circle. In one there was some coarse meal cooked in fat broth, in another boiled deer-meat and in a third roasted deer. Between every three dishes there was a space of two feet to leave a passageway by which the dog-meat could be carried out. No war-feast was begun without it. The meal was coarse because warriors ought not to be delicate and the eating of the dog was to indicate the care with which a warrior ought to follow his war-chief. They ate the deer because of their belief that they would then become swifter.

Before beginning the feast all the warriors assembled and the oldest warrior who, because of his great age, could no longer go along, took the war-calumet in his hand and made the following speech:

"My comrades, oh, that I were young enough and strong enough to accompany you to this war and to do to our enemies now what I did to the nation from which I have taken three scalps, or to that from which I have taken five. And how many blows of the war-club have I made against our enemies in order not to be taken? I made so many efforts that I allowed time for the other warriors to succor me, set me at liberty and take me away with them. For I much prefer to die fighting than to allow myself to be taken and die at home.

"So, my comrades, go with great courage; always have strong hearts; walk on your toes; keep your eyes open; never shut your ears; have no fear of the cold. Do not hesitate to throw yourselves into the water in order to escape if it is necessary, and thus conceal your retreat well. Do not, particularly, ever fear the arrows of the enemy. Let it be seen that you are men and true warriors. Finally, if you find the occasion for it, use all your arrows on the enemies and afterward strike, and kill, until your war-clubs are drunk with their blood."

When this speech was finished, the old warrior filled the calumet-pipe with tobacco. He gave it to the great war-chief to smoke and then to all the other warriors according to their rank. The youths who have never yet been to war also come to smoke as if to signify that they were enrolling themselves for future warpaths. The old warrior smoked last and replaced the calumet on the pole.

After this ceremony the war-chief took a piece of dog-meat. Others did the same thing and placing themselves outside the circle of plates, ate, walking continuously at the

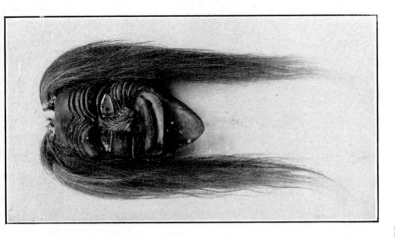

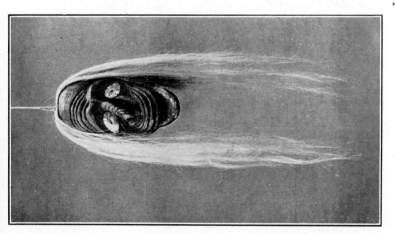

IROQUOIS WOODEN MASKS

MANDAN INDIANS HUNTING HERD OF BISON UNDER MASK OF WHITE WOLF SKINS
(*After Catlin*) (*Upper*)
MANDAN VILLAGE (*after Catlin*) (*Center*)
MANDAN SURROUNDING A HERD OF BISON (*Lower*)

same time, to signify that a good warrior ought to be continually in motion and on his guard.

When the meal was begun one of the young people went behind a thicket two or three hundred paces off and uttered the death cry. At once all the warriors took their arms and ran in the direction from which the cry had been heard. When they were near, the young warrior came out uttering the death cry anew to which all the other warriors then replied.

They then returned to take up the meat which they had thrown on the grass. Each young man repeated the same thing twice. After that they brought the war-drink. It was made of a large quantity of the leaves of a certain herb boiled in enough water to be cooked in spite of their hardness. By pressing these strongly the intoxicating drink was extracted. Then the meal was finished and they went to the post behind which was planted the pole and the calumet.

All the warriors assembled in a group fifty paces from this post, which was made to resemble a man as much as they were able, especially in the size of the head. They painted it red and each warrior in turn struck this post. Each person took his war-club and ran with all his might and gave the death-cry when he arrived there. Then he struck the post with the war-club and recounted his military deeds with emphasis, always casting insults upon the post which was supposed to represent the enemy. At the end of his speech he took great care to pronounce the last syllable with all the strength he possessed, and the other warriors replied by a great "hao." Then all these warriors, one after another, recounted their exploits before this post, and although some, heated by the war-drink, often claimed more than they had actually done, this boasting was always complacently pardoned.

Here, in this account of the Natchez war-dance, there are many customs still functioning that among the northern tribes have lost all their significance and are meaninglessly and mechanically repeated.

In order to obtain a better insight into the variegated culture of the Gulf tribes, we must now turn to a tribe which belongs to this region only secondarily, the Cherokee. Among them we find a very specialized development of medicine formulæ used in the curing of disease. Though the particular form found among the Cherokee is probably a local growth, the evidence at our disposal indicates that formulæ of analogous nature were common throughout this region as well as among the tribes north of the Cherokee.

Each formula consists of two portions, an invocation to the spirits to help drive out the disease and the prescription proper, showing how the medicine is to be used. The invocation consists of a very dramatic monologue in which the whole progress of the curing of the disease is symbolically portrayed. Take for example the formula for curing rheumatism:

"Listen! Ha! In the Sun Land you repose, O Red Dog, O now you have swiftly drawn near to hearken. O great *adawhei*, you never fail in anything. O, appear and draw near running, for your prey never escapes. You are now come to remove the intruder. Ha! You have settled a very small part of it far off there at the end of the earth.

"Listen! Ha! In the Frigid Land you repose, O Blue Dog. O now you have swiftly drawn near to hearken. O great *adawhei*, you never fail in anything. O, appear and draw near running, for your prey never escapes. You are now come to remove the intruder. Ha! You have settled a very small part of it far off there at the end of the earth.

"Listen! Ha! In the Darkening Land you repose, O Black Dog. O, now you have swiftly drawn near to hearken. O great *adawhei*, you never fail in anything. O, appear and draw near running, for your prey never escapes. You are now come to remove the intruder. Ha! You have settled a very small part of it far off there at the end of the earth.

"Listen! On Wahala you repose, O White Dog. O, now you have swiftly drawn near to hearken. O great *adawhei*, you never fail in anything. Oh, appear and draw near running, for your prey never escapes. You are now come to remove the intruder. Ha! You have settled a very small part of it far off there at the end of the earth." . . .

The explanation is even more fascinating. The disease is called the intruder and is supposed to be brought by the chief of the deer and put into the body of the hunter. These chief animals are really animal-deities located at the four cardinal points and these four cardinal points are known respectively as the Sun Land (the east), the Frigid Land (the north), Darkening Land (the west), and Wahala. Their symbolical colors are red, blue, black and white. The white or red spirits are commonly invoked for peace and health, the red alone for the success of an undertaking, the blue for defeating the wiles of an enemy and the black for causing his death.

In the case of the formula before us the medicine-man is represented as first invoking the Red Dog in the Sun Land to whom nothing is impossible. He is implored to come immediately. Then the supplication changes and we are to suppose that the great spirit has already arrived and carried away part of the disease. Now the blue, black and white dogs are called who bear away another part of the disease and finally the white terrapin is called to carry off what little still remains. The patient is now declared cured.

One problem still remains. How can we properly appraise all these customs of the Indians of the southeast of the United States in attempting to reconstruct the history of aboriginal America? We know that they are the customs of tribes who dwelt in this region when it was first discovered by Europeans, but being so far away from Mexico, students of the subject have always been loth to see any connection between them and the great civilizations of Central America and Mexico, preferring to regard whatever similarities exist as due to chance. To this we cannot assent. The economic, social and ceremonial life of these people contains so many of the features that are fundamental in the civilizations of the Mayas and the Aztecs, that it is surely not overshooting the mark to claim that there must have been some very vital and fairly direct connection. Admittedly our task would be hopeless if it were necessary to bring the Mayas directly into connection with these distant people. But, fortunately, there is no need for this, for these people lived in the midst of the Mound-Builder area and surely it is not too much to expect that something, perhaps even a good deal of the culture of their illustrious predecessors, was passed on to them. . . .

With an account of the worship and sanctity of fire our chapter began and it is only proper that it should end with what the Natchez regarded as the greatest calamity that ever befell their nation, the extinction of the sacred fire in their temple due to the carelessness of one of the attendants. It happened in this way:

Once in the dim past, one of the two guardians of the fire went out for some purpose or another, and while he was away his companion fell asleep and let the fire go out. When he awoke, seeing the fire extinguished he was naturally seized with fright. But as his companion had not come back he determined to conceal his fault, an easy thing to do, so that he might escape the death which he so justly merited. So he called to the first passer-by and begged him to bring him some fire with which he could light his calumet. This the stranger willingly did although he well knew that it was not permitted to touch the eternal fire except to tend it and that no other use could be made of it.

Thus the fire was relighted with profane light. Immediately sickness fell upon the great nobles, the Suns. In a few days they were seen to die in rapid succession and it was necessary, so custom ordained, to send into the world of spirits many people to serve them. Four years this frightful mortality lasted without any one being able to guess what had occasioned it. Nine great Suns who succeeded each other died in this interval as well as a large number of other people. Finally at the end of this time the faithless guardian himself fell ill. This evil man, feeling that he was not able to live much longer, had word sent to the great Sun that he had something to communicate to him of such great importance that if he died without revealing it all the Natchez would die. The great Sun went to see him as quickly as possible. As soon as the wicked man perceived him his whole body trembled and he appeared unable to speak. However, he spoke these words, although with difficulty:

"I am going to die, so it makes no difference to me whether sickness or a man kills me. I know that I am a bad man for having, for so long a time, concealed, in order to preserve my life, what I am going to tell you. I am the cause of the death of my nation, therefore I merit death; but let me not be eaten by the dogs."

The great Sun understood by these words that this man was guilty of some great crime and that it was necessary to reassure him in order to draw from him his secret, which appeared to be of such vast importance. He therefore told him that whatever he had done he might be assured that he would not be put to death and that he would be buried properly, that what he had promised him was as true as it was true that the Sun, their father, lighted them every day. He should hasten, therefore, to speak before death prevented him. On this promise the faithless guardian confessed all that he had done.

Immediately the great Sun assembled the old men and by their advice it was resolved to go that very day to wrest fire from the other temple. That was accordingly done and the Suns ceased dying.

CHAPTER X

FROM CLIFFS TO PUEBLO

As we have seen, the direct trail that connected the Indians of the United States with the Mayas stopped at the mouth of the Mississippi. But there was another trail, indirect, tortuous and circuitous, yet nevertheless, a trail clear-cut, well-trodden and broad; and it led to The Seven Cities of Cibola, and the arid tracts of Arizona and New Mexico.

In the year 1540 the viceroy of the New Spain, Mendoza, dispatched Vasquez de Coronado upon a journey of discovery and conquest. He was to find the Seven Cities of Cibola. The journey was arduous. A long and difficult country had to be crossed, and what with a failure of provisions and the attack of savage tribes, Coronado and his men approached the coveted cities disheartened and in the worst of spirits. Nor did their spirits appreciably change when they finally reached their destination. For what did they find? Let Castañeda, the chronicler of the expedition, tell us:

"When they saw the first village, which was Cibola, such were the curses that some hurled at Fray Marcos that I pray God may protect him from them. It is a little, unattractive village, looking as if it had been crumpled all up together. There are mansions in northern Spain which make a better appearance at a distance."

Castañeda was right. There were even many aboriginal mansions belonging to the Aztecs that looked and were much finer. In fact, there were even ruins of mansions scattered

233

throughout the territories of Arizona, New Mexico, southern Colorado and southern Utah that in their desolation, looked finer and more imposing. And it will be our purpose to discover what history lay behind the relative unattractiveness of Cibola, and the superior beauty of the ruins scattered around this Pueblo. It is a fascinating journey we shall make and, like everything else in aboriginal America, it will lead us back over devious and diverse paths to the glory that was Maya.

The culture of the Pueblos is so old, so complex, and so specialized, and our knowledge of it is still so fragmentary in spite of all the excellent work that has been done, that scholars hesitate to reconstruct its history even tentatively. Much of this hesitation, we cannot help feeling, is unwarranted for three fundamental facts definitely emerge: first, that agriculture is the very lifeblood of their civilization; second, that there is a specific break in the continuity of their development as revealed by the superimposed culture layers; and lastly, that at least five distinct languages are spoken by the Indians inhabiting these pueblos to-day. All this clearly bespeaks endless migration and invasion. No one can seriously question this. Indeed we can obtain some suggestive clues as to the direction from which these migrations came, from the natives still inhabiting the pueblos and from the tribes immediately surrounding them. What we discover is obviously an epitome and a repetition of what must have happened again and again in this region for at least two thousand years.

To-day as we survey the distribution of aboriginal culture in southern California, Utah, Colorado, Arizona and New Mexico, we discover certain faint elements that clearly belong to the culture of the Pueblo Indians. They manifestly represent the result of slow infiltrations. At the same time, in Colorado and New Mexico, we also encounter tribes like the Apache and Navaho, who have been thoroughly saturated with Pueblo traits, even although it is quite clear that they have watered them, misunderstood them, transformed them, and adapted them to new uses. Yet this is only one aspect of the situation. Let us turn to another phase.

What are the affiliations of the actual inhabitants of the pueblos themselves? The Hopi are the kindred of the wild Utes and Comanches; the people of Taos, not far from Santa Fé, are the kindred of the comparatively simple Kiowa Indians of the prairies. Linguistically the Hopi and the Tanoan—the latter represented by the Pueblos of Taos, Jemez, San Ildefonso, etc.—are also related, even if distantly. Borrowings from Siouan languages also seem likely. In other words, everything suggests that the Pueblos were repeatedly invaded from without by barbarian and semi-barbarian tribes, and that these assailants were consistently absorbed into the older and more stabilized culture. To-day the gulf between the Pueblos and the Apache and Navaho is great enough. At one time it was as marked as that between the Pueblos and the Utes. And complex as the present Pueblo culture seems to us, there was a time in the not remote past, when it too would have seemed simple as compared with the culture that had preceded it. Thus do the present gradations of culture help to visualize those of the past, those that the stratified remains disclose to us.

At the very bottom we find a non-agricultural, non-pottery-making people. Slowly the simpler elements connected with agriculture seeped through to them. The knowledge of making rude, stone houses was also learnt, and together with these two fundamental traits, must have come many customs and beliefs. Then came a break. A new race entered, a race that was round-headed in contradistinction to the older peoples who had been long-headed, and a race that practiced head-deformation. They came in such numbers that they soon submerged the former inhabitants. With them appeared a number of cultural traits, like cotton, the habit of grouping houses into more or less compact communities and a special kind of pottery out of which the typical Pueblo pottery of to-day was eventually to emerge.

All these early so-called pre-Pueblo villages were grouped around the Colorado River, in that area where to-day the states of Utah, Colorado, Arizona and New Mexico meet. What happened then must have happened hundreds of times in the history of the southwest, namely, the region north of the Colorado River had to be abandoned, owing to the pressure of the wild, marauding tribes from the plateaus and plains of the north. Yet on the whole, only a little was lost, for additional hosts of these round-headed people soon swarmed in again from the south and eventually conquered the entire eastern half of Arizona and the western half of New Mexico. This conquest was to be of momentous consequence for the aboriginal history of the United States, for it inaugurated the only renaissance of aboriginal culture that took place there. It was a true renaissance, even if we must regard it as a tired and a belated one.

It was then a tired civilization that eventually attained its greatest efflorescence in the valley of the San Juan River in the north, and along the Rio Grande, Little Colorado and the upper Gila Rivers in the south. So firmly, however, was it entrenched, and so favorable was the inaccessible region in which it had taken refuge, to its growth, that not only could it hold out tenaciously against attack from with-

out and dissensions from within, but it even possessed sufficient vitality to fuse the disparate elements which it was continually absorbing into a highly specialized and integrated
whole. In one respect, nevertheless, it was unhealthy. It
was always on the defensive. Populations shifted from one
place to another; pueblos were abandoned and reoccupied.
The arid desert, deceptive and treacherous, threw its alluring
shadows over it all, and the war-whoops of the Utes and the
Apaches were never completely silenced. Doggedly and
stubbornly, these ancient dwellers in that glorious land hung
on, and when the pressure became too unbearable, they hid
themselves in canyons or, better still, hugged the cliffs
and fattened unhealthily in a proud isolation. And there
in the nineteenth century the remains of one of their greatest
triumphs were found, the cliff-palace of Mesa Verde.

Who were the builders of these and similar ruins, and
where did they come from? It is not merely the lucky find
at Pueblo Bonito of an object belonging to the Toltec civilization that furnishes us with a clue. There are suggestions
everywhere—in the practice of head-deformation, cremation, the worship of the turkey, the use of turquoise, the
community house, details of architecture, etc. They all
bespeak the Toltec. But tired Toltecs, Toltecs who have
completely lost touch with their motherland, yet who have
zealously preserved and guarded what they could, and who
have had at times spurts of new inspiration whenever a
temporary lull, or a protected spot gave them a long breath-
ing space and the necessary leisure. Compared with what
they accomplished, the American pioneers were pigmies,
and compared with their task the Winning of the West was
a child's play.

But we must not suppose that the southwest owed all its

civilization to these Toltecs. At best that invasion could not have taken place much earlier than the eighth century. Though the most decisive of the invasions from the south it was clearly not the latest. We must, in fact, assume a whole series of such overland incursions, all probably of a discontinuous kind, i.e., an invasion followed by a break, then another invasion, etc. Nor must we forget the early attenuated Maya culture which spread over the valley of the Mississippi. That none of this Mississippi culture should have spread westward it would be ridiculous to assume. Indeed there is even some corroborative evidence for such an hypothesis in the linguistic affiliations of the most easterly group of present day pueblos—the so-called Keresan group, to which the pueblos of Acoma, Laguna, Cochiti and Santa Domingo belong. The language they speak is quite distinct from that of Taos and Hopi, and leans perceptibly toward that great group, the Hokan, to which the Creek, the Natchez, and their remote kindred, the Sioux belong.

These Keresan Pueblos are both the most conservative and the most generalized, culturally speaking, of all those to be found in this area, and it is not at all inconceivable that their ancestors may have come from the southeast and brought with them something of the culture that flourished as early as the beginning of the Christian era in the valley of the Mississippi.

But let us follow the evolution of Pueblo culture. After the great revival, the edifice collapsed and the immediate descendants of the people who had built Mesa Verde and Pueblo Bonito were driven back on all sides and compressed into a small T-shaped area extending across northern central Arizona and eastern northern Mexico. What happened culturally and spiritually to them during this period we can only surmise, but, in a way, our surmise can be controlled by what we know of Pueblo life to-day. They did what all hard-pressed people do; they retired within themselves and attempted to find solace and happiness through an inward adaptation. They became introverts of the most pronounced kind and reorganized their old life in terms of ritualism and symbolism. Individualism was almost eradicated; priests, secret fraternities and the bureaucracy reigned supreme. To accomplish this the world had to be renounced and with it all expectations of conquest and the spread of their specific culture to other regions. They paid the price and preserved what they had. But they were to have no great influence on the further cultural life of aboriginal America with the possible exception of the Pawnee.

The ritualism and conservatism which permeates every corner of Pueblo life to-day is based upon two factors— the consecration of the past that was in the process of ceasing to function and whose original meaning had long been forgotten, and the fixity that had grown out of isolation and passiveness. It represents a drawing-in on all sides, a going into retreat. And this historical development has been illuminatingly symbolized by a cardinal fact in the Pueblo ritualistic system—the going into retreat of the fifteen sets of priests who are, *par excellence*, the spiritual guides of the people. In fact, the constitution of these sets of priests and the order in which they go into retreat will serve as a convenient summary for the symbolical reconstruction of Pueblo culture.

Each one of these sets of priests consists of five individuals, the priest proper, his associates and prospective successor, two assistants, and an aged female associate. They take little interest in human affairs. They do not dance and they go into fixed retreats for fasting, penitence and meditation. By the blamelessness of their conduct, their concentration of mind and the sacredness of their office, they are supposed to keep peace, bring prosperity to the community and bring the rain so greatly needed. As an authority on this region has well said, "Public ceremonies are largely only an exoteric accompaniment of the still more important esoteric activities of the priests."

At the head of fifteen sets of priests stand, as we might have expected, the rain-priests. They make up the first four divisions. We can easily visualize what rain must have meant to the early Mexican invaders who had come from the coast of Vera Cruz where it is so plentiful and falls with such regularity. What it subsequently signified to people who had first to traverse a rainless, arid desert, and then to become dependent upon agriculture for subsistence, we need not add. But the rain-priests themselves tell us, for as they go into their winter retreat, they chant this poignant prayer, in low weird tones, to the Rain-Makers:—

I.

Come you, ascend the ladder; all come in; all sit down.
We were poor; we were poor; we were poor; we were poor;
    we were poor; we were poor,
When we came to this world through the poor place,
Where the body of water dried for our passing.
Banked-up clouds cover the earth.
All come, all come, all come, all come, with your showers.
Descend to the base of the ladder, and stand still;
Bring your showers and great rains.
All come, all come, all ascend, all come in, all sit down.

2.

I throw out to you my sacred meal that you may all come.
Hold your gaming-stick; throw it forward. All come,
That the seeds may be strong and come up,
That all the plants may come up and be strong.
Come you, that all trees and seeds may come up and be strong.

3.

Cover my earth-mother, four times with many flowers.
Let the heavens be covered with the banked-up clouds.
Let the earth be covered with fog; cover the earth with rains.
Great waters, rains cover the earth. Lightning cover the earth.
Let thunder be heard over the six regions of the earth.

4.

Rain-Makers come out from all roads, that great rivers may
    cover the earth;
That stones may be uprooted and moved by the torrents.
Great Rain-Makers come out from all the roads;
Carry the sands of our earth-mother of the place.
Cover the earth with her heart, that all seeds may develop,
That my children may have all things to eat and be happy.
That we may have all kinds of seeds and all things good;
That we may inhale the sacred breath of life.
Send us the good south winds;
Send us your breath over the lakes, that our great world
May be made beautiful, and our people may live.

5.

There, far off, my Sun-Father arises, ascends the ladder,
Comes forth from his place.
May all complete the road of life, may all grow old.
May the children inhale more of the sacred breath of life.
May all my children have corn,
That they may complete the road of life.
Here sit down; here remain; we give you our best thoughts.
Hasten over the meal-road; we are jealous of you.
We inhale the sacred breath through our prayer plumes.

Of all the fifteen sets of priests, these first four are the most sacred and the oldest. Is it simply chance that they are associated with the oldest ritualistic units of aboriginal America, the gods of the four cardinal points, the gods who hold up the world, the great gods who play so fundamental a rôle among the Maya? These four sets of priests are the first to go into retreat just as the early Mexican influences can be said to have been the first to have gone into retreat in the history of Pueblo culture.

The fifth set of priests follows. But what a strange set is this, consisting, as it does, of but one priest? And what is the name he bears, what are the functions with which he is associated? His names are "the speaker of the Sun," the regulator of the calendar and the guardian of public sanctity. Above all others, he is expected to be furthest removed from worldly affairs. He is the "above." Sanctified above all men, who is he? Where did he come from? Let us hazard a guess. He is the symbol of that great invasion, call it Toltec or whatever you wish, that brought the round-heads to the southwest, that hugged the cliffs of the San Juan valley, that built the temples to the Sun-god, and that set its imprint for all time upon the land. He follows the rain-priests to a retreat where penitence and a contrite heart are the essential qualifications of man. Just so, did the Toltec civilization follow the Maya to retreat.

In this land of turquoise skies and luminous yet mystical mountains, set in a frame of burning sand, symbolisms pile upon symbolisms. Here we can always feel certain that what is sacred and enshrined in the hearts of the people is the glorified past that sometimes extends into the present, but more frequently looks backward toward the beginning of things. Nowhere else north of the Rio Grande do we find ancestor-worship, nowhere else do we find feather-sticks—the visible embodiment of prayer—or elaborate altars. These feather-sticks consist of short rods to which feathers are tied according to fixed rules. They are then set out in shrines or buried in the ground, "planted" before every ceremony for the dead. The altars are even more unusual. Paintings are made on the floor in colored earths, behind which is set up an elaborate screen of slats, covered or painted with symbols. Deposited on or above the ground-paintings are animal images, stone concretions, sacred ears of maize, offerings in bowls, etc. To complete the picture, we must mention the numerous masks. More than a hundred were worn by dancers to impersonate the dead.

But all this fades into insignificance before that veneration paid to the past which is both living and dead, to the most sacred of all objects—the tribal fetishes called *ettonne* among the Zuñi, *mile* in the other Pueblos. These *ettonne* consist of reeds bundled together and filled with materials that are either precious in themselves or symbolic of the precious things of life. The whole is wrapped in native cotton. And what are these precious things of life that need a covering of reeds and an envelope of mysticism? Meal, pollen, seeds and turquoise. In the dim remote past these *ettonne* were brought up in their present physical form from the lower world. They belong to the priesthood, the societies and the clans and must be handled with extreme care. In ritualistic language, they are "fed" with offerings. They are never exposed except when ritual definitely provides and even the room in which they are kept is taboo.

All this belongs to the old Mexican stratum. To preserve it, even in its greatly transformed shape, it had, as the Pueblo area shrank to its present proportions, to be sanctified and semi-deified, wrapped in native cotton, and kept hidden from the reach of an annihilating reality.

In addition to the *ettonne* the Zuñi have another fetish called *mili*. This *mili* is simply an ear of maize, sheathed in feathers, and otherwise specially prepared, to be used as a badge of membership in the curing orders of the society. In other words, what was originally a sacred fetish has become a mere badge. And that this badge should actually consist of an ear of maize ritualized, is profoundly significant.

Only one more element in this ritualization of the past has still to be emphasized, the ritualization of war.

When in 1680 the Zuñi arose against their Spanish oppressors, this must have constituted an unusual event in the aboriginal history of the Pueblos. Certainly for centuries Pueblo history had meant retreat, defense and passivity. During all these centuries war had lost much of its virility, and was slowly becoming something of a ritual, and this is symbolized in the Zuñi warrior-societies, particularly in the famous Bow-Priesthood. It is quite distinct from the other fraternities to which it belongs. Instead of membership being open to all, it is limited to individuals who have taken a scalp. But this is the only red-blooded thing about it. The fraternity has two heads, the descendants and the representatives of the War Gods, the Children of the Sun who lead mankind out of the bowels of the earth to daylight, heroes whose fortunes can be followed from Central America to the Great Lakes. The functions of these warriors, however, have changed. They, too, have become ritualized and now act simply as the guardians and the physical executors of the decisions of the religious officials. Their prime duty is to enforce the decrees of the all-powerful theocracy and to guard the masked dancers. One of their members is delegated to protect the altar and keep out intruders.

The one real reminiscence of war is the requirement for initiation. That the Zuñi made occasional raids upon the hated Navaho, even within the last century, we know and this slight indulgence in warfare has kept alive in the Bow-Priest society the older rôle that war once played. Everything else has become formalized and non-functional.

This, of course, had not always been the case. The Zuñi, too, had once been great warriors. Their ancestors had come to the land as invaders from the distant south and they had had to fight their way foot by foot, not only to obtain a hold upon the newly-discovered land, but to protect and retain their most precious possession of the culture they had brought with them. This precious possession was maize. According to legend, it was the two great War Gods who rediscovered and recreated maize. War and maize were thus united, and it is not strange consequently if the sacredness of the latter contaminated the former and contributed its share towards the inevitable ritualization of war.

Hand in hand with the ritualism that grew out of the consecration of the past went the ritualism and bureaucracy that arose out of isolation and out of the forced concentration of Pueblo culture upon itself. Organization was imperative, and organization accordingly they developed to an amazing degree.

At the head of the Zuñi state stood a civil official, the governor, with whom were associated other minor officials.

These latter were chosen by a supreme council of six priests called significantly enough the "daylight people." They consisted of the chief priests of the first four sets, and two additional priests from the first priesthood. The Bow-Priests sit with the council as guardians and execute all decisions. The head of the council is the house-chief proper with practically unlimited power. He can, in fact, be said to stand at the head of the whole Zuñi hierarchy.

The high point of intricate and elaborate organization, however, was attained in ceremonial life. There are three types of organization: first, a group of thirteen societies or fraternities, mainly concerned with the curing of disease; secondly, a very extensive group of communal organizations, conducting dances in which the participants are masked and impersonate the gods; and, thirdly, a series of fifteen priesthoods devoted to the spiritual welfare of the nation. Between the first and second group there exists a fundamental difference; membership in the second being limited to men, whereas it is open to both sexes in the first, and initiation into the second being compulsory, whereas it is optional in the first. Their functions, likewise, are different, one being connected with rain-making, and the other with the curing of disease. To this second group belong some of the most famous of Pueblo ritualistic exhibitions.

Among the Zuñi, as well as in all the other Pueblos, the year is, for ceremonial purposes, divided into two seasons, the winter and the summer solstice. The winter solstice, according to Zuñi calculation, begins when the rising sun strikes a certain point at the southwest end of Corn Mountain. As the sun then moves to the north it passes the moon, and, continuing around to a point northwest of Zuñi, reaches the mountain called Great Mountain, where it sets consecutively for four days at the same point. The last day is the summer solstice.

The winter solstice ceremony begins with an interesting rite called "cleansing the earth," which is followed by an extensive series of dances in which the members of six *estufas* synchronously dance on six occasions for one to eight nights. At about the same time occurs the rabbit-hunt, participated in by masked dancers and the people at large. Every four years there is an initiation associated with the image of the sacred horned snake.

Here we see the great plumed serpent that plays so tremendous a rôle among the Maya, significantly enough transformed into a fetish. Among the Zuñi, the figure of the horned snake presents a remarkable appearance. It is constructed of deerskin about five feet long and eight inches thick. The under-portion is painted white, and the back black and covered with duplicate curves in yellow and blue-green to designate its scales. A rod of cottonwood extends through it symbolizing the spinal column. A miniature stick with plumes attached representing the heart, is secured at the middle of the rod. Hoops of slender pieces of cottonwood representing the ribs of the serpent extend from the neck to the lower end. A deerskin tongue, colored red, hangs from the mouth, which is provided with teeth. Plumes decorate the top of the head which is made of a gourd. And thus has the great god Quetzalcoatl degenerated to make a Zuñi holiday!

The summer solstice begins with an impressive and solemn visit to the sacred lake of the dead who mean so much to the Zuñi. One of the best authorities on the tribe, Mrs. Stevenson, describes how she discovered an old Indian near the water engaged in prayer. He stood erect, his hair blowing in the breeze. His right hand was extended toward the setting sun and with it he was scattering prayer-meal toward the lake. He had approached the lake on foot as this sacred place must not be desecrated by the tread of beasts. As he caught sight of strangers, his eyes brightened, and he exclaimed: "I am very happy, and yet I know that I must die. I shall be contented to die, for I have looked upon the waters of the house of my departed fathers."

On the return from the sacred lake, a series of ceremonies takes place, of which the most important are an elaborate ceremony for rain, an impressive thanksgiving festival for the crops and the dance of the *kianakwe*, ghost people, who are supposed to be angry with the Zuñi for their destruction. This rite is performed in order to propitiate them.

But now we must leave the Zuñi and turn our attention to two groups of barbarian tribes, who at widely separated periods, were drawn into the charmed circle of Pueblo influence—the Hopi and Navaho. Beginning as marauders and destroyers both became fascinated victims. The Hopi had probably been drawn into the charmed circle centuries before the Pueblos had even heard of the Navaho. The memory of their migrations from their original home, however, remained ever present in their minds and their legends fairly reek of it. To-day, they are, culturally speaking, a typical Pueblo tribe, but their specialization has not gone to anything like the extreme that we find among the Pueblos proper. In a sense, they seem to have preserved the Toltec impress much better than the other Pueblos, a fact that is most illuminatingly illustrated by one of their ceremonies called The New Fire rite.

As we peruse the descriptions of that remarkable rite among the Hopi, the Aztec ritual comes vividly to our minds, and we know that the Aztec Fire ritual was but a transformation of that of the Toltecs. Among the Hopi, this transformation has perhaps gone much farther, but it has preserved the fundamental emphasis that it had among the Aztec, the Toltec and the Maya. It is still the central fact of their ceremonial, in fact, of their whole life.

Here among the Hopi, the foremost, most important and most sacred religious fraternities take part in it, and their life can be said to center around it. The prayer to nature announcing the rites, indicates the tremendous significance which the kindling of the new fire possessed as the prelude for the life-giving rains:

All people awake, open your eyes, arise!
Become as the Child-of-Life, vigorous, active, sprightly.
Hasten, clouds, from the four world quarters.
Come, snow, in plenty that water may be abundant,
When summer comes.
Come ice, and cover the fields,
That after planting they may yield abundantly.
Let all hearts be glad.
The *wuwutcintu* dancers will assemble in four days.
They will encircle the villages, dancing and singing their lays.
Let the women be ready to pour water upon them,
That moisture may come in abundance and all shall rejoice.

All the dances and songs reach their culminating point in the rite performed when the new fire is actually to be kindled. The societies enter in a definite order. Then come the individuals connected with the actual details of the lighting. North of the fireplace rests the fire-stone, two priests kneeling by it and holding each end firmly pressed down to the floor. It was set on a bed of shredded cedar bark upon which six radiating lines, representing the cardinal points, west, north, east, south, the zenith and the nadir, had been drawn with pollen. The fire-board was placed south of the fireplace, and like the fire-stone, was held in place by two kneeling priests. The fire-drill was manipulated by the leader and a companion. It, too, was laid on the shredded bark. Arranged in a semi-circle between the chiefs and the fireplace were the four baskets containing meal and the stringed pine needles of the different societies.

As soon as all the priests had entered the ceremonial chamber, the fire-makers fitted their fire-drills into the impression of the fireplace, and the other priests arose while the leader recited a short prayer. There was silence for a little while, and then the members of two of the societies began to sing, while those of the two others accompanied the song with the clanging of their bells and the rattling of tortoise shells and deer hoofs. Simultaneously with the beginning of the song, the fire-makers began to rotate their drills, corn pollen having been dropped into the slots of the fire-board and fire-stone before the spindles had been inserted. A second fire-maker relieved the first at intervals. A spark was soon produced and after a while, a smudge could be detected in the cedar-bark. Blowing upon this, a flame was soon produced, the fire-makers standing so that all might see the new fire. The songs continued and the burning cedar-bark was placed in the fireplace where it ignited the pile of greasewood which had previously been put there. Then when the fire had burnt down somewhat, the leaders of two

(75)

QUEZTALCOATL—FROM AN ANCIENT AZTEC CODEX

of the societies took basket trays, and standing before the fire offered up a prayer. After the prayer, each chief dropped six stringed pine-needles into the flame, one for each cardinal point. Then after some more prayers had been uttered, pine-needles were brought to the lips of the worshipers and dropped into the flame. Slowly the priests left the ceremonial chamber, some staying behind longer than the others, in order to obliterate the meal from the floor of the chamber where the rites had taken place, and in order to sprinkle the walls with medicine-liquid, a purifactory precaution to offset evil influence. The New Fire ceremony was over.

Nothing of the ancient barbarism of the Shoshonean tribes, this being the group to which the Hopi belonged, clung to the Hopi in any form. They are as steeped in Pueblo culture as the Aztecs and their Nahuatl predecessors were in Toltec civilization. Not so the other tribes that terrorized the Pueblos, like the Apache and the Navaho. The Apache, but more particularly the Navaho, possessed a tremendous capacity for assimilation, and innumerable elements of Pueblo culture have become part and parcel of their life. Yet at heart they remained strangers to the culture they had gobbled up so voraciously. They never quite understood it, never quite adjusted it to their own needs, never quite knew what to do with it. Always somewhat perturbed and muddled yet fascinated, puzzled and overcome by that feeling of inadequacy that only nomads and hunters have when they raid an agricultural community, they entered the charmed circle and yet were never of it. In a way this was fortunate, for when people do not understand they are apt to become poets, and mysticism and symbolism become their handmaids.

So it was with the Navaho. Their origin-legend tells in mystical confusion how whiteness arose in the east from the middle of the first world, and how they regarded this as day. Blue rose in the south, and this, too, seemed day to them and they moved around. Then Yellow rose in the west and showed that evening had come, and finally Dark rose in the north and they lay down and slept. Streams flowed in different directions to the east, to the south, and to the west. In the east there was a place called Corn, and in the west, one called Standing-Reed. Indeed, there were many places—They-Come-often-for-Water, House-Made-of-Red-Mountain, Underground-House and Among-Aromatic-Sumac. And who are the beings that lived there? The dark ants, the red ants, dragon-flies, yellow beetles, bats, and locusts.

Now, this is simply a version of the origin myth common to all the Puebloes, but it has been drawn through the mystical skein of a barbarian's bewilderment. In a similar fashion did the rude barbarians of northern Europe deal with the inheritance of Rome and Greece to produce the mysticism and symbolism of medieval Christianity. The Navaho are not content, for instance, with simply giving the cardinal points definite colors. They must also have jewels associated with them. Thus the east has white shell beads and rock crystals; the south, turquoise; the west, haliotis shells, and the north, black stone. Nothing is ever said in ordinary language. When the two heroes are born and come to the Sun-Carrier to ask for weapons with which to fight the beings destroying mankind, they cannot at first discover their enemies, but Sun-Carrier discovers them and he unrolls "the robe of dawn with which they were covered; then the robe of blue sky; next the robe of yellow evening light; and, lastly, the robe of darkness." It is always poetical language of this kind that is employed. The heroes save mankind, and change the contours of our earth. "Surely the monsters are all gone," the great goddess of mankind exclaims. But no, the Navaho poet-priest exclaims. "Old age, cold, poverty and hunger still survive. Indeed, they must live on; for how then would man prize life, or the warmth of the upper air, or food, or the goods of the earth?" When Black Body and Blue Body built the seven mountains of the Navaho country, they built them in such a way that there would be one at each cardinal point and three in the center. They ran a bolt of lightning through Tsinadzini and fastened it to the earth. Then they decorated it with white shells, white lightning, white corn, dark clouds and he-rain. They set a big bowl of shell on its stomach, and in it they put two eggs of pigeon to make feathers for the mountain. The eggs they covered with a sacred buck-skin to make them hatch. All these things they thereupon covered with a sheet of daylight, and they put the Rock-Crystal Boy and Rock-Crystal Girl into the mountain to dwell.

They are excellent poets, these bewildered Navaho. Throughout aboriginal America, the Sun-god journeys from east to west. But only among the Navaho does he sing a song like this:

> In my thoughts I approach
> The Sun-god approaches,
> Earth's end he approaches
> Etsanatlehi's heart approaches,
> In old age walking the beautiful trail.

All their ceremonies deal with the curing of disease. And that is all they could do with those wonderful rites and ceremonies developed for every conceivable purpose that are to be found among the Zuñi and even among the Hopi! But curing, too, could become steeped in mystical feeling and poetry. Prayer escapes from the bondage of a formula and soars into realms where but few can follow. Not a mere delight in mysticism can here explain everything. The blood of ancestors whose ideal was war and wild adventure is still in them, and they must have a haven of rest if not without, at least, within themselves. All warrior-civilizations seek that haven, and we shall see the warlike Pawnee, the Osage, the Omaha, the Winnebago, develop ceremonies where the mention of war was taboo. The Navaho found this haven in mystical prayers, and surely rarely has a lovelier poem-prayer been intoned than this:—

> House made of Dawn!
> House made of Evening Light!
> House made of the Dark Cloud!
> House made of Male Rain!
> House made of Dark Mists!
> House made of Female Rain!
> House made of Pollen!
> House made of Grasshoppers!
> Dark Cloud is at the door.
> The outward trail is Dark Cloud.
> The zigzag Lightning stands up in it.
> Male Deity!
> Your offering I make.
> I have prepared a smoke for you.
> Restore my feet for me!
> Restore my legs for me!
> Restore my body for me!
> Restore my mind for me!
> Restore my voice for me!

This very day take out your spell for me,
Your spell remove for me!
You have taken it away for me,
Far off it has gone.
Happily I recover.
Happily my interior becomes cool.
Happily I go forth.
My interior feeling cold, may I walk,
No longer sore, may I walk.
With lively feelings may I walk.
Happily may I walk.
Happily with abundant Dark Clouds may I walk.
Happily with abundant showers may I walk.
Happily with abundant plants may I walk.
Happily on a trail of Pollen may I walk.
Happily may I walk.
Being as it were to be, long ago may I walk.
May it be happy before me.
May it be beautiful behind me.
May it be beautiful below me.
May it be beautiful above me.
May it be beautiful all around me.
In beauty it is finished, in beauty it is finished!

Thus did barbarians again achieve distinction. The reflection of Pueblo culture rested upon them. To the Navaho, the Apache, the Mohave, the Zuñi Priests might have applied the closing blessing given at the ritual-chanting of their sacred legend: "In a short time our fathers who reside there at Kothluwalawa, the sacred spring, will meet you on the road. You will meet together. They will come and will give to all their children more of the great breath, the breath of Awonawilona; the breath of the light of day."

CHAPTER XI

THE GREAT MOTHER

DEIFICATION is generally the beginning of the end, the first stage of the journey that is to lead to death. When a man is deified he dies, and similarly when an element which forms the economic basis of a nation's life is raised to the skies, it has ceased to function in its proper way. This truism has been exemplified time and time again, but nowhere in so symbolical and transfigured a fashion as among those Indians whose habitat lay between that of the Pueblo and the heirs of the Mound-Builders and whose most representative tribe was the Pawnee.

Maize, in this sign we shall conquer! Such was the battle-cry of the Pawnee; conquer life materially, symbolically and ethically. And thus we find in the principal ceremony of the Pawnee, the Hako, an ear of white maize with its tip painted blue to represent the sky, the dwelling place of the spirits, and four blue equidistant lines running halfway down the ear, to symbolize the four paths along which the spirits descend to minister to man. So, too, a deified ear of maize is here to lead man to a revivified conception of peace and good-will.

Prefiguring the journey that is to unite father and son, in the Hako ceremony of peace—to merge the old with the new—the Great Mother, maize, consents to lead, and as the procession solemnly winds its way, a chant arises:

256

1.

Mother Corn, Oh hear! Open your way!
Lo! As we draw near, let our souls touch thine
While we pray thee:
Children give to us! Mother Corn, hear!

2.

Mother Corn, Oh hear! Open your way!
Lo! Our heads we bow, while our souls touch thine;
Then as one mind
Make the choice of Son. Mother Corn, hear!

3.

Mother Corn, Oh hear! Open your way!
Lo! With head erect Mother stands, and then
Moves she through air
On her mission bent. Mother Corn, hear!

4.

Mother Corn, Oh hear! Open your way!
Lo! Now over hills, over streams, we go
Taking our way
Toward the children's land. Mother Corn, hear!

5.

Mother Corn, Oh hear! Open your way!
Lo! Our journey's end now is near, we look
O'er the strange land,
Seeking children there! Mother Corn, hear!

6.

Mother Corn, Oh hear! Open your way!
Lo! Our eyes behold where they dwell. In their
Village we walk
Seeking there the Son. Mother Corn, hear!

7.

Mother Corn, Oh hear! Open your way!
Lo! His lodge we find, through the door we pass.
Sleeping he lies,
Knows not we are there. Mother Corn, hear!

8.

Mother Corn, Oh hear! Open your way!
Lo! Now at her touch comes a dream; then a
Bird calls, "My Son!"
While his soul responds. Mother Corn, hear! . . .

The Hako is a prayer for children, a prayer that the tribe
may increase and be strong, that the people may have long
life, enjoy plenty, be happy and be at peace. Not a breath
of the spirit of dissension, not the slightest whisper
of war, invades this ritual. The calm is almost oppres-
sive, a calm of suspicious presage, especially when its ministers are symbolism and mysticism. Numerous ceremonies
of the Pawnee were pervaded with these same elements.
Yet what was it that reigned supreme outside of the sacred
precincts of the Hako sanctuary? War in its most intensive
form. The Pawnee were the terror of their neighbors.
Among the adjacent tribes mothers would terrify their infants by saying: "The Pawnee are coming."

Never did a people need such an oasis of peace as did
the Pawnee. In this they are at one with many of the
northern tribes with which they came into contact. To all
these people—the Omaha, the Winnebago, the Sioux, the
Ojibwa—war was as the breath of life. Yet all fled to the
peaceful atmosphere of some such ceremony as the Hako.
Only in such introspective rites could they gain peace of
mind and rid themselves of the evil effect wrought by too

great a preoccupation with bloodshed. Only thus could a warrior civilization become balanced and save its soul. The Aztecs did not have it, and terror is the predominant note of their culture, despite all its splendor.

But the symbolism and mysticism, the conservatism and the puritanism of the Pawnee, possessed another significance likewise. Situated between the Mississippi and the south-west they became the meeting-point of all the influences emanating from these directions. To the north, at the same time, extended the great plains, and this meant individualism and adventure. Their great and fundamental problem, therefore, was to develop some method by which they could achieve an adjustment and an integration. A true external adjustment they were not destined to achieve. For that they were too open to alien influences and for that the allurement of the open prairie was too strong. Stability and an internal adjustment they did attain. The first essential for this was the consecration of the past—the consecration of maize, and the deification of the stars. The second essential was to allow free play to the individual and yet prevent anarchy. To achieve this, they developed an ethical reinterpretation of life and religion. They were thus to become traditionalists and individualists. The future belonged to individualism. North of the Pawnee, individualism was to reign supreme, and even among themselves traditionalism had to become reinterpreted in mystical and symbolical ways in order to remain intact. And surely mysticism and symbolism are blatant forms of individualism.

But let us turn to the consecration of the Great Mother and the deification of the stars.

In the Hako one of the most important rites is the painting of the ear of maize. The priest mixes blue clay in a wooden bowl with water taken from a running stream, and paints with it an ear of white maize while the following song is sung:—

1.

Tirawa, hearken! Mighty One
Standing we wait thy bidding here.
The mother corn standing waits,
Waits to serve thee here;
The mother corn stands waiting here.

2.

Tirawa, hearken! Mighty One
Behold! We in thy dwelling stand,
The mother corn standing there,
Leader she is made;
The mother corn is leader made.

3.

Tirawa, hearken! Mighty One
The downward path we take again,
The mother corn, leading us,
Doth her symbol bear;
The mother corn with power leads. . . .

Thus is symbolized the journey of the Great Mother from the earth to the vault of heaven, where the Sky Father dwells. Having arrived there she is sanctified and returns to the earth to lead the wonderful procession which is to bring peace and good-will to all. Everything connected with this consecrated ear of maize is replete with symbolism, the official symbolism of the priests. The ear of maize represents the supernatural power that dwells in the earth, which brings forth the food that sustains us, and that is why it is called "mother-breathing-forth-life." The power in the earth which enables it to bring forth, comes from above; for that reason, the ear of maize is painted blue. The bowl is round like the dome-shape of the sky and holds the blue paint, which also represents the sky.

This association of maize with a peace ceremonial serves as an excellent index of the changing rôle of agriculture among the Pawnee. They remained a maize-growing community, but the plains and the prairie were rapidly disintegrating and remodeling their whole social structure. Other interests were in the ascendant; and so, maize was fittingly assigned the new and symbolical rôle of mystical leader in a ceremony of peace. Peace had already become an anomaly on the plains, and agriculture was rapidly becoming a purely secondary means of subsistence. To save them, both had to be consecrated, and that the Pawnee succeeded in doing admirably. For an understanding of the tribes to the north and the northwest of them, it is imperative to bear the Pawnee solution clearly in mind, for it was their formula that became disseminated among the northern peoples, always, of course, accompanied by the steady diminution in importance of maize.

Not a little of this veneration for maize must have come from contact with the Pueblo culture, probably at a very early period of its history. It was possibly contact with the same Pueblo culture that brought the Pawnee their fetishes or bundles. We must, however, be careful not to ascribe too much to influences from the Pueblos. They were, after all, pretty far away. It seems more reasonable to think of these ritualistic bundles that play so tremendous a rôle in Pawnee life as being derived from that same Toltec invasion that brought most of the civilization to the Pueblo.

But it is idle to speculate on this point. The Pueblo did unquestionably influence the Pawnee, and the Pawnee bundles have striking analogies in many ways with the Zuñi *ettonne*, the reed-bundles containing the precious things of life.

The basis of the social and political organization of the Pawnee is their sacred bundle. What among the Zuñi is simply a very sacred religious fetish, merely one part of an intricate and complex life, has become reinterpreted and invested with a new function. The part is taken for the whole. The name given to the bundle still betrays its ancient affinities—"mother" and "wrapped-up-rainstorms"; "mother" in reference to the two ears of maize kept within it, and "rainstorm" because of the belief that important powers of the world reside in the west, the home of the thunderers. The bundle can, in a way, be taken to symbolize the various cultures that have here met among the Pawnee. The maize recalls the most ancient and most persistent of all influences that emanated first from the early conquerors of the Mississippi valley, then from the Toltecs, and much later from the Pueblos. The whole idea of the bundle markedly suggests the Pueblos, the rôle of the rainstorm suggests the southeast again, while the importance of the thunderers bespeaks the open plains to the north and its barbarian inhabitants. The star-names for the main bundles are again eloquent of the southeast. How all these elements merge, yet never unite, a cursory glance at some of the traits of Pawnee culture will disclose.

In the most important division of the tribe there are thirteen villages and every village has a bundle. Let us look at the names of some of these villages. We find the following: Center Village, to which belongs the primary bundle, that of the Evening Star; Old Village; Stretching-out-in-the-Bottom-Lands; Village-on-Branch-of-River; Big-Antlered-Elk-Standing; Village-in-a-Ravine; Village-in-Thick-Timber; Skull-painted-on-Tipi; Fish-Hawk; Black-Ear-of-Corn. What a medley of sites and what a medley of economic pursuits these names foreshadow! The breath of the open spaces of the prairie is upon them. It announces itself everywhere. When at the sound of the first thunder in the spring the keeper of each bundle opens it, he makes an offering of dry buffalo meat to the powers in the west. And the four great star-deities are pictured sitting with a *parfleche* filled with dried buffalo meat.

But the prairie and the plain, adventure and individualism, are disintegrating influences for old cultural values. So the villages unite just as the Siouan Dakota did as they traversed the northern plains. Authority is invested in the Center Village where the Evening Star bundle resides. Yet authority must at times be delegated. And so there arose, surely on an old mythological and religious background, an additional four main bundles, which served as the basis of the governing power:—

Yellow Tipi, or Yellow Star bundle, pertaining to the powers of the northwest.

Mother-Born-Again, or White Star bundle, pertaining to the powers of the southwest.

The Leading Cornstalk, or Red Star bundle, pertaining to the powers of the southeast.

The Big Black Meteoric Star bundle, pertaining to the powers of the northeast.

These four were all kept in the second of the villages,

Old Village. But there were more villages. It is typical of the new spirit that two refused to join the federation— The Squash-Vine Village and The-Wolf-Standing-in-Water-Village, and that some bundles, for instance, the Human-Skull and the North-Star bundles, belonged to no specific village.

Such is the picture presented by the social organization of the Pawnee—centralization and localism, traditionalism and individualism, the comfortable and settled south and the uncomfortable but romantic north.

We have already had some intimation of the rôle played by stars in Pawnee life. We must now proceed to show how the stars became deified, and how this deification and sanctification was reflected in every phase of their life.

The position of the villages with reference to each other was as a reflected picture of the stars in the heavens. "The Skidi Pawnee," said one of their leaders, "were organized by the stars; these powers above made them into families and villages and taught them how to live and how to perform their ceremonies. The shrines of the four leading villages were given by the four leading stars and represent those stars which guide and rule the people. The shrine of the village at the west was given by Tirawa, who is above and over all the stars. Tirawa sent this shrine by the star in the west. But it was not to represent that star but Tirawa, who gave to the mysterious beings standing below that star, the power to put life into all things, to set the people in order and to give them knowledge."

According to their poetic symbolism the Evening Star resides as chief power in the west, and the four other stars in the west represent the clouds, the thunder, lightning and the winds. These four stars sit there in the west acting as priests; they sit there with a hill of maize, the stalks always green, and a place in front of them to serve as an altar.

The stars and maize, such is always the Pawnee formula. Everywhere we find the stars. They were visible even in the construction of their peculiar habitations, the earth-lodge. The circular floor symbolized the earth, the dome-shaped roof the arching of the sky, and the four posts which supported the framework of the roof the four stars of the leading village. The sequence of the ceremonies, likewise, had reference to them. The rites began with the star in the west, to which the life-giving power of Tirawa passed, coming from the west to all living forms. Then one passed from the west to the east, and closed with the rites of the shrine of the Morning Star, which included a sacrifice typifying the conjunction of the east and the west, the below and the above.

The stars had not always occupied this position of greatness, they had not always been sanctified and deified above all things. Second in the order of created things, they had once lived underground and only subsequently been translated to the skies. To-day the deification is complete. Nothing can exist without some connection with a star. All the numerous societies had origin-legends and in most cases they go back to some star-deity founder. Let us quote one, which will both exemplify the obsession of Pawnee society by the stars and also indicate the nature of their very remarkable mythology:

Before the creation, the stars were human beings. Certain of them were given great powers. Tirawahut gave stars the power to create all things. When the earth was created, the stars agreed to send Paruxti, the wonder being, to the earth, to see if it were ready to be peopled. The stars held a council, but forgot to invite

Fools-wolves star. Whenever this star comes up, the wolves howl because they think it is the morning star.

Paruxti was sent to the earth in the form of a long-haired giant. He was daubed all over with the sacred red paint. He wore large moccasins with the hair inside and big flaps. Over his shoulders he wore a buffalo robe which covered him completely. Around his waist was tied a buffalo hair rope with several pendent loops at the back which represented rain.

The council caused a thunderstorm which was followed by a rainbow. This they broke in two, placing one-half in front and the other behind the giant as a companion. The north star and the south star each furnished a man to carry the rainbow. The evening star provided a bag. The council discussed what these people should take with them. Morningstar said: "I will supply a sacred bundle and I wish eveningstar to contribute some one to carry it and four men to care for it."

Eveningstar brought an ear of corn which was transformed into a girl, the bearer of the bundle. First the four men were put into the bag, then the girl with the bundle, then the people, and finally, the two lance men. The bag was tied so the man could carry it on his back.

It was now time for Paruxti to visit the earth. Eveningstar commanded the four powers in the west, clouds formed, lightning and thunder were placed into the clouds. Paruxti was placed upon the clouds and the wind slowly blew them along toward the earth. Soon the clouds rested on the earth and Paruxti stood upon it. He went towards the east leaving footsteps so the gods knew he was on his way.

One time when he was tired and lonesome he remembered what the gods had told him about the bag. He sat down near a stream, placed the bag in front of himself, and opened it. First the two lance bearers, carrying the lances, jumped out. They stopped some distance off, one standing at the south and one at the north side. Soon people sprang out and took their places behind the two lance men. Then came the girl with the sacred bundle on her back. Behind her the four men walked abreast.

The two lance men led the people to some level ground. They

stuck the lances into the ground while the rest of the people put up their tipis. The first one was set up facing east, for the bundle girl and the old men. The bundle was hung up inside the tipi on the west wall. The girl sat beneath it. Two of the old men sat on the north and two on the south side of the tipi. Throughout the village all was bustle and confusion. The boys, young men and old men were playing with their sticks and rings. For the boys the ring was small and the sticks had two hooks on one end. The sticks used by the older men were hooked at one end and had two cross-bars while the ring was smaller than that used by the young boys. The oldest men played with large rings and straight sticks. The women sat in circles and played a game with plum seeds and a basket, while others played shafts.

Messengers were sent through the village to call out the men to look for game. The runners notified the people that they had seen many buffalo. The men went out to hunt and returned with the meat. The first buffalo killed was taken to the holy tipi.

They stayed at this place four days when the holy being told the four old men that it was time to move. Camp was broken and every one returned to the bag, the two lance bearers last of all.

Again Paruxti went on his way. Several times he opened the bag; camp was pitched. He rested only when the bag was opened. He had traveled far to the east and had returned by the north.

Fools-wolves, the wolf star, had seen Paruxti on his journey and said. "I will undo what the others wish to do. I will send a being to the earth who will ruin what the others have accomplished." He put a wolf on the earth who became hungry and ran hither and thither until he discovered the tracks of Paruxti, which he followed. The wonderful being who had become tired and sleepy, lay down. As he lay there, the wolf came up to him and noticed the bag. He thought, "There must be something to eat in the bag. I will take it away and open it and find something to eat." He dragged it to some prairie where there was neither water nor timber and untied it.

The two lance men jumped out first. Wolf was frightened and jumped sidewise. Soon people came out of the bag and he heard them say that they were going to camp and get something to eat. The two lance men selected a camping place and as usual stuck their lances into the ground. The people played their games, but found no buffalo. The men shouted: "Something is wrong. Our wonderful being must be in an ill-humor. Take him something to eat."

Some men carried dried meat to the wolf, which he ate. The people marveled at this and did not know what to make of it. The wolf was brought to camp and given a place in the tipi where the wonderful man sat. Just as they were about to burn incense in his honor some one shouted, "Our wonderful being is coming over the hills, crying. Watch the being in our tipi, for he is not our wonderful being." The wolf tried to get away, but the people surrounded the tipi and killed him.

The four men then burned some incense before the wonderful being and anointed him with red ointment, buffalo fat mixed with red earth. All the people were gathered around the tipi and the wonderful being asked what had become of the wolf. They replied, "We killed it." Then Paruxti said, "Bring it and skin it. When the skin is dry, put it on the bundle where it must remain. You will always be known as the *skiri*, or wolf people. Because you killed the first animal on earth you will die, too. The gods in the heavens intended that you live forever. You will always have lances. Those who carry them will be soldiers. . . ."

We have just seen how that mystical pair, the stars and maize made for conservatism and solidarity. It only remains for us now to point out how war, the spirit of adventure and the far-stretching prairie made for a new individualism. It was an individualism hallowed by religion, and one upon whose basis there was to be built up a new ethical revaluation of life. The individual was to mean more than he had ever done before. Yet the dangers attendant upon his liberation were such that only by the inculcation of his duty to the group and to the gods was license to be prevented. Thus there arose the clearly-defined doctrine that every man had an alienable right to free expression, but that he must learn to bear the consequences of his conduct if this free expression brought him into conflict with the group and with reality. Out of this medley of interacting forces emerged a new stoicism and a new puritanism. To be strong of purpose, to accept unflinchingly whatever fate had in store, to have a personal relation to the supernatural powers, and to stand abashed in the presence of the gods—that became as great an ideal as loyalty to the group. This is particularly well illustrated in war.

Here is the account given by a distinguished Pawnee warrior named Curly Chief of one of his war expeditions:

"I started on the warpath with a number of young men. From the camp we went south to the Arkansas River. When we reached that river it began to snow, and the snow fell six feet deep. One day as we were going along we saw far off three Indians on foot. They were Kiowas. Probably they had been on the warpath and had lost their horses. We attacked and killed them. They did not fight. We killed them like women. Then, indeed, we divided the scalps and made many of them. From there we started home. When we reached home, there was great joy, and we danced the Scalp Dance.

"I sanctified the scalp to Tirawa. I felt that he had given me the victory over my enemies, and for this reason I wanted to give him something. I wanted to make an acknowledgment of his goodness to me. It was a sacrifice greater than the sacrifice of the buffalo meat. Not many men had made it, but once in a while you see some one who has been noticed by Tirawa."

Here we have that braggadocio and supreme self-confidence that always accompanies a marked individualism, linked with a religious awareness and humility that effaces self before God. And this was the formula that the Pawnee were the first to elaborate, and which subsequently became the dominant note of the culture of the prairie and the plains. Nowhere has this formula been more poetically and completely expressed than in the ceremony connected with the changing of a name. A man could take a new name only after performing an act indicative of ability or strength of character, and such a new name had to be assumed openly before the people to whom the act it commemorated was known. Miss Fletcher has given a rhythmic rendition of it:

1.

Hearken! 'Twas thus it came to pass.
In ancient days, a Leader and his men
Walked this wide earth, man's vast abode
Roofed by the heavens, where dwell the gods.
They reached a place, the spot no man can tell,
Faced dangers dread and vanquished them:
Then, standing as if born anew to life,
Each warrior threw away the name
That had been his ere yet these deeds were done.

2.

Hearken! The Leader and his men
Made there the Victory Song, and set the mark
Ye must o'ertake, if ye would be like them!

3.

Hearken! the Leader and his men
Turned then toward home. Their Victory Song
Proclaimed them near; the village rose,
Looked toward the hill, where on the top

Stood the brave men singing their Song,
Heralding thus the favor of the gods
By which they had surpassed all former deeds,
Made new their claim to be accounted men.

4.

Hearken! This poor man's prayer went on,
Speeding afar into the blue
Heavens above, reached there the place—
Hearken! Where dwell the lesser gods—
Hearken! And great Tirawa, mightier than all!

5.

Hearken! And thus it was the prayer
Sent by this man won the consent
Of all the gods. For each god in his place
Speaks out his thought, grants or rejects
Man's suppliant cry, asking for help;
But none can act until the Council grand
Comes to accord, thinks as one mind,
Has but one will, all must obey.
Hearken! The Council gave consent—
Hearken! And great Tirawa, mightier than all.

6.

Hearken! 'Twas thus it came to pass:
The Leader grasped the help sent by the gods;
Henceforth he walked steadfast and strong,
Leading his men through dangers drear,
Knowing that naught could strike at him
To whom the gods had promised victory.
Attend! Once more I change his name!

7.

Hearken!   Riruts' katit, it was
We used to call him by, a name he won
Long days ago, marking an act
Well done by him, but now passed by.

Hearken! To-day all men shall say—

Hearken!   His act has lifted him
Where all his tribe behold a man
Clothed with new fame, strong in new strength,
Gained by his deeds, blessed by the gods.

CHAPTER XII

WHERE THE WOMEN RULED

THE crusaders of the stars and maize were destined to spread their gospel far and wide, from Texas to North Dakota. East of the Mississippi, however, we hear nothing of them. Yet along the course of the upper Ohio River and farther to the north and east, there dwelt a tribe who in language were distantly related to the Pawnee—the Iroquois. Between them and the Pawnee lay a solid wedge of Siouan and Algonquian peoples. Pawnee influence profoundly altered the culture of these Sioux, but it penetrated no further. All the cultural affiliations of the Iroquois were with the southeast and with the descendants of the Mound-Builders.

The connections with the southeast are manifest. But new features also obtrude themselves that we have not encountered before, some of which, such as the organization for war and peace, the militant expansion and the forging of a confederated state, we are justified in regarding as essentially special developments. Others like the remarkable position held by the women and the elaborate condolence ceremony given on the occasion of the death of a chief and the installation of his successor, one is more than inclined to ascribe to an old inheritance. Naturally, we turn for their origin to the Mound-Builders and the Toltecs. The Iroquois were, indeed, at one time within the radius of Toltec influence, although surely it was only at the fringe. But even after we allow for such possible Toltec influence, where even south of the Rio Grande do we find women exercising any real power in the government of the state? Nowhere. But if this is a specific Iroquoian development can we hazard any guess as to how it had come about? Dangerous as it may seem we shall attempt one.

The Iroquois, to a far greater extent than the Pawnee, were faced with the problem of how to escape disintegration, for their policy of audacious expansion was a direct challenge to the old order of things. They too were, therefore, forced back upon some type of consecration of the past.

There are numerous indications in their ceremonies that agriculture was, so to speak, their first line of defense. But the channels into which their aggressive expansion and their policy of fire and sword had forced them, coupled with the inevitable necessity of incorporating into their ranks an increasingly large number of non-agricultural people of the north, must have overwhelmed this bulwark fairly early. Whatever crystallization it was still possible to achieve had to be largely adventitious. This explains, in part, why the two elements around which much of the veneration and consecration of the past clustered, should have just been the position of women and the Condolence rite.

The Iroquois reckoned descent in the female line. But though the rôle of women in determining descent is, among primitive people, undoubtedly important, it never signifies any active participation on their part in the affairs of government. This distortion was introduced among the Iroquois, we may assume, wholly because of their endeavors to hold on to as much of their old heritage as they could. The Condolence ceremony, too, was raised to the position of commanding importance which it held among this tribe not because of any intrinsic significance it possessed but through chance, in obedience to that "law" of historical transformation, which we see so often exemplified, according to which an unimportant element in one culture becomes a fundamental trait in another. And so it came about that a mere incident in the complex life of the Aztecs—the set speeches of congratulation and condolence—was transformed into the ceremony *par excellence* of the Iroquois.

But let us join the ladies. Here among the Iroquois they have come into their own and occupy the seats of the mighty. In the Condolence ceremony, for instance, we are told:

"He who has worked for us has gone afar off; and he also will in time take with him the whole body of warriors and also the whole body of men, they will go with him. But it is still harder when the woman dies because with her the line is lost."

At first blush, the woman's rôle does not seem so important after all. Like other Indian women, she cooked, made the dresses, attended to the agricultural pursuits and took care of the children. That the household goods belonged to her and were inherited by her relatives and not by those of her husband is known elsewhere likewise. Nor is the complete equality of the sexes in social estimation and general influence uncommon in aboriginal America. What is unique here among the Iroquois is the formal manner in which this estimation was expressed and a woman's right, when she happened to be the oldest matron in the family of one of the more important grades of chiefs, to select a successor of a deceased chief of that family.

Now if the Iroquois woman can thus be said to have attained so large a measure of equal suffrage long before her white sisters had gained that coveted honor, it must not be supposed that this was due to any long evolution of the rights of women. In contradistinction to what is the case for Western Europe it was simply an accidental crystallization of the past. The attitude taken toward women was merely one of the means of erecting defenses around the old cultural heritage, a heritage which included the worship of the League, of the kindred, of the warriors, and of the ancestors. In fact, women were in a fashion sandwiched in between the warriors and the ancestors. No wonder then that in the Condolence ceremony the participants chant:

> I come to greet and thank the League;
> I come to greet and thank the Kindred;
> I come to greet and thank the Warriors;
> I come to greet and thank the Women.
> My forefathers—what they established—
> My forefathers—hearken to them!

As we have just seen that it is in connection with the selection of a successor to the chief that the importance of woman looms greatest, and it is in connection with this same selection that Iroquois ceremonial life attains its most dramatic moment. This is as it should be. For the Iroquois chiefs were the visible incorporation of the greatest achievement to the credit of their nation, the formation of the famous League of the Five Nations—the Mohawks, Oneidas, Senecas, Cayugas and Onondagas.

Fact and fiction are so inextricably intermingled in the accounts that have come down to us of the founding of the League, that it is well-nigh impossible to disentangle the skein now. Still, this much seems clear, that at one period in their history the various nations belonging to the Iroquois group were engaged in fratricidal conflicts for the possession of the rich valleys of central New York, a struggle quite analogous to the conflicts that had taken place in the valley of Mexico between the different branches of the Nahuatl-speaking peoples. There, too, the earlier arrivals had found it necessary to unite against the common enemy, the earlier occupants of the land. A number of the Iroquois tribes finding themselves in a similar dilemma, united in a league for mutual protection. Now it so happens that this league originated at a comparatively late period in their history, and the facts connected with it, as well as the particular individuals to whom the league seems to have owed its origin, became enshrined in tradition and ritual. Nay more. The various steps leading to the formation of the League were dramatized and were thus preserved from generation to generation, always of course with the usual additions and transformations.

Most of us know the story: It is the story of Hiawatha. It is narrated of him that he was already past middle age when meditating over the evils which were afflicting his people, he elaborated the scheme of a vast consideration that would not only ameliorate conditions in his own tribe but ensure a universal peace. From the very beginning he had to contend against an evilly-disposed rival chief Atortaho, the "Entangled-One." Naturally, we are immediately reminded of Quetzalcoatl and Tezcatlipoca. Indeed some of the mythical details woven around the persons of Hiawatha and Atortaho may very well be survivals of the older myth. The events of Hiawatha's life, as the Iroquois love to recall them, fairly bristle with analogies to the Mexican legend.

Hiawatha, after he had matured his plans, first endeavored, of course, to enlist his own people, the Onondagas, in his cause. He met with the usual opposition toward the reformer. Wherever he turned the sinister figure of Atortaho opposed him. Finally, defeated on all sides, he decided to present his scheme to other tribes. The journey on which he then embarked was looked upon with religious veneration by the Iroquois, and embellished with mythical detail subsequently, was ever after commemorated in song and story. He is represented as plunging through the forest, climbing mountains, crossing lakes, floating down rivers in a canoe, until he finally reached the town of a chief who was congenial to his plans, Dekanawidah. It was early dawn when he approached the village of the latter. Seating himself on a fallen trunk near a spring he waited until some one would see him. Soon a woman spied him and immediately went to Dekanawidah. "Seated at the spring is a man or, at least, a figure like a man," she said, "and his breast is covered with strings of white shells." "It is a guest," said the chief to one of his brothers, "go and bring him in. We will make him welcome."

From that moment on the success of the League was assured. Dekanawidah secured the allegiance of his own tribe—the Caniengas—and the kindred Oneidas. The Onondagas, where Atortaho still ruled supreme, were again approached. But the answer was the same as on previous occasions. So the two friends, now always united, journeyed on to the Cayugas. These consented and there a plan was finally devised whereby Atortaho could be won over. The Onondagas were to be the leading nation of the confederacy, their chief was to be the chief of the league, their main town the capital where all the great councils were to be held, and they were to have fourteen representatives as opposed to the ten representatives possessed by the next most important member of the confederation. Atortaho thereupon consented and himself suggested that the Senecas be included.

Thus did the great confederation arise according to the semihistorical account. We need not take this account too seriously. If the Onondagas had the chieftainship, two chiefs as special counsellors and fourteen representatives, we can be certain that this leading position was not obtained in the idyllic and peaceful manner the legend intimated. And it is quite clear, likewise, that the figure of Hiawatha is a mixture of the mythical culture-hero and some historical personage. Yet it is also evident that, owing to its development into a formal ceremony, not a few of the actual facts that occurred at the time of the formation of the League have been preserved to us in this interesting medley.

The League, as it is pictured to us, represents an attempt at preserving the old structure of the state by remodeling it to meet the necessities of the new conditions that confronted the Iroquois. Yet so thoroughgoing was the transformation that it is by no means easy to determine exactly what that old structure was. We know that the Iroquois had clans, that these were grouped into two phratries and that descent was reckoned in the female line. It seems highly probable, likewise, that either a caste system had once prevailed or at least a number of chiefs arranged in a definitely graded series had existed. In consolidating its powers and assigning official functions to its various members the new League played havoc with these old distinctions. To speak of fifty permanent sachems being created at its institution, as the older authorities on the Iroquois do, following the native Iroquois tradition, is preposterous. These sachems were simply former chiefs invested with new functions and new dignities.

The fifty sachemships of the League had, as we know, specific names, were hereditary and were unevenly distributed over the five nations—the Onondagas receiving fourteen, the Oneidas, Cayugas and Mohawks nine each, and the Senecas eight. They were all equal in rank and authority. Each sachem had to be "raised up," as the phrase ran, and invested with his title by a council of all the sachems. No one could become a full-fledged ruler until so confirmed. The sachems in each tribe composing the confederacy were furthermore grouped into classes and, in the main, each class belonged to a certain clan. Thus, for example, among the Mohawks the sachems of the first class belonged to the turtle clan, those of the second to the wolf clan and those of the third to the bear clan. Among the Onondagas there were five of such classes but with the exception of the first class, all of whose members belonged to the bear clan, the clan affiliations of the individual members differed. These classes practically formed a kind of graded nobility.

But let us see what powers the league actually possessed, how these were distributed, and how the league itself worked. Originally the general councils had undoubtedly no other purpose except that of filling the vacancies to sachemships as they arose, and that of discussing general intertribal matters. In the course of time, however, it assumed greater and greater powers. It declared war and made peace, sent and received "embassies," entered into treaties of alliance, regulated the affairs of the subjugated nations, received new members into the league, etc., in short, usurped many of the powers that must have formerly belonged to the individual tribes themselves.

In spite of its attempts to declare war and make peace the League never really succeeded in controlling the war activities of the individual tribes composing it. For this there were two reasons: first, because war remained more or less an individual matter and secondly, because it was inextricably associated with the group of so-called inferior chiefs with whose powers the League had not been able to interfere. In fact, although treating them as an inferior class, the League found itself compelled to give these inferior chiefs a definite status. The titles awarded them were not hereditary and everything was done to hold them down. But in this the League was unsuccessful, because these chiefs represented the democratic element, where rewards were obtained through individual merit, in an otherwise oligarchical constitution. Do what they would the sachems could not prevent them from gradually encroaching upon the rights and prerogatives that these fifty best families felt belonged only to themselves.

One of the real problems with which the League, like every other confederation, had been confronted at its incipiency, was that of deciding how to distribute the various powers and privileges among the Five Nations in such a way that no one would be absolutely supreme and yet that no one could justifiably complain. Why certain powers were assigned to specific tribes we no longer know. It seems likely, however, that a number of functions which had once belonged to specific clans in one of the Five Nations were generalized and given to the tribe as such. Thus chieftainship always remained the prerogative of the Onondagas as also the office of "keeper of the wampum"; the Senecas became the "door-keepers." These latter officials were rather important. One of these door-keepers had an assistant whose duty it was to stand behind the sachem on all public occasions and to act as his runner or attendant. The two supreme military chieftainships belonged to the Senecas.

Thus the League, both in its make-up and in its functioning, was a very remarkable creative remodeling of the older social structure of the Iroquois. Only a few new ideas were actually introduced but the older ones were so reinterpreted that, to all intents and purposes, the Iroquois could feel that a new order of things had begun with the work of Hiawatha. One of the new ideas which developed was the willingness to incorporate other tribes into the League, whether these were linguistically kindred or not. Thus the Tuscarora of North Carolina, who were only distantly related, were adopted as the sixth nation, and the Delaware, of Algonquian, and the Tutelo, of Siouan stock, were given almost this much-coveted honor. Indeed the confederation functioned as an asylum for almost any nation and even fragments of tribes who had once been the most bitter enemies of the Iroquois, like the Erie and Huron, were received into the fold.

Peace and unification were the two avowed purposes animating the League and these are best illustrated by what might be called the three fundamental laws of the realm: first, that though a chief die his office shall not perish with him; second, that no personal revenge was to be taken individually for the murder of any member in the League but that the whole matter was to be referred to a general council; and thirdly, that the elaborate and ruinous mourning ceremonies which prevailed should be reduced to one simple rite in which a few individuals, delegated to represent the whole League, were to address words of comfort to the bereaved.

All these provisions suggest definitely that the Iroquois, unlike the Pawnee, for instance, sought refuge and a haven of rest from the spirit of war, not in a ceremony replete

with mysticism and symbolism like the Hako, but in a political assembly and in the League.

That the breaking-up of such a league meant practically
the destruction of the nation, is not to be wondered at and
we can enter into the feelings of the litany in which its
weakening was deplored:—

> Woe! Woe!
> Hearken ye!
> We are diminished!
> Woe! Woe!
> The cleared land has become a thicket.
> Woe! Woe!
> The cleared places are deserted.
> Woe!
> They are in their graves—
> They who established it—
> Woe!
> The Great League.
> Yet they declared
> It should endure—
> The Great League—
> Woe!
> The work has grown old.
> Woe!
> Thus we are become miserable.

The tendency toward systematization which was illustrated
in the various enactments of the League, must have been
an old trait of the Iroquois, for it is also present in their
pantheon and in their unusually comprehensive prayers.
All the various spirits were classified and arranged in groups

of assistants and subordinated to the Great Good Spirit and the Great Bad Spirit. It is this same tendency toward unification that we meet in the semideification of the spirits of agriculture, conceived of as an inextricable triad, the Three Sisters,—Corn, Bean, and Squash. All nature is grouped and formed into a confederation on the model of its earthly counterpart, a confederation where each deity is distinct but where, as in the League, each spirit derives increased powers from its association with the whole. And so a great prayer arises:—

Hail! Hail! Hail! Thou who hast created all things, who rulest all things, listen to our words. We now obey thy commands. That which thou hast made is returning to thee. The smoke of the tobacco is rising to thee by which it will appear that our words are true.

Continue to listen: The united voice of the people continues to ascend to thee. Forbid all things which shall tempt thy people to relinquish their ancient faith. Give us power to celebrate at all times the sacred ceremonies which thou hast given us.

Continue to listen: Give to the keepers of the faith wisdom to execute properly thy command. Give to our warriors and our mothers strength to perform the sacred ceremonies of thy institution.

We return thanks to our mother, the earth, which sustains us, that she has been caused to yield so plentifully of her fruits. May she not withhold them next year and may we not suffer want.

We return thanks to all the herbs and plants of the earth; we thank them for giving us strength to preserve our bodies in health and for curing us of the diseases inflicted upon us by evil spirits.

We return thanks to the Three Sisters, the main sustainers of our lives.

We return thanks to the bushes and the trees; we thank the winds which banish disease as they move.

We thank the thunderbirds who give us happiness and comfort by having the rain descend on the earth, causing all plants to grow.

We thank the moon and the stars and the sun. May the latter never hide his face from us in shame and leave us in darkness. . . .

But the really significant and dramatic moment in Iroquois life centered around the Mourning rite for a deceased sachem. It was more than a condolence ceremony, more than the preparation for the installment of his successor. It was a composite gesture, like everything else among these people; an act of reverence for the remote past, a semi-deification of the great ancestors and the culture they had inherited and upon which the last faint reflection of the great Mound-Builders still lingered. It was also a chant of victory for the recent past, for the spirits and the heroes who had made the great adjustment to the new conditions and had founded the great League. Lastly, it was a *Te Deum* for the future, that the nation should survive and meet the changing conditions of time and place with the same courage and ingenuity that it had done in the past and with the same results—to retain the past within the present and extend the present into the past. A part of this faith in the future was amply justified, for of all the American Indians the Iroquois were the only people who succeeded in forging a new workable religion out of the mixture of the old faith of their fathers and the new faith of their conquerors.

The Condolence ceremony begins with the welcoming of those who are to take part in it and is referred to symbolically as "At the Woods' Edge" in reference to the fact that it was there that the council-fire was first kindled:—

"Friends" [so the solemn rite begins], "I have been greatly startled by your voice coming through the forest to this opening. You have come through the forests to this spring. You have come with troubled mind through all obstacles. You kept seeing the places where they met on whom we depended. How, then, can your mind be at ease? You kept seeing the footmarks of our forefathers; and all but perceptible is the smoke where they used to smoke the pipe together. Can, then, your mind be at ease when you are weeping on your way?

"Great thanks now, therefore, that you have safely arrived. Now, then, let us smoke the pipe together. Because everywhere around us there are hostile glances which are each saying, 'I will frustrate their purpose.' Here there are thorny ways and here there are fallen trees and here there are wild beasts lying in ambush. Either you might have perished, my offspring, or, here by floods you might have been destroyed or by the uplifted tomahawk in the dark, outside the house. Every day these are wasting us. Deadly invisible disease might have destroyed you, my offspring."

It is in this elevated and symbolical strain that the whole rite continues. Addressing the mourners the official consolers speak as follows:—

"Come, let us wipe away your tears so that in peace you may look about you; let us remove the obstruction carefully from your hearing that you may hear the words spoken; let us remove the obstruction in your throat that you may speak freely in our mutual greetings; let us wash off the blood-marks from your seat that the place whereon you sit will be clean and that you will look happily upon us."

Then the speaker launches upon a preliminary account of the creation of the League, full of figures of speech and symbolical allusions now lost. When that is finished the great and famous chant celebrating the League, its founders and their descendants, is intoned:—

Continue to listen,
Thou who wert ruler!
This was the roll of you
You who were joined in the work,
You who completed the work,
The Great League. . . .

Ye too were principals
Father and son,
Ye too completed the work,
The Great League.
Ye too added each other
Ye too founded the house.
Now therefore hearken!
Thou who wert ruler. . . .

These were his uncles,
Now hearken!
Thou who wert ruler—
These were his cousins
These were his brothers thenceforth.
Then his son.
He is the Great Wolf
Thus were combined the many minds.

This befell in ancient times.—
They have their children.
These the two clans;
He the high chief.

This put away the clouds:
He was a war chief,
He was a high chief,
Acting in either office—
This was the roll of you!

Then in later times
They made additions
To the great mansion.
These were at the doorway
They who were cousins,
These two guarded the doorway.

Now we are dejected
In our minds. . . .

From the recital of the deeds of the great founders they then turned to the more specific act of consolation, addressing those who were mourning "in the deep darkness." The sky is to become clear and the clouds to be dissipated; the sun is to shine upon them. "Yeh! the sun shall seem to be hanging just over you; you shall look upon it peacefully as it sets. We are full of hope that you will yet see the pleasant days."

That a civilization capable of such achievements, of such true progressiveness, should have shown a tenacious resistance to the inroads of the whites not known elsewhere in North America was to have been expected. A bitterness commensurate was engendered in the hearts of their leaders when they saw the edifice tottering and when they contrasted the constructiveness of their heroes with the destructiveness of the puny leaders of their conquerors.

"Friends and relatives," said one of their noted leaders, "we have reason to glory in the achievements of our ancestors. I behold with sadness the present declining state of my race. Once our fathers were strong and their power was felt throughout the land. But we have been reduced and broken by the cunning and the rapacity of the white-skinned race. Many winters ago our ancestors predicted that a great monster with white eyes would consume our land. This monster is the white race and the prediction is near its fulfillment. Our ancestors advised their children when they became weak, to plant a tree with four roots branching to the north, south, east and the west; and then collecting under its shade to dwell together in unity and harmony. This tree, I propose, shall be this very spot. Here we will gather, here live and here die."

CHAPTER XIII

THE GREAT ADVENTURE: THE CONQUEST OF THE PLAINS

MOST of the energy of so-called civilized peoples has been expended in holding on as best they could to their past cultural heritage. New needs and new conditions have, it is true, necessitated the introduction of changes and transformations in which they were often enough profoundly interested, but the preservation of the past has always been their main concern. How else indeed could any of them have possibly survived? So it is everywhere and so it was also among the American Indians.

The pursuit of the buffalo and the warlike ambitions of tribe upon tribe, often brought disruption in its train and frequently imperiled temporarily the old ideal and the old order of things. But nowhere among the aboriginal peoples we have so far passed in review was the energy of any tribe ever completely diverted from the preservation of the glorious heirloom which had come to it indirectly from southern Mexico, even if it had come to them in shreds and patches. Wherever this old heritage could still be made to function the old order somehow persisted and when this was no longer possible, then the old order was consecrated and enshrined in ritual and mythology, to blossom forth again with new meanings and derived functions.

In the case of the tribes so far discussed circumstances had, on the whole, been favorable to the preservation of the basic traits of the culture implanted by the Mayas, Toltecs and the Mound-Builders north of the Rio Grande. The tribal movements that took place, were generally on a large scale and the land traversed was fertile and inviting. As long, likewise, as these tribes still clung to the middle and lower Mississippi they were in the midst of an unbroken tradition difficult to forget. The pursuit of the buffalo, and the marauding expeditions which brought them to the very fringe of the plains stretching to the west and the north of the Great River, did unquestionably weaken the force of this tradition, but as long as they did not actually settle in the plains the old order was still upon them.

Some day, however, it was clear that the die would have to be cast, that the plains and the buffalo would lure these people from safety and tradition, and spur them on to true adventure where the outcome was unknown and mysterious. What would then happen? No one could possibly tell and no one could possibly have foretold what actually did result. All we know is that when the Europeans first came to the northern plains along the Missouri they encountered a strange medley of tribes who had come from all points of the compass, and a culture as conglomerate. All these tribes had certain traits in common but they also possessed a number of societies and ceremonials which apparently had no affiliations with those of any other tribe.

As we scan the names of these tribes old friends or, rather, the relatives of old friends appear. Here are the Arikara, brothers to the Pawnee, and the Mandan, Hidatsa, Crow, members of the far-flung Siouan peoples. Some members of this latter group we might have expected here for they are present everywhere, whether it be in the region of the Great Lakes, the valley of the Mississippi and Ohio, the lower Mississippi, the southeast, or the northeast. Here, too, we find the Arapaho, the Cheyenne, the Blackfoot and the Gros Ventre, in speech Algonquians and therefore cousins of the Ojibwa and the simple tribes north and east of the Great Lakes, although completely different in culture. So much for the tribes of the center of this area. Close to these, and sharing some of their traits, was a veritable hornet's nest of tribes—the Pawnee themselves, the Dakota, Ponca, Omaha, the last three all Siouan tribes; then the Kiowa, linguistically related to the Tanoan group of the Pueblos. On the fringe finally hung the Sarsee and the Kiowa-Apache, the kindred of the Apache and Navaho, the Algonquian Cree and the Ute, and the Shoshone and Comanche, distant cousins of the Aztecs.

In short, every one had converged upon the plains—from the south, from the east, from the north and from the west. We no longer know what spurred these tribes on to such dangerous adventure and we do not know at what widely separated periods of time they arrived there. This much, however, we do know—that the tribes of the most complex type of culture live approximately in the north-central and the extreme northwest parts, and that a perfectly legitimate method exists of reconstructing both the development of the specific features of the Plains culture and the approximate contributions and distortions made by the more important tribes.

As in the case of most civilizations when torn from their native soil and from the surroundings endeared and congenial to them and to their ancestors, the habitat in which the newcomers found themselves and to which they in turn had to adapt themselves economically and psychically, produced profound and far-reaching changes. But all this was as nothing compared to the disintegrating effects—

i.e., where there was anything to disintegrate—of the long and tedious migrations, some of them lasting generations, that had to be undertaken by the various tribes who were eventually to be included in the culture denominated the plains. Old identities were lost or transformed beyond recognition and out of the collision and impact of these converging masses there emerged a new spirit, if not a new culture, whose chief characteristic was its loose-jointed stability and its many-faceted plasticity.

But let us examine these various tribes more closely and endeavor to see whether even at this late date, the all-consuming cauldron that is adventure and the monotonous leveling that is the plains, have not left some trace of old affiliations.

As we have already pointed out the very heart of the Plains culture lay far to the north, in the north-central part of what is to-day North Dakota. There, along the shores of the Missouri River, on soil made fertile by the yearly overflowing of that fickle stream, dwelt three tribes who practiced agriculture fairly intensively, the Siouan Mandan and Hidatsa, and the Arikara, a fairly recent offshoot of the Pawnee.

Now the fundamental feature of the old Siouan civilization was the division into two halves between whose members marriage was prohibited; clans and special functions for the clans; sacred bundles; warrior-societies, and religious fraternities, membership in the latter being determined by a vision-experience in which a deity was supposed to communicate to the dreamer the details of the ceremonials he was to establish.

Of all these traits the Siouan Hidatsa and Mandan have lost certain old cultural possessions completely, and others have become either badly obliterated or transformed. The clan and the dual division have stood the test of adventure and of economic and environmental pressure fairly well. The dual division has, however, lost its main function, that of regulating marriage, a function that was at best always an unstable one. Of the older customs one, the ceremonial rivalry between the two halves of the tribe, has persisted although in very much altered form. Agriculture which it might confidently have been predicted, should have been doomed, has, on the contrary, not only survived but taken on a renewed vigor, due possibly to the proximity of the Arikara.

To explain the persistence of these very old cultural traits we must suppose that the Mandan and Hidatsa had reached their present habitat at a time when the great plains were still sparsely, if at all, settled, and long before the general migration toward this region had taken on portentous proportions. These two tribes, more specifically the Mandan, constituted the basic core of the eclectic culture that was to develop here and they, more than any of the other tribes, were destined to be the determining element in transforming, creating and diffusing it. In so far as common elements in the Plains culture exist, in so far as any welding and integration has taken place, it is the work of these two tribes. But before their achievement can properly be assessed, let us glance at some of the other tribes.

Four Algonquian tribes—the Arapaho, the Cheyenne, the Blackfoot and the Gros Ventre—have practically lost all their old identities. They must have come into contact with the Mandan and the Hidatsa fairly early in their career, for their whole ceremonial and most of their social life has been manifestly derived from them. In fact even their original tongue was almost submerged. The dialects they speak are so divergent from typical Algonquian, that we must suppose that numerous elements of alien origin have been incorporated into them. Especially is this true of the Arapaho and the Cheyenne. In two respects only have they retained their older social structure, first in their refusal to adopt the clan organization—although even in this respect the Cheyenne, at least, seem to have wavered—and secondly, in their refusal to adopt agriculture.

Of the Siouan tribes of the area the Crow, who are linguistically quite close to the Hidatsa, occupy something of an anomalous position. They have retained their clan organization but lost the old clan designations and all recollection of the dual division. Agriculture has become markedly attenuated. In their ceremonial organization they are like the Hidatsa and the Mandan but without certain striking features of the latters' system. On the other hand, they have retained much of the typical old Siouan religion, such as the curious specialization of the religious fraternities.

The Arikara although the most intimately associated of all the Plains tribes with the Mandan and Hidatsa, had lost comparatively little of their old culture, a phenomenon easily explained by the fact that they probably did not split off from the Pawnee before 1700. Yet in one respect they have very emphatically shown the disintegrating effect of their journeys and the isolation from their kindred, namely, in the complete loss of the sacred bundles without which, as we have seen, Pawnee culture is unthinkable. The Pawnee, themselves, lost practically nothing from their association with the Plains culture but they, too, felt its effects although in a more diffuse sort of fashion.

The tribes on the margin, the Kiowa, Shoshone, Comanche

and Cree, were even less touched except in one respect, the influence of that famous and entirely new creation—the Sun Dance.

This leaves us with a few Siouan tribes not yet mentioned the most important of whom are the Omaha, Ponca, and the Oglala Dakota. The first two were only secondarily affected and retained their old fundamental Siouan traits to a remarkable degree, but the latter tribe was completely transformed by the great adventure which had brought them to the Plains.

It is not at all clear why this should have happened for they were very late arrivals in this area. Well into the eighteenth century, in fact, they still possessed villages in northern Michigan and Wisconsin. Something of very unusual nature must have occurred, for when we find them on the Plains these Dakota possessed neither clans, dual organizations, agriculture nor sacred bundles. Of their original culture only the religious fraternities survived. Everything else was either fairly thoroughly obliterated or markedly transformed.

Loss of old identities and disintegration—these stand out as the salient facts of the Plains. Yet this was only the negative side. There was a positive side, too, shown in the transformation of old cultural features and in the development of new combinations and permutations. The initiators and the organizers of these new changes were the Hidatsa and the Mandan and the essential transformation they wrought, consisted fundamentally in the specialization of a type of dancing-society which had been from time immemorial a very characteristic trait of most Siouan tribes—the military associations. Upon the basis of this old and comparatively simple unit was built up a perplexing array of graded societies, each with its own specific paraphernalia, privileges and customs. They were all dominated by the possession of a few peculiar traits such as, for instance, the part played by purchase, the ceremonial relationship of sons and fathers in which the buyers and sellers of the privilege of entering a society stood to each other and, finally, the rivalry and antagonism that existed between certain of the societies.

Among the Hidatsa and Mandan these societies were graded in a definite way and it was the ideal of every man to pass from one to the other until he had reached the enviable condition where there were no more left that he could join. Such a man was strangely enough called a "Stinking Ear." He began as a boy and passed from one society into another provided, of course, that he and his friends and relatives had the requisite purchase price. The names of these societies in their proper order were Notched Stick, Stone Hammer, Crazy Dogs, Lumpwood, Kit-Foxes, Little Dogs, Dogs, Half-Shaved Heads, Black Mouths or Soldiers, Bulls and, lastly, Ravens. Membership in each society was secured through a simultaneous purchase of membership by one group of people of approximately the same age from an older group, and the purchase was always collective, inasmuch as all members of the purchasing class contributed to the initial payment. It also had an individual side, however, for each purchaser selected one of the sellers to be his ceremonial father and to this person he was expected to give special gifts and to entertain for a certain number of nights prior to the final acquisition of the membership privileges. This purchasing factor is so fundamental to a proper understanding of these societies and yet so peculiar that we shall give a typical example. It refers to the acquisition of membership in the Stone Hammer society.

The prospective buyers filled a pipe, and after choosing a spokesman proceeded to the Stone Hammer lodge, where they sat down between the door and the fireplace. The leader went to the rear and deposited the initial gifts, packed in four or five bundles, and a pipe. Facing the Stone Hammers who were seated in a semicircle in the rear, he said: "Fathers, we want to buy your songs! See all these goods. They are all that we have been able to get together. We ask you to take them, and to light this pipe. We want to have your songs. Light this pipe that we may know that you accept." Then he sat down with the rest of his group. A Stone Hammer replied that the goods were not sufficient to purchase his society.

The would-be buyers then debated among themselves whether it was possible for them to get more property from relatives or friends. Several thought they could, left the lodge, and came back with additional gifts, which were laid down with the rest. The spokesman of the sellers said the presents were still hardly enough, but as the buyers had done the best they could he would consent to sell and asked his group whether they agreed with him. When they had expressed their consent, he lit the pipe and carried it to the Stone Hammer on the right end of the semicircle, who smoked it and passed it to the left. When the pipe had been smoked dry, the Stone Hammer spokesman returned it to the buyers' spokesman, then went back to the rear, and thus addressed the younger group: "Our sons, to-morrow evening you must give a feast and the members will make ready to give you your stone hammers and teach you the songs. Four nights they will teach you the songs and you shall give a feast to them each night. By that time you will have learned all the songs and they will be yours." The boys then left and returned to the lodge from which they had started.

Those who had special gifts to give to their ceremonial fathers as payment for the stone hammers then decided whom they were going to choose for their father. About eighteen of the forty were able to do this. Then, in accordance with the sellers' instructions, the boys selected six officers to hold the four lances and the two rattles the society was to receive on the last night of the purchase.

The next day, before sunset, the novices assembled in the same lodge as before. The parents of some had already prepared food with which to feast the sellers, so the boys who were going to have ceremonial fathers went home to get it, returning to the lodge with their kettles. All went to the Stone Hammers, and the boys with food arose and offered it to their fathers, each saying, "Father, make me my stone!" The food was passed along the semicircle, all the Stone Hammers helping themselves. The buyers who had no ceremonial fathers remained seated. Some women and children came in, and sat at the right of the door, while the novices were at the left. Three of the older "friends" of the buyers sat with the sellers and shared the food.

When the fathers had done eating, they called to their sons to take back their dishes. Wolf-Chief's father thus addressed the people: "Listen, my friends, to what I have to say. To this son I now give my name, hereafter he shall be called Deer-Head." Then to Wolf-Chief, he added: "Son, I will make you your stone. I will begin to-morrow. You shall receive it when we get through the four nights' feasting." Those boys who had relatives among the women spectators then asked them to take their kettles home.

After the feast, the sellers smoked from the one pipe owned by the society, but a few of the buyers had brought pipes with them and offered them to their fathers. Finally, one of the sellers arose and said: "Our sons, we are now going to sing. You who want to learn, listen to us. You must learn these songs. When we get through we will go, expecting to gather here again to-morrow evening, and you must again give us a feast as you have to-night. So also for the third and fourth nights. When we are all through, then on the following day, by daylight, we will take you out in the village to dance. You shall be the ones to dance that time. As I have said, we are going to sing. You may listen, or you may join in the singing if you wish. And now, friends, let us begin our singing."

Two musicians with hand-drums and seven other singers sat in a circle in the rear of the lodge, between the semicircle and the two rear main-posts, and began to sing and drum. Some of the fathers rose and danced. Finally the gathering broke up. The buyers went back to Wolf-Chief's lodge, practiced some of the songs heard, and at last went home. . . .

These Stone Hammers were boys, yet they had strong military ambitions. They regarded themselves as of stone and accordingly did not fear their enemies. The most distinctive of their activities, however, was the licensed theft of food which they practiced. Before they could start on their pilfering expeditions a public announcement had to be made so that the villagers could hide their food. The following is an account given by an Indian himself:

After the completion of the purchase we marched through the village, and made this announcement: "We are going to steal to-night. Hide your *parfleches!*" We went about, repeating the words of this song many times. Finally we returned to our lodge. One of the older members spoke to us as follows: "Go in pairs, all of you!" I selected Wounded-Face for my partner. We went together to the village and saw light in one of the earth-lodges. As soon as we got to the door, we looked in and saw a woman making bread. We said, "We'll try to steal that, it has a pleasant smell." We watched all night. When done, the woman put her bread into a dish-pan, placed it inside a box and hid it. We noted the place. "Friend," said I, "we shall surely get it." She covered the box with a dry skin and put some heavy object inside. We saw all her attempts at hiding the food.

We ran off some little distance to watch the smoke-hole in order to see when the fire would be out. Then we returned. Wounded-Face removed a log far enough for me to crawl in, then I en-entered. As soon as I was inside, he called me back, and whispered, "Unbar the door!" Wounded-Face continued, "Be careful, go very slowly, or they will catch us." I went ahead. At every step I heard my arms and leg-joints creaking. I raised the bar with a noise. "Be careful, grasp it at the bottom, and lift," said my partner. I obeyed. Wounded-Face entered and both of us advanced towards the food. Our bones were creaking. We proceeded very quietly along the edge of the earth-lodge. Part of the way I took the lead, until we got to the biscuit box. We were in a hurry to get the food. I raised the hides, and reached down for the biscuits. The top one I gave to Wounded-Face, who began eating it then and there. He found that it was as yet uncooked. The flour covered his mouth and breast with white. He said to me, "You run faster than I, take the pan. I'll lift the door and give you a sign when I am ready. Then you must run out." So I got ready, raised the cover, and lifted the bread.

When I had done that, I pushed the cover off, no longer caring what noise I made, and ran off. I ran towards the river. Wounded-Face said, "Run hard! If they catch us, they will take away all our clothes." So we ran hard and reached the river. We jumped from the bank into the water and waded along the bank for a while, then we climbed up a hill and continued to run. We got back to the lodge of the society. Each pair of members had stolen something—sugar, dried meat, or other provisions. After the feast, towards daylight, we went home.

The following morning the owner of the lodge I had stolen from summoned me to his home. Though I was afraid, I went. When I arrived, I looked around and saw Wounded-Face already seated there. I sat down near him, expecting to be questioned regarding the meat. Our host gave us each a platter with food. When we had eaten, he filled a pipe for us. When we had smoked, he said nothing, and I thought he was going to reproach us for the theft. All three of us smoked, laughing and talking at the same time. I was glad at his not making mention of the last night's doings. But when we had done smoking, I knew he was going to ask us about the stolen food, and I got frightened again. At last he said, "Last night some one stole all our baked biscuits. You are my friends, perhaps your society did this, and I wish you to tell me who were the thieves." I did not answer, but Wounded-Face, pointing to our host, said, "You are not acting as you should. You ought to say to your wife, 'Give these boys some biscuits and coffee.' Yet you did not say so. I know you can afford to entertain us in this way: it would not kill you at all." "Very well," said our host, "I am very glad, my younger brothers, that you tell me what I ought to do. The matter is now settled. You must not have any bad feelings against me." Then we went from the lodge, and thereafter no longer were afraid of the man whose meat we had stolen. . . .

Now all these societies which attain their most complex expression among the Hidatsa and Mandan have a double interest for us. Not only do they represent the most characteristic feature of the culture of the Plains but they symbolize at the same time all the various elements that have combined to create it. The Plains culture is a triumph of eclecticism and the graded military societies constitute its greatest single achievement. These societies themselves are an old heirloom of the Siouan people and we find the germ of this highly differentiated grading in quite a number of southern Siouan tribes where it probably represents the last stages in the disintegration of what had once been a caste system. The second element, the father-son relation is patently a variant of a fundamental feature of the Pawnee Hako ceremony. How it came to the Plains we no longer know precisely, but there are a number of possibilities from which we can choose. Either the Arikara, the Pawnee themselves, or the Oglala Dakota introduced it. We suspect that it was the latter for they possess a ceremony which is a palpable borrowing of the whole Hako and it would have been a comparatively easy task for a single feature like the father-son relation to have spread independently. The third feature, the purchase element, finally, is a contribution of the northern barbarians, probably the Blackfoot.

Thus did these diverse peoples unite to contribute feature upon feature toward the formation of the new culture that was to arise out of their great adventure, and thus did the indirect descendants of the Mayas, Toltecs and Mound-Builders join hands with the children of the northern barbarians, like the Blackfoot, the Arapaho and the Cheyenne, to catch for one passing moment something of that creative impulse which was so conspicuously absent in most of the other cultures north of the Rio Grande.

We have just seen what the Plains meant to so highly civilized a tribe like the Mandan or the Hidatsa. Let us see what it signified to a tribe that entered from the north, with but a modicum of culture—the Blackfoot.

When the Blackfoot emerged from the cold and dreary forests of eastern Canada and began their long and tedious struggle for some share in that civilization which the Hidatsa, Mandan and Arikara had brought with them to the

Plains, they themselves possessed a very simple, undifferentiated democratic culture. Like all the Algonquian peoples they had an especially rich assortment of personal fetishes and medicines. The contribution which they were destined to make to the Plains culture was, in fact, to be the elaboration of certain of these fetishes.

From time immemorial it had been an Algonquian custom to gather certain charms and medicines together into a small bundle. There had originally been little system connected with the manner in which this was done and, of course, even less ritual. The first result of contact with the Plains culture was the development of a marked organization of everything connected with these medicine bundles. They became sacrosanct and were guarded by their owners according to definite rules. Songs were always associated with the new ritual that thus arose. Two main types of bundle developed called respectively the Medicine-Pipe and the Beaver.

Each bundle contains an enormous number of objects each possessing a definite significance and function. To give some idea of their diverse nature let me give the contents of one of them:—a tanned elk-hide; a bear-skin; a decorated pipe-stem, the chief object in the bundle; a head dress of mountain goat; an eagle wing feather; a rattle; a bag of muskrat skin; a flageolette; the head of a crane; the skin of a loon in the form of a tobacco pouch; the fœtus of a deer; the skin of a prairie dog; the skin of a squirrel; of a mink; of an owl; a raw-hide bag with accessories; a small bag of roots used for making a smudge; various bags containing red paints; muskrat skin for wiping the sweat from the face of the owner; a bag of pine-needles; necklaces; tongs used for placing fire on the smudge place; a tobacco cutting board; pipe stokers; a wooden bowl for the owner's food; a whip for the owner's horse; a thong lariat and a painted buffalo robe.

There are four occasions on which the pipe-bundle can be opened; first, when the sound of the first thunder is heard in the spring; second, when the bundle is to be transferred to a new ruler; thirdly, when the tobacco within the bundle is to be renewed, and lastly, in accordance with a vow. The ritual connected with it is voluminous but fairly simple. There are two main divisions, the rites connected with its opening and the so-called "dancing with the pipe." Before the bundle is opened a smudge is made with sweet pine-needles. Then a burning coal is taken from the fire with the wooden tongs and placed in the smudge square. The so-called pipe-man now picks up some of the sweet pine and slowly drops it on the fire. As the smoke rises he and his wife hold their hands in the smoke and sing two songs:

1.

That which is above; it is powerful.

2.

That which is below; it is powerful.

As this is sung the woman rises and taking the bundle down from its position between herself and her husband, holds it throughout the period that the third and fourth songs are sung. The woman then takes off the outer wrapping and lays the bundle down between herself and her husband. Another series of songs is now sung:

1.

You stand up; you take me.
You untie me; I am powerful.

The woman now unties the cords.

2.

We are still of the same place sitting; it is **powerful.**

The woman puts the bundle down.

3.

This here man, he says, my robe, take it; it is **powerful.**

This last is sometimes called the antelope song and while it is sung the woman makes the movement of hooking and poking at the bundle in imitation of this animal.

Then a fourth song is sung:

4.

Man, you must say it; buffalo robe, I take it; it is **powerful.**

While this is sung the woman takes off the outer thong. The pipe is considered to be addressing the owner as if he were his son.

Then follows the fifth song:

5.

My robe, I take it; it is **powerful.**

This last is called the elk song. The pipe is supposed to be speaking of his own robe and the woman shakes her head, etc., and like an elk charges upon the bundle and knocks off the outer wrapping of the elk's skin.

Then both the owner and the woman pull their robes over their heads and sit like beavers. At the very end the woman makes four passes toward the bundle, and bringing both hands down on it, in imitation of a bear, removes the bear-skin covering, which is the robe referred to in the song. And so it goes on *ad infinitum* and *ad nauseam*.

But now we must leave the Blackfoot. Their culture illustrates remarkably well the unlimited possibilities that the entry in the Plains and the contact with more highly civilized peoples, meant for the barbarian north. The Blackfoot participated in everything that they found there, but yet we always have the feeling that they did not know exactly what to do with the sparks flying all about them. One thing, however, they were taught—how to organize their simple shamanistic performances and how in this way, to give them a corporate significance that they had never before possessed.

Two other Algonquian tribes were to achieve a far greater triumph in the reinterpretation and organization of their old, simple and undifferentiated cultural background—the Cheyenne and the Arapaho. These two seem to have almost completely absorbed most of the distinctive achievements of the Hidatsa and the Mandan in the realm of ceremonialism. Yet something of the bewildered newcomer still clung to them too and this is shown in the enormous development of symbolism pervading their whole life, a symbolism utterly different from that of the Pueblo and the Pawnee, for its roots lie in the individual and it is steeped in mysticism. Apparently they felt the need of tempering the fierce individualism and egotism which the adventure in the Plains had brought with it, by falling back upon the protection of that vague, awesome and undifferentiated world of the mysterious.

We must turn to the last of the great tribes that set their impress upon the new culture, the Oglala Dakota. They are the great individualists *par excellence*. The difference between their individualism and that of the simple tribes of the north is that they achieved it, whereas among the northern barbarians it was simply a passive corollary of an undifferentiated culture. And because it was an achievement and a rather late one in their complex history, they were conscious of it, felt its implications at every point of their life, played with it as does an artist when he has mastered a technique. It is exhibited everywhere but nowhere so much perhaps as in their remarkable vision-experiences. Let us give an example, one that will illustrate at the same time the approved method of entering one of the numerous mystery-societies which play so great a rôle in the life of these people. It is the account given by a man sixty-eight years old:

"One time when I was about thirteen years old, in the spring of the year, the sun was low and it threatened rain and thunder, while my people were in a camp of four tipis. I had a dream that my father and our family were sitting together in a tipi when lightning struck into their midst. All were stunned. I was the first to become conscious. A neighbor was shouting out around the camp. I was doubled up when first becoming conscious. It was time to take out the horses, so I took them.

"As I was coming to my full senses I began to realize what had occurred and that I should go through the *heyoka* ceremony when fully recovered. I heard a herald shouting this about, but was not sure it was real. I knew I was destined to go through the *heyoka*. I cried some to myself. I told my father I had seen the thunder. 'Well, son,' he said, 'you must go through with it.' I was told that I must be a *heyoka*, if so I would entirely recover. If I did not go through the ceremony, I would be killed by lightning. After this I realized that I must formally tell in the ceremony exactly what I experienced.

"I also saw in the dream a man with hair reaching to his heels, while all over his back were many birds moving about. He was painted red; on the arms and legs were longitudinal marks with forks at the ends. On his face were live tadpoles and dragon-flies. He carried a sinew-backed bow with four red arrows. In one hand he carried something covered with horse-flies; it seemed afterward to be a deer-claw rattle.

"In the *heyoka* I was ordered to array myself as nearly like this dream man as possible. So I had a long-tailed bonnet made and covered the tail with feathers. On my face and body I painted tadpoles and dragon-flies. In one hand I carried a deer-claw rattle and a string of the same over the shoulder." . . .

All societies among the Oglala have a supernatural origin. But this in no way makes for formalism. Each man stands on his own feet and never allows any stereotyped formula to interfere with his spiritual freedom. Almost any individual could found a society and that is why among these people societies arose and disappeared with remarkable rapidity. All that an Oglala would consent to do in the way of conforming to some general type was to frame his vision and his newly founded society in the external dress that was an old heritage of all the Sioux. Take for instance, this account given of the founding of one of the most famous of the Oglala societies, the Dog Society.

The founder of the society is represented as having gone up a high hill to fast for four days. Then he goes home. As he approaches his camp he is seen to carry a bundle wrapped in sage-grass. Outside his tipi he takes a pile of buffalo chips and on them he places his bundle. Then he

orders a sweat house to be prepared on the following morning and his tipi to be taken outside of the camp. It is his
object to demonstrate the medicine, that is, the power he has
received from the spirits during his fasting.

The next day he directs that the floor of his tipi be cleared
off and that a bed of sage-grass be arranged in the center, and
then when this is done he places his bundle there. As it is
unwrapped the bystanders notice that it contains the body of
a crow. "Bring me four coyote skins and four whistles of
eagle bone," he orders. Then he takes four roots of medicine and pulverizes them, and when this operation is finished
he pulls the tail feathers out of the crow and throws its
body out of the tent. Seven men are now invited to join him
in the ceremony and another man to act as his assistant.
Some of the pulverized roots are then tied up in small buck-
skin bags and fastened to the quills of the crow feathers and
these in turn are attached to the necks of the coyote skins.
Then he takes up a black pipe, fills it and begins to sing.
As he passes from one song to another the coyote skins are
seen to move of their own accord. "Now," he exclaims,
"you are to go on an expedition with me. I shall select four
of you to carry the coyote skins and four others to take the
plumes."

They set out on the warpath and after two days are joined
by four men, making fifteen in all. Two men are detailed
as scouts and after a time report that the enemy are near.
Then the leader addresses them, "All the horses of the
enemy were promised to me before. Now you are to get
them." So that night they all proceed to the enemy's camp
and run off all the horses successfully.

It is in this way that societies are founded. A general

scheme is adhered to but everything else is individual and
personal.

The account of the founder of the Dog Society brings us
to the last fundamental trait of Plains culture, war and the
horse. Little could these ferocious individualists have
imagined that the Big-Wolf, as so many of them called the
strange animal that the Whites had introduced, was but the
first intimation of their undoing, the shadow of death. Had
they known it they might have rejected the horse in spite of
all its implications for them. But they did not know. On the
contrary, they took the strange and lovable animal to their
hearts and it became so integral a part of their lives that
they almost forgot that they had not known of its existence
before the arrival of the avaricious Whites. Not only, indeed, did they accept it but it became the instrument of one
of the most remarkable and most interesting of all their
creative achievements, the Sun Dance. The Sun Dance is
par excellence the Oglala contribution to that strange disjointed but yet spiritually unified cultural potpourri which
we call the Plains culture. It is a fascinating medley of customs of the most various kinds all subordinated to the two
great obsessions that the tribes of this area developed—the
supplication to the deities for power, and war. Let us see
what it was like.

Although the Sun Dance differs in many details from
tribe to tribe, it is still possible to give a generalized description of it. It is most frequently initiated by an individual in fulfillment of a vow made at some critical moment
in his life when supernatural aid was needed. Immediately
after he has made his vow a camp-circle is formed and a tipi
pitched near its center and in this the preliminary rites,
which are always of a secret nature, take place. Here in

this tipi both the pledger and whatever associates he happens to have, are instructed in the hidden and mystical significance of the ceremony by specially qualified priests. Then the regalia are prepared and a general rehearsal follows.

While these secret rites are taking place a number of more public preliminary activities are going forward. What these are differs in the various tribes. In general the tribes prepare buffalo tongues to be used during the dance and special hunters are often sent out to obtain a buffalo bull hide. Others are engaged in gathering the necessary wood for the structure in which the dance is to take place. Then come the more spectacular public performances, such as the ceremonial setting out to fetch the center-pole for the dance lodge. This is done in a definitely ritualistic manner. A great mass of people leave the camp and scout for a tree much as if it were an enemy for whom they were looking. When the proper tree is found they strike it, exactly as a Plains warrior does when he has killed an enemy. Then it is felled and brought to the camp.

After that the man who has taken the vow and the priests, leave the sacred tipi and enter the dance lodge. A bundle of brush, the buffalo bull hide, and various other offerings are tied to the forks of the center-pole, the pole is raised and the structure complete.

Only after these ceremonies does the real dancing commence. In this dancing every one may participate. The warriors dance in the lodge itself where an altar has been erected. The pledger and his associates who have refrained from food and drink throughout this period only now begin to dance. Steadily gazing at the sun or at the offerings on the center-pole they make their supplications for supernatural power. Day and night this continues. Then comes the dramatic climax so well known to every one—the self-inflicted torture. Skewers are thrust through the flesh of the breasts or the back and by these the men are tethered to the center-pole, dancing and tearing against these bonds until the flesh gives way. Captain Bourke has left us a very vivid description of one of the Sun Dances he witnessed in 1881, which will give the best idea of what it was like. Let us begin with the ritual connected with the securing of the sacred tree.

An advance party is sent out to look for the tree as soon as it has been selected. The medicine-men then tell the young warriors that they must now act just as if they were going to war. When the signal is given, the whole party dash off at full speed on their ponies, and as soon as they arrive at the tree, they break into song and distribute presents to the poor.

Next, a band of young men steps to the front and each in succession tells the story of his prowess, each reference to the killing or wounding of an enemy being corroborated by thumping on the skin-drum used by the medicine-men.

The first young man approaches the sacred tree, swings his new ax, and cuts one gash on the east side; the second follows precisely the same program on the south side; the third, on the west side, and the fourth, on the north side, each cutting one gash and no more.

They are then succeeded by a young girl, against whose personal character not a breath of insinuation could be brought, and she is decked in all her finery—a long robe of white antelope-skin almost completely covered with elks' teeth and with beads. She seizes the ax and, with a few well-directed blows, brings the tree to the ground.

In carrying the tree to the camp it is placed upon skids, no one being allowed to place a hand upon the tree itself. Upon reaching the summit of the knoll nearest the camp the tree is left in charge of its immediate attendants while the rest of the assemblage charge at full speed upon the camp itself.

When the tree has been erected in place, each one of those who is to endure the torture provides himself with an esquire. The camp is filled with all kinds of officials, an armed force of men to preserve order, criers to make proclamations, and heralds and water-carriers armed with long staves tipped with bead-work and horse-hair. These water-carriers do not carry water for the men attached to the tree, for these were not allowed to drink. But if they happen to faint the medicine-men will take a mouthful of water apiece and spray it upon the body of the sufferer.

On the particular occasion when Captain Bourke was present, all the Indians were attached to the tree itself by long ropes of hair or by thongs, fastened to skewers run horizontally under the flesh. One young woman, named Pretty Enemy, took part on this occasion. She, however, was not tied up to the tree, but danced with the others, her arms scarified from the shoulders to the elbows. All this scarification was done by a medicine-man.

The young men were scarified in the following manner: Their attendants seized and laid them on a bed of some sage-brush at the foot of the sacred tree. A short address was then made by one of the medicine-men. Then another, taking up as much of the skin of the breast under the nipple of each dancer as could be held between his thumb and fore-finger, cut a slit the length of the thumb, and inserted a skewer to which a rope was fastened, the other end of the rope being tied to the tree.

Young men placed what they called eagle pipes in their mouths, this being simply a ceremonial term for flutes made from one of the bones in an eaglet's wing. They had to be sounded throughout the time the young man was dancing. This dancing was done in the manner of a buck jump, the body and legs being stiff and all movements being upon the tips of the toes. The dancers kept looking at the sun, and either dropped the hands to the sides in the military position of "attention" with the palms to the front, or else held them upward and outward at an angle of 45 degrees, with the fingers spread apart, and inclined towards the sun.

When laid on the couch of sage-brush, each young man covered his face with his hands and wailed.

Before approaching the tree the victims were naked, with the exception of blue cloth petticoats and buffalo robes worn with the fur outside. The buffalo robes were, of course, thrown off when the young men were laid on the sage-brush preparatory to the scarification.

"One young man," so writes Captain Bourke, "was unable to tear himself loose, and he remained tied up to the tree for an hour and seven minutes by my watch. He fainted four times. The medicine-man put into his mouth some of the small red, bitter, salty seeds of the *Dulcamara,* while the women threw costly robes, blankets, articles of bead-work and quillwork and others of the skin of the elk and antelope upon the rope attaching him to the tree, in the hope of breaking him loose. The articles thus attached to the rope were taken away by the poor for whom they were given. There was any amount of this giving of presents at all stages of the dance, but especially at this time, and the criers were calling without ceasing. 'So and so has done well. He is not afraid to look the poor women and children in the face! Come up, some more of you people! Do not be ashamed to give! Let all the people see how generous you are!' or words to that effect. . . ."

The Sun Dance is not one single ceremony but a series of them. Indeed, it is a frightful conglomeration of rites and customs that have been here merged into the semblance of a unified whole. Such an artificial unit could only have been attempted by a people, or by peoples, who were making one last desperate effort to keep the disjointed elements of their old heritage from flying to the four ends of the world. Most of their old corporate life had already become completely disrupted—the dual organizations, the clan, the method of reckoning descent. That they should have succeeded in achieving so high a degree of success in this reorganization of their ceremonial life was due, we cannot help feeling, first to an external accident, the horse, and secondly, to the need that even the most blatantly individualistic of people must feel for some place where they can for a brief period of time forget their egotism and subordinate themselves to a less vacillating and less nerve-racking unit. It must consequently have been with relief that they welcomed the severe discipline that prevailed during the ceremonies connected with the Sun Dance, and the strict subordination of their personal desires to the group.

And so we see eclecticism reigning supreme throughout the Plains. But the danger of eclecticism lies in the fact that the borrower does not always know what destruction may lurk in the new object he has incorporated into his own culture. So the Plains Indians adopted the horse and completely reorganized their life and many of their cultural values in terms of it. Little did they realize that this strange animal was but the precursor of annihilation.

CHAPTER XIV

THE CAPITALISTS OF THE NORTH

THE northwest coast of Canada has always been an enigma to ethnologists. Here in this land of forbidding inlets and fjords, the best that one might have hoped for was a simple indigenous culture with interesting survivals from the dawn of aboriginal civilization in North America. Yet, instead, we find one of the most complicated and specialized cultures to be encountered anywhere.

The northwest coast shows, however, points of similarity, on the one hand, with the region to the southwest, *i.e.*, with the northwest Plains, particularly with those aspects of its culture that seem disconnected with the influences coming from the tribes who had inherited the memories of the Mound-Builder civilization—the Hidatsa, the Mandan and the Crow. At the same time, we find marked resemblances to the cultures directly to the east, across the inhospitable tracts of Canada and as far as the Great Lakes, and beyond. Indeed there are echoes, even throughout the Atlantic seaboard, among the Algonquians, the Iroquois, the Mushkogean and, still farther south, among the natives of the Caribbean and northeastern South America.

How are we to explain these far-flung resemblances? Are they accidental or are we in the presence of an old cultural substratum, that which the Asiatic ancestors of the Indians brought with them from their old home? Everything points to the latter supposition. It is this culture, or something approximating to it, which the Mound-Builders encountered when they swarmed in all directions from the Lower Mississippi and overwhelmed the original cultures.

But all this would only explain one part of the northwest coast culture. Certain significant higher elements still remain unaccounted for, elements that bear a striking resemblance to the customs, art and rites of Melanesia and which have led some scholars to predicate a direct contact between the two regions.

But let us turn to less hypothetical matters. In whatever manner the higher elements of culture were brought to the northwest coast we are justified in stating that they were at first restricted to a small and definitely circumscribed section. Upon this cultural oasis there then burst, first the tribes of the interior belonging to the Athabascan stock, a stock which oddly enough also includes the southern Apache and Navaho. Following them came the Salish known to many Americans perhaps best through the Flathead Indians. Other tribes with other linguistic affiliations also thrust themselves into this melting-pot, so that the final product was a culture with a marked family resemblance but with an incredible number of variations in detail. There are, of course some major dissimilarities too, but these must all be regarded as having arisen in a very simple fashion and as representing the particular degree to which various tribes from the interior of Canada and the region immediately south of Puget Sound, were able to absorb and digest an alien culture found originally in a very restricted area.

The outstanding feature of the northwest coast civilization is its interest in names. Everywhere, especially among the American Indians, do personal names possess great significance both for their social implications as well as for their value in contributing toward personal vanity. But rarely has their purchasing power been so assiduously cultivated and catalogued as among these ranting best families of the northwest coast. What price, indeed, would a man not pay there either to hold on to the purchasing power his name possessed, or to give it increased monetary value? Let us see.

At the well-known ceremonial of the Kwakiutl Indians of British Columbia called the *potlatch* and which is to all intents and purposes an auction sale of names, privileges and property, one of the auctioneers, or shall we say pullers-in, is described as delivering the following speech:

"You all know, Kwakiutl, who I am. My name is Yaqat-lenlis. The name began at the time when our world was made. I am a descendant of the chiefs about whom we hear in the earliest legends. This ancestor of mine came down to the place called Xopa and took off his bird-mask and became a man. Then he took the name that I now bear. Such was my ancestor. He married the daughter of the first chief of the clan Wewamasqem. That is the reason why I speak. I know how to buy great coppers. I bought this copper that I hold now for four thousand blankets."

This chief was immediately followed by another who exclaimed: "Now you have seen my name. This is my name; this is the weight of my name. The mountain of blankets rises through our heaven. My name is the name of the Kwakiutl and you cannot do as we do, tribes."

What did these people imagine belonged to a name that

it could have such weight? It is a long, but nevertheless fascinating story.

To the Kwakiutl names mean everything. First of all they carry legendary and historical significance for they refer to an adventure that a man's remote ancestor had with the animal from whom his clan derived his appellation. Secondly, they indicate the wealth and position of a family, for in addition to the clan animal ancestor, other animal guardians may be acquired through purchase and then be handed down from one generation to another. The ceremonies connected with acquiring a name or names, are consequently identical with those associated with the acquisition of rank and prestige in the community. A short sketch of the life of a child will bring this out vividly.

When a boy is born he is given the name of the place where he is born. He keeps this name until he is about a year old. Then one of his parents, or some other relative, gives a paddle or a mat to each member of the clan and the child receives his second name. When the boy is about ten or twelve years old he obtains his third name. When he is about to take this third name he must borrow money, in their currency, blankets, for blankets and coppers are the units of wealth. This loan he must repay after a year with a hundred percent interest. There is a definite scale of interest, in fact. For a period of a few months six blankets must be returned for the loan of five; for six months seven must be returned for a loan of five, and for a year or longer, ten. If a person has poor credit he may even pawn his name for a year; then during that period the name must not be used. For, let us say, the thirty blankets which he had borrowed he must then pay the enormous sum of one hundred if he wishes to redeem his name.

Such is the significance and the purchasing power of a name. It has brought us face to face with the peculiar characteristic of this and all northwest coast culture, a trait that sets it off against every other region in North America. Yet it falls in very nicely with the fundamental principles of the economic life of some of the people living in far-distant Melanesia across the Pacific.

Names are thus merely part of a definite ritual of wealth and this ritual is one of the most blatant crystallizations of human vanity, self-aggrandizement and snobbery that can very well be pictured. To appreciate it in all its implications we must first say a few words about the social organization of this region.

All the tribes of the Pacific coast of America are divided into three classes, a nobility, common people and slaves. Only a definite number of families, however, are recognized. The ancestor of each of these families always possesses a tradition of his own quite apart from that of the clan. He thus possesses a certain crest and certain privileges that are all his own. Tradition, crests, and privileges together with the name of the ancestor, descend in the male line, at least among the Kwakiutl, first to his direct descendants or, through the marriage of his daughter, upon his son-in-law, and then through him upon his grandchildren.

Only one man nevertheless can at any given time impersonate the ancestor, and only one man consequently has his particular rank and privileges. This it is that limits and fixes the number of noblemen in the group.

These noblemen are not equal in rank but range in the manner in which their ancestors were supposed to range and they sit in this order at all festivals. The noblest clan, and among them the noblest name, is the Eagle.

CHIEFS OF A WOODLAND TRIBE

HIDATSA DOG DANCE   MANDAN CHIEF

NORTHWEST COAST HOUSE (*Upper*)   HAIDA TOTEM POLES (*Lower*)

The personal name borne by a noble is his certificate and his property mark. The names are all reminiscent of the things a Kwakiutl likes to talk about—his ancestor, his property and his greatness. Take, for instance, the following: Giving-Wealth; Whose-Body-Is-All-Wealth; The-Great-Only-One; About-Whose-Property-People-Talk; Throwing-Away-Property; Making-Potlatch-Dances-All-the-Time; Satiating; Envy; Too-Rich; From-Whom-Presents-Are-Expected; Always-Giving-Away-Blankets-While-Talking; To-Whom-People-Paddle; etc.

An added complexity is given to the caste system by the fact that these names, although acquired by different individuals, are not necessarily retained through life, for with every new marriage a new name may be obtained from the new wife's father.

The ideal of the Kwakiutl is to possess wealth and then make as great a splurge about it at festivals as possible. The economic system has been so built up that no man loses anything by his ostentatious display of his possessions. Whatever may have been the case once, to-day rivals fight with property only. One of the main objects in life, especially for the rich man, is to show himself superior to his rival and this he does by inviting him, his clan or his tribe to a festival and there bestowing a considerable number of blankets upon him. Then the trouble begins. This invitation must be accepted and custom dictates that the rival place an equal number of blankets on top of the pile offered to him. Then he receives the whole pile and finds himself a debtor to that amount, thus obligating himself to repay the gift with a hundred percent interest. Now the highest denomination of currency used is that called the "copper." A copper is a T-shaped plate covered to-day with black lead upon which a face representing the crest-animal of the owner is outlined. These coppers possessed names of their own and were valued at different prices. For instance, one was appraised as being worth seventy-five hundred blankets, another six thousand blankets, and still another five thousand blankets. It is in connection with the offer of a copper to a rival that the curious ritual of weath, the *potlatch,* has been most elaborately developed. Prof. Boas has admirably described such a sale. The ceremony attendant upon it is filled with innumerable speeches and songs celebrating property and extolling the virtues of the rich. Let us quote some of the dialogue that takes place:

First Speaker: "Let me speak of my ways. Go on, tell the whole world that this was given to our ancestors at the beginning of time."

Second Speaker: "You, my tribe, I have nothing against the way, Kwakiutl, in which you treat me and my tribe. Here is this copper. It has a great price and its name is The-One-of-Whom-All-Are-Ashamed. Now I am going to lay it down before you. Do not let me carry it."

First Speaker: "I will buy this copper. Now pay me, Kwakiutl, what I loaned to you, that I may buy it quickly, in order to keep our name as high as it is now. Don't let us be afraid of the price of it. Tribes, I buy the copper for one thousand blankets."

Second Speaker: "Did you say this was all you were going to give for the copper? Do you think you have finished? Come, chief, give twenty times ten pairs more so that there will be two hundred more! You were not provident when you resolved to buy this great copper. My heart is well inclined toward you. You have not finished; you will give more. The price of the copper will correspond to my greatness, and I ask forty times ten blankets, that is four hundred blankets more." . . .

And so it goes on until the number of blankets is deemed adequate. Between these speeches songs are sung in which rivals scathe each other most mercilessly:

1.

"Do not look around, tribes! Do not look around, else we might see something that will hurt us in the great house of this really great chief.

"Do not look around, tribes! Do not look around, else we might see something formidable in the great house of this really great chief. His house has the Tsonoquo. Therefore, we are benumbed and cannot move. The house of our double chief, of the really great chief, is taking our lives and our breath.

"Do not make any noise, tribes! Do not make any noise, else we shall precipitate a landslide of wealth from our chief, the overhanging mountain.

[Another chief responds.] "I am the one from whom comes down and from whom is untied the red cedar-bark for the chiefs of the tribes. Do not grumble, tribes! Do not grumble in the house of the great double chief who makes that all are afraid to die at his hands; over whose body is sprinkled the blood of all those who try to eat in the house of the double chief, of the really great chief. Only one thing enrages me, when people eat slowly and a little only, of the food given by the great double chief."

2.

"I thought another one was causing the smoky weather. I am the only one on earth, the only one in the world, who makes thick smoke rise from the beginning of the year to the end, for the invited tribes.

"What will my rival say again, that Spider-Woman? What will he pretend to do next? The words of that Spider-Woman do not go a straight way. Will he not brag that he is going to give away canoes, that he is going to break coppers, that he is going to give a grease feast? Such will be the words of the Spider-Woman and therefore, is your face dry and moldy, you who are standing in front of the stomachs of the chiefs.

"Nothing will satisfy you. Yet sometimes I treated you so roughly that you begged for mercy. Do you know what you will be like? You will be like an old dog and you will spread your legs before me when I get excited. So you acted when I broke the great coppers 'cloud' and 'Making Ashamed.' This I throw into your face, you whom I always tried to vanquish; whom I have maltreated, who does not dare to stand erect when I am eating; the chief whom even a weak man tries to vanquish. . . ."

Such a ritual could have of course only developed in an atmosphere pervaded by the spirit of capitalism, an atmosphere where everything can be purchased. We should therefore expect marriage and the marriage dowry to play a considerable rôle. It does. Many privileges of the clan descend only through marriage upon the son-in-law of the possessor. He, however, does not use them himself but acquires them simply for the use of his successor. He becomes entitled to them only by paying a certain amount of property for his wife. This property is then repaid to him. There are two installments. The woman herself is regarded as the first installment. The second is made later

when the couple have children, and consists partly of a
certain amount of property, partly of the crest of the clan
and its privileges. The percent of interest paid depends
upon the number of children born. For one child it is two
hundred percent; for two or more, three hundred percent.
Legally, after this payment has been made the marriage has
been annulled, that is, to the extent that the wife's father
is regarded as having redeemed his daughter. If the latter
then continues to stay with her husband she does so of her
own free will. To avoid this situation the husband frequently makes a new payment to his father-in-law so that
he may have a hold on his wife.

Just as these capitalists ate up everything—property,
crests, privileges, wives—so they were possessed of the
violent desire of eating men, of being, on occasion, cannibals
in the strict sense of the term. The Kwakiutl have a fairly
large number of spirits who initiate men into their rites.
One of the most famous of these is a deity called the First-
One-to-Eat-Man-at-the-Mouth-of-a-River. He is a cannibal always in pursuit of man. His immediate *entourage* is
most delightful. First, there is his wife, who like a dutiful
spouse, procures food for him. With him also lives a female
slave who does the same by catching men and gathering
corpses, and another slave, the raven, who eats the eyes of
the people whom his master has devoured. The last member of this family is a fabulous bird with an immensely
long beak who lives on the brains of the men whose skulls
he has fractured. But we must not forget, likewise, the
cannibal grizzly bear. He may be a terrible animal to
approach but the privileges to which a man is entitled when
he meets him amply make up. These are the privileges:
First, he may become an orthodox kind of a cannibal

obsessed with the desire of devouring whomsoever he can lay his hands upon; second, a cannibal of less violent character; third, an individual who can devour and touch fire with impunity; fourth, the grizzly bear of the cannibal-spirit who delights in killing people with his strong paws; fifth, simply a person who procures human flesh for the orthodox cannibal; and sixth, one who can break the skulls of men.

Here we thus find a most enviable specialization in the gentle art of eating man. Let us see how it works in practice, in the initiation into the cannibal society. The novice is supposed to be taken away by the great cannibal-spirit and to stay at his house for a long time, possibly over three to four months. During this time he actually secludes himself in the woods. About the middle of this period he reappears near the village. He can always be recognized by his whistle and his cries of *hap, hap, hap* (eating, eating, eating).

The purpose of his first appearance is to get the person who is to impersonate the mythical cannibal being and who is supposed to procure food for him. This individual is always one of his female relatives.

Finally he returns and attacks every one whom he encounters. In fact, he bites pieces of flesh out of the arms and chests of individuals. He is met by "healers," for the whole purpose of the ceremonies that are to follow is to cure him of his cannibalistic propensities. These "healers" run up to him swinging rattles carved with designs representing the skull, and the sound of these rattles is supposed to pacify the cannibal. To-day modern conditions have thrown a mild haze over certain parts of the ceremony. In olden days when he returned in a state of ecstasy, slaves were killed for him, which he devoured. In those days, too, after the cannibal novice had succeeded in biting a piece

out of the arm of an individual, preferably one of his enemies, he gulped down the flesh and drank hot water with
the laudable object of thus causing an inflammation in the
wound of his victim. Corpses as well as living slaves were
devoured. Indeed, Prof. Boas was told that dried corpses
were preferable to fresh human flesh, the latter being in
fact rather difficult to eat.

This brings the first part of the ceremony to an end.
Part two is concerned with the attempts to cure him. The
"healers" take him by the head and drag him to the salt
water. They wade into the water until it reaches up to
their waist and then facing the rising sun they dip the
cannibal man four times under it. Every time he rises
again he cries *hap!* Then he returns to the house cured of
his excitement. In the dances that follow he no longer
shouts *hap!* but seems downcast and embarrassed. Finally
at the end of the ceremonial, true to Kwakiutl capitalistic
form, he indemnifies those whom he has bitten and the
owner of the slaves whom he has killed.

Thus ends this drama of capitalists and cannibals to the
complete satisfaction of all concerned, the participants, the
onlookers and the system.

This ceremony takes place in winter. Now in winter,
among the Kwakiutl, contrary to usage among the civilized
communities of Europe and America, a curious phenomenon
takes place. The ordinary organization of the tribe into
clans, etc., ceases to function and society, in fact, breaks up,
that is, it becomes transformed into an entirely different
kind of society where dances and ceremonies reign supreme.

To understand these ceremonies a number of things must
be remembered. It is one of the customs of the guardian
spirits to give new names to the men to whom they appear

and it is one of the peculiarities of these new names that they may only be used when the spirits are supposed to dwell among the Indians, that is, during the winter. The summer names which each individual possesses are consequently discarded and winter ones substituted. But a name, we have just seen, is not a purely decorative detail among the Kwakiutl. A change of name means a change of the foundations of society. The clan is accordingly packed away and society blossoms out into a new type of organization where people are grouped solely according to the spirits that have initiated them. This means that secret societies reign supreme. These societies, and their number is quite large, have all the same basis of organization, that is, all the people upon whom the same or almost the same power or secret has been bestowed by the same spirits, belong to a single society. The various fraternities thus formed are arranged in two principal groups, the Seals and the Quequtsa. The former is the higher in rank. But each of these two main divisions is still further subdivided in a most curious fashion, according to age and sex. The Seals have the following subdivisions:

Males	*Females*
1. Boys	1. Girls
2. Killer whales (Young men)	2. Hens (Young women)
3. Rock cods (Young men about twenty-five years old)	3. Cows (Old women)
4. Sea-lions (Old men)	
5. Whales (Chiefs)	
6. Old Men	
7. Eaters (Head chiefs)	

The Quequtsa, on the other hand, have the following subdivisions:

Males	Females
1. Puffins (Little boys)	1. Eating first (Girls)
2. Mallard ducks (Boys)	2. A species of bird (Women)
3. Sea anemones (Sick and lame people)	3. Albatrosses (Old women)
4. Halibut hooks (Young chiefs)	
5. Red cod (Third-class chiefs)	
6. Sea-lions (Men about thirty years old)	
7. Anchor lines of chiefs (Old chiefs)	

No more complex breaking-up of a society can very well be imagined. What it implies historically it is difficult to say. But surely it must go back to some complete substitution of one type of social organization by another. This would naturally suggest that we have here possibly another illustration of that onslaught by the barbarian tribes of the interior upon the new nucleus of higher civilization that had developed along the coast. While apparently these barbarian invasions were fairly successful, on the whole, they never succeeded either in completely destroying the higher culture nor yet merging with it. This explains in part why the civilization of the northwest coast never really became a well-rounded and integrated whole. In fact, certainly from the viewpoint of the organization of society, it was a sad mess and it is this messy side of its make-up that has produced the undoubted number of cultural anomalies so characteristic of it.

But let us return to one of the accessories of capitalism, the delight in genealogies and the commemoration of ancestors. Since a man's name was his fortune he naturally delighted in everything associated with it, particularly in those ancestors who bore the same name, and the deities associated with them. He painted representations of them on the walls of his house and on his various receptacles; he carved them in wood and he set these statues in front of his house. These totem poles thus commemorated his ancestors and blazoned his family history before an envious world.

In order to understand a particular drawing or totem pole we must delve into a person's genealogy and know the origin-legends of his family. In one case, for instance, the following details have to be known in order to explain the figures on the pole: that the owner was a descendant of a man named Gyote, the son of Kyepusalaoqua, the youngest daughter of Kuexagyla, the son of Hataqu, the daughter of Oneatl; that they have six family dishes with specific designs that have come down to them through marriage, and that the owner had been told to unite all these dishes and to carve them on his totem pole. In another case the figures on the post are to be explained by the following legend. The name of the house in which the post stood was given by an individual called the Great Transformer, who, it is said, made two houses of dirt, one for himself and one for his brother. He blew upon them and they grew large. He called the first So-large-that-one-cannot-look-from-one-corner-across-to-the-other and the other The-wind-blowing-through-it-all-the-time. He carved four men of cedarwood and gave them names; then he instilled life into them and they lived in his house. Three of these men are represented on the posts.

Since so much had to be represented on a pole, box, or what not, it was necessary to introduce all kinds of conventionalizations when carving or painting family histories. To

WHALE MONSTER SHOWN AS IF SPLIT IN TWO

accomplish this, specific features of the animal were selected as symbols and as indications for the whole animal. Animals, for instance, could be distinguished from human beings by having erect ears placed above the eyes surmounting the head. Birds could be recognized by their beaks, irrespective of the type of face to which they were attached. Various birds, in turn, could be identified by the shape of the beak. It was straight for the raven, curved for the eagle, and curved until the tip rested on the mouth or chin for the hawk. The beaver was indicated by his large incisor teeth, a scaly flat tail and a stick held to his mouth with his fore-paws; the grizzly bear by a large mouth full of teeth, a protruding tongue and large paws; the killer-whale by the dorsal fins and by a blow-hole; the shark by a vaulted fore-head on which there were three crescents; the sculpin by two spines over its mouth in addition to gills.

PAINTING OF SHARK CUT APART AND SPREAD OPEN

All this implied an organization of design of both an elaborate and a very specific nature. Many utensils were carved in the form of men or animals and the natural pro-portions of the animal had always in such cases to give way to the requirements of its use as a vessel. This fact, plus the principle mentioned above, of representing animals by parts of their bodies, while it overcame many technical difficulties, led to a type of decorative art which impresses us as highly grotesque. This grotesqueness was still further heightened by an artistic convention which insisted on leaving no spaces undecorated and treating the parts of a given object as though they corresponded to the parts of the animal to be depicted. Thus, for example, the square boxes were so covered that the front aspect of the animal was represented on one end, the rear parts on the opposite end and the sides on the sides. A still greater freedom was taken with the relative size and the relations of the body-parts to each other. But the most unusual feature of the artistic theory of the northwest coast was the curious analysis to which they subjected the human and animal form and which amounted practically to an anatomical dissection of

WATER MONSTER WITH RAVEN'S HEAD AND A
KILLER WHALE'S BODY

its various parts. An animal was not infrequently repre-sented as if it had been split from the rear to the nose and then spread out in two profiles joined in front only. In bracelets, for example, we actually find representations where the two parts of the animal, longitudinally bisected, encircle the wrist.

The art that thus results is neither realistic nor symbolic, but a mingling of the two. From a broad point of view it again illustrates or, if you will, symbolizes, both the com-posite nature and origin of northwest coast civilization and the lack of true unification, in spite of all appearances to

the contrary. No one can study the customs, read the
legends and the songs, stand bewildered by the art of this
much-discussed region, without feeling its unutterable raw-
ness, its lack of subtlety, its messiness and its blatant and
unrelieved egocentricity. In few other portions of the globe
could we find a song like the following:

That is the only cause why I laugh, the cause why I always
laugh at the one who is hard up.

The one who looks around here and there, the silencer,
the one who points about for his ancestors who were chiefs.

The little ones who have no ancestors who were chiefs, the
little ones who have no names coming from their grandfathers.

The little ones who do many kinds of work, the little
ones who work hard, who make mistakes,

Coming from insignificant places in the world and who
try now to go to high places;

They are the cause why I laugh for they speak in vain to
my chief.

But he does not work and plan at all, the great real one,
the great one whose voice is true;

He continues as one from one generation to the other in
this world, he continues as one who is made to be the highest in rank with his real father,

The one who named himself Having-Food.

And that is why I laugh, the cause why I always laugh,
at those who rush against pieces of copper that are thrown
against my chief.

CHAPTER XV

THE GREAT GOD HARE

ONCE upon a time there lived in a wigwam an old woman and her daughter. One day the old woman spoke to her daughter and said, "I beg of you, my dear daughter, to be on your guard and listen to what I am going to tell you. Verily, I am greatly afraid, I am in fear that something will happen to you. Never let it happen when you go out that you sit facing the west."

But daughters are notoriously not very obedient, especially only ones, and so it happened that one day the young girl, unmindful of what her mother had told her, left the lodge and walked towards the west. Suddenly she heard the sound of wind coming toward her—and she was chilled. Not long after that she knew that she was pregnant. The old woman scolded her, but there was nothing to be done any more.

In the course of time the old woman heard the sound of children quarreling with one another in the womb of her daughter. And so without ceasing did she weep, for she knew that her daughter would die. As she listened to the beings quarreling she became suddenly aware of one saying to the other, "I wish to be the first brought forth." And then another saying, "No, you cannot be the first born. I am to be the oldest."

Not content with the idea that one was to be born before the other, these unborn children decided that they would all try to emerge from a different place so that no one could

337

precede the other. So finally they were born and destroyed their mother.

After a while as the old woman looked around for indications of her daughter and her unborn children, she discovered a clot of blood. Thereupon she peeled some birch-bark from a tree and upon this bark she put the blood-clot and laid it aside. When she looked at it again not long after, much to her surprise, she beheld a babe who immediately addressed her saying, "Do you know who I am? Why I am Hare, Nanabushu." But let us follow the story as told by a native himself:

So accordingly then did the old woman bring him up.

And so by and by he said to his grandmother: "Don't you know of a place where there are some people?"

"Yes," he was told by his grandmother. "In yonder direction on the farther shore of the sea are some people."

"I am curious to know if they do not possess fire."

"Yes," he was told by his grandmother; "truly, they do possess some fire."

Now, this was what he said to his grandmother: "Please let me go fetch the fire," he said to his grandmother. And this was what he was told by his grandmother:

"Not will you be able to succeed. Truly, a very careful watch do they keep over it there where they dwell. An old man abides at the place. And all the while, as often as the day comes round, upon a net he works. Never anywhere does he go, but always there indoors he remains. Now, two are those daughters of his, and only they are continually out of doors."

And this he said to his grandmother: "Nevertheless! I will go," he said to his grandmother.

"Very well," he was told by his grandmother.

Now, this was what he then said afterwards: "I will that the sea shall freeze, as thick as the birch-bark covering of the lodge so let this sea freeze."

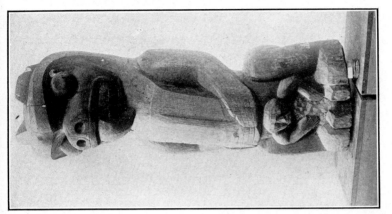

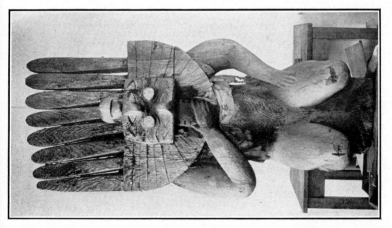

GRAVE POSTS

BLACKFOOT CHIEF

ALIGNMENT OF BLACKFOOT TIPIS

It was true that it happened according as he had said.

"Now, this is the way I shall look," he said. "I will that I become a hare." So accordingly that truly was the way he looked. Thereupon he then started on his way over the ice. It was true that he did not break through (the ice). Of course it was so that he knew that at yonder place the people were abiding. And so after he was come at the place where they drew water, this then he thought: "I wish that for water some woman would come," he thought. And this he did there where she intended to dip up water: that after he was washed up by the waves of the sea, then he was tossed rolling to the place from which the woman was to draw water. And this he said: "I wish that she would take me for a plaything." So thereupon he lay in wait for her to come for water. Lo, truly he beheld her walking hitherward.

Thereupon soon was she come at the place where he was, at once she dipped out the water.

As soon as he was discovered, forthwith was he seized upon. And after the water had been rubbed from him, then was he taken over there to her home; in the bosom of her garment she put the creature. And after he had been carried inside, truly he saw an old man that was seated (there). Sure enough, he was at work making a net.

And this said the woman to her elder sister: "I say," said she in secret to her elder sister, "see this creature that I have found, a little bunny! Oh, such a cunning thing is this dear little bunny! I wish you would also think it cunning, elder sister, this little bunny."

Now this was she told by her elder sister: "We shall be scolded by our father; on account of it shall we be taken to task," she was told by her elder sister; and in secret she was told by her elder sister.

Accordingly, after she had searched in the bosom of her garment, then was he placed there beside the fire, that from the heat his hair might become dry. Thereupon laughed the women as they made a pet of the little bunny.

Then they were found out by their father. "You are noisy," they were told by their father.

And this they said to their father: "See this," they said to him, "see this little bunny!"

"Beware!" they were told by their father. "Have you not heard of the manitous how they were born? Perhaps this might be one of them. Go put it where you got it," they were told by their father. "Truly, indeed, were you foolish to take it."

And this said the woman: "Such a precious pet do I think this little bunny!" And this she said to her father: "How is it possible for a manitou to be a little bunny?" she said to her father.

And this he said: "Truly, indeed you are not heedful of what is told you. Do you not behold me, how far in years I am?"

Now, this the woman did: in spite of what she was told, she exposed the little bunny to the heat of the fire; that she might dry its hair, she turned it over with its other side near the fire.

And this thought Nanabushu: "By this time surely must I be dry from the heat."

Yet at him laughed the women.

And this he thought: "I wish a spark would fall upon me." Sure enough, a spark fell upon him. After he was set on fire, then out of doors he leaped.

And this said the women: "Look at him, out of doors is he running with the fire!" they said to their father.

"Too bad!" said the old man. "Truly, indeed, are you unheedful of what is told you. Doubtless it is one of the manitous that has come to take away this fire of ours." Then, leaping to his feet, the old man ran to his canoe; but it was of no use, for it was frozen with ice. And all they could do was to watch (the hare) till they beheld him pass out of sight. Of course they were helpless to do anything.

And then presently he was coming in sight of his home. Now, this he had said to his grandmother before he started away: "Be prepared if perchance I truly happen to fetch the fire," he (thus) had said to his grandmother. Afterwards he addressed her when he was coming in sight of their home, and this he said to his grandmother when he came flying in: "Rub the fire off from me, I am burning up, my grandmother!"

Whereupon truly off from him did the old woman rub the fire. Therefore such was how they there came into possession of fire.

And this said Nanabushu: "Therefore such shall be the look of the hare in the summer-time. . . ."

It is thus, through the death of his mother, that the Great God Hare comes into the world. He is a true hero, born of a virgin and attaining maturity miraculously and instantaneously. Some scholars would have us believe that he is but one of the incarnations of our old friend Quetzalcoatl, who, in one of his aspects was both a wind and a fire god. Perhaps there is some truth in this contention. In any case, even if this were true it would be but the dimmest reflection of the great Toltec hero and deity that we would have before us, a barbarian conception and misinterpretation, more disturbing than helpful to our understanding of these simple people of the eastern woodlands.

The tribes where Hare was worshiped were a simple, essentially non-agricultural and unorganized people and the roots of their being were still closely bound up with the woods and streams. A naïve form of individualism was manifest everywhere. The relation between man and nature was real and personal, that between man and man direct and unsophisticated. The world of nature was organized on a democratic plan and pristine virtues reigned supreme—self-restraint and a home-spun ethical conception of the meaning of life. They were children of nature in the strict sense of that much-abused term and the fawn and the satyr still peeped at them from around the trees. Delightful tales are told. Take, for example, the following three that the author obtained from the Ojibwa of south-eastern Ontario:

I.

Once an Indian shouted, "I hear a bad owl!" His friends exclaimed, "Do be careful; that owl is challenging you!" Then the owl was heard to hoot. But again the Indian shouted, "Bad owl!" Again the owl was heard to hoot, and this time the sound was just outside the wigwam. But the Indian, undaunted, came out of the wigwam and sitting in front of it shouted, "Bad owl! Bad Owl!" And so the two of them shouted and hooted at each other all night.

2.

Once an old man said to his children, "In two days he is going to pass, the white animal." The children were very glad that they were going to see this animal and one of them asked his father, "Father, is this the animal who brings the morning?" And the father answered, "Yes. After a while you will hear him coming along and singing."

So within two days' time he told his children, "Remember, to-day you will hear him just before dawn. Look! Look! He is coming now."

"*Awihihi, awihihi.*" Thus he passed along toward the west singing and it was morning.

And surely Pan stalks unconcernedly through a woodland scene where the following could take place:

3.

Once an Indian while hunting came upon a deer. But before he could shoot he saw a lynx sneaking up toward it. He did not shoot for he wanted to see what the lynx would do. When the lynx got close enough he jumped on the deer and dug his claws deeply into its back. The Indian followed. The poor deer ran as swiftly as it could and as it was making its way under the limb of a tree, the limb struck the lynx so hard a blow that it fractured its skull and the animel died. The Indian did not shoot the deer.

We are not surprised, therefore, if in an atmosphere like this we find the bear both a staple of food and a demigod. Bear ceremonials pervade the whole area. But none are so interesting as those connected with the bear hunt.

When a bear is caught, particularly a black one, it is treated with all imaginable veneration and respect. First the hunter addresses a few words of apology and explanation to the animal. It is then killed and dressed up in all the finery obtainable and is made to look like a human being. It is believed that the bears have a chief and that the orders of this chief must be obeyed. Sometimes this chief orders a bear to go to an Indian trap so that, in a way, every bear that is caught has come as a willing sacrifice.

When a dead bear is dressed up this is done as an offering or prayer to the chief of the bears that he may send the Indians more of his children. If this were not done then the spirit of the bear would be offended.

After the bear has been eaten a pole is erected upon which are hung the skin of the animal's muzzle, his ears, skull, offerings of tobacco and ribbons. The bear's bones are never given to the dogs but always hung far out of their reach. In gratitude for the treatment accorded him the bear forgives his slayers and enters their traps a willing and fascinated sacrifice.

Something of their attitude toward animate nature is

extended to the inanimate world, particularly to their beloved birch-bark canoe.

In certain regions each canoe has its own name and everywhere its various parts all possess special designations. Indeed it is treated very much like a pet. In its construction men and women play an equal share.

The largest and smoothest birches are selected, so that the pieces of bark may be as large as possible and prevent too much sewing. The inner side of the fresh bark is cleansed and scraped by the men and then handed over to the women, who thereupon sew the pieces together and make a large cloak which can be wrapped around the whole canoe. While the women are thus engaged the men prepare the framework of the boat, employing for this purpose the elastic branches of the Canadian cedar tree. As a rule a kind of frame of the figure and the size of the canoe is made and around this the ribs are bent. In the center the arches are larger and they grow smaller towards either end. In shape they are practically semicircular. The ribs are peeled very thin in order to make the canoe light and easy. Between the upper end of these ribs is fastened a thin crosspiece to keep the ribs in a horizontal position. Both the ribs and the crosspiece are tied to a piece of wood on top.

When the framework has thus been prepared the bark-covering is spread out on the ground and laid over the wood. The bark is drawn as tightly as possible around the frame and the edges are turned down over the piece of wood on top and firmly bound to it. The interior is often lined with thin boards laid across the ribs.

All the woodwork, as well as the material for the cords and strings, is obtained from the white cedar. The cord that is made of this material is particularly satisfactory, for it lasts a long time and resists the influence of water much better than hemp cords.

Then the canoe is completed and the material is left to dry. For this purpose pieces of wood are inserted in every part to keep it well extended. Then it is hung up in the air. The final process is that of covering with pitch all the little holes, seams and stitches. This is done with resin of the pine or fir. The canoe is then ready and can embark on its numerous errands. Of these, none is perhaps so interesting as that connected with one of the main pursuits of these Algonquian tribes, the gathering of the wild rice.

Wild rice, so the legend runs, was first discovered by Hare. While living with his grandmother he was once reprimanded and ordered to go out and learn how to obtain food and get accustomed to the hardships of life.

So he left and taking with him his bow and arrow wandered into the forests. After traveling around for some time he came to a lake full of wild rice, the first he had ever seen. But he did not know at the time that the rice could be eaten. He continued on his journey into the forest and there found a large pine tree. From its bark he made a canoe so that he could gather the wild rice. First, however, he returned to get his grandmother, for he needed help. Both then started for the lake and after gathering some of the rice they sowed it in another lake. There he left his grandmother and started for the forests alone.

As he wandered along some of the little bushes spoke to him and whispered, "Sometimes they eat us." Hare paid no attention. Again these bushes spoke and then Hare turned around and said, "To whom are you talking?" "To you," they answered. So he stooped down and dug up the plant. He found a root as long as an arrow and it tasted so good to him that he ate too many of them and became very ill. At first he could not move, but after a while he was able to get up and he wandered through the woods faint and hungry.

All at once he noticed that he was passing along a river and that there were little bunches of "straw" growing in the water. These spoke to him and said, "Hare, sometimes we are eaten." So he picked some and ate it and said, "Oh, but you are good! What are you called?" "They call us wild rice," he was answered. Then Hare waded out into the water up to his breast, beat off the grain and ate and ate and ate. But this time he did not become sick.

Ever since then the Indians of this region have gathered the wild rice. First, they go into the "standing corn," as they call it, with their canoes, and taking as many stalks as they can into their hands, they give them a twist and kink. Then they turn the bunches downward, leaving them to ripen on the stalks. At times the heads of the rice are tied with bark-strings into sheaths, care being taken as they are drawn together gently, not to break the stems or the roots. The next process is that of gathering the matured rice. As a rule this is done by two women passing around in a canoe, one sitting in the stern and pushing it along while the other with two small pointed sticks about three feet long collects it by running one of the sticks into the rice and bending the rice into the canoe, while with the other stick she threshes out the grain. This she does on both sides of the canoe alternately and while it is moving.

The next stage is that of curing and drying. After being gathered the grain was brought to the shore and spread on a long rack. A pole was placed with its lower end on the blanket while the other end was held at a slight angle above. Over this pole the stalks with the now dried fruit heads were held and the grain was beaten with a stick. Before hulling it was again cured.

To thresh the grain a number of types of treadmill were used. One of the common type was that which consisted in making a hole in the ground and then inserting a skin in the hole filled with ears. A man then treads out the grain. The winnowing is a simple process. A blanket or a birchbark is spread on the ground and with the help of a good stiff breeze the grain is fanned out. Then the grain is stored and the work is finished.

Even in this none too simple cycle of processes connected with one of their main staples we see the inhabitants of this region insistently refusing to organize on any elaborate plan. A simple division of labor suffices for all they need. This same lack of adopting any but the loosest kind of organization is also apparent in one of the most characteristic elements of their culture, namely the shamanistic practices connected with conjuring.

Conjuring among these simple tribes is one of the necessities of life. The varieties of conjurors are infinite. We shall mention only one, the most important, the conjurors concerned with discovering the cause of all the major and minor ills that beset the community. Is a man sick? Then one resorts to a conjuror to find out whether his sickness has been caused by the machinations of some enemy, whether his soul has voluntarily wandered away, or whether it has been seized by some evil-intentioned member of the community. Has a person not returned from a hunt or a fishing expedition? Then again, one consults a conjurer and he informs the anxious inquirer whether the individual in question is dead or where, if alive, he is to be found. Nothing can give as vivid an idea of the rôle played by the so-called conjuror as examples given by the natives themselves. Let us illustrate.

On one occasion an Indian woman came to one of the author's informants and begged her to help in trying to find out the condition of her parents whom she had left home sick. The author's informant went to her brother-in-law, who was a well-known conjuror, and together they built one of the little lodges in which such ceremonies always were performed. The lodge itself was built of four poles, one of pine, one of balsam, one of spruce and one of cedar. Then basswood bark was wound very tightly around the outside of the structure. The top was covered with the same material.

When this was finished, the woman, for whom her brother-in-law was doing this came toward him, but stood quite a distance off. The brother-in-law took his shirt off, sang a song and threw the shirt inside the lodge. Soon the lodge began to shake. Then the man's voice was heard saying, "The turtle has come." The turtle said, "What do you want?" The man answered, "A woman wants to speak to her sister and ask about her parents. She wants you to go after her sister." The turtle left and the lodge started to shake again. He was not gone long and when he came back he said, "Here is the sister." Then the woman who had been standing at some distance came nearer and asked about her parents, and the sister in the lodge said that they were all well and that the mother had become much better since she had left. Then the man told the turtle to take the sister home. The lodge started to shake again. Afterward the turtle came back and the man said, "Won't you take a glass?" and put a glass full of whiskey inside the lodge. After a while, the glass was thrown out. Then the little lodge shook again as the turtle left.

In other instances the conjurors, so an Indian told the author, could locate the whereabouts of people who had gone astray or of things that had been lost or stolen. A man at Wallaceburg, Ontario, for instance, had been drowned. His canoe was found overturned. In order to find his body a conjuror was called upon. He made a little lodge about six feet in height with an opening at the top just as large as that on the bottom. Special kinds of poles were used in making it. These were tied with grape-vine. A fire was kept burning on the outside all day.

In the evening the conjuror entered the lodge, stark naked. After a while the lodge began to shake. He had entered singing and continued after he was inside. Then some one was heard to whistle at the top of the lodge and the man inside was heard saying, "Who comes?" The voice at the top of the lodge answered, "Turtle comes." Then a hoarse voice was heard speaking in a whisper within the lodge. This continued for some time. After a while the man said, "Who will go and look for the drowned man?" and the answer came, "I will." It was the turtle's voice. The turtle then went out and was gone for quite a time. Again a whisper was heard and one recognized the words of the turtle saying that the dead man's body was to be found below a certain clump of trees, on a straight road from the place. Afterwards, they found the body of the man at the exact place where they were told to look.

As a final example let us quote the fate of an unfortunate girl to whom the moon had appeared in a vision:

Once there was a young girl who was sick, and the parents did not know what was the matter with her. They used to give offerings to a medicine-man and beg him to cure her, but he always found that his method of curing was not strong enough for the purpose. Then they called in a conjuror to find out if any one was making this girl sick. But the first one they called could not find out. Many of these conjurors attempted and failed.

Finally they heard of a man who was a wonderful conjuror. There never was anything he failed to know when he was asked. So they sent for him. They offered him a horse, broadcloth and tobacco if he could find out what ailed the young woman. He said he would try, but he told them what he wanted them to do. First to get twelve very strong poles and stick them in the ground about four feet, for if they did not have them deep, the poles would not stand the strain. Then they were to tie a strong grapevine around the poles. They were told to put up three of these little structures, having four poles in each. When they had those structures up, they told the conjuror that they were ready for him to come.

That night there were many people who watched him try to find out why the girl was sick. He sang a song at the first little structure, then threw his shirt inside, for the structure was open above.

Suddenly a gust of wind blew and the little structure started to shake. Soon they heard a noise. This was when the animals and insects were arriving who had come to tell why the girl was sick. Then the man went to the next house and sang a song. Then he threw some of his clothing inside again. Soon the wind became stronger and the house started to shake again. They heard more noises, for more of the animals were arriving. Then he went to the last one and sang a song. Finally he went in. The wind blew still harder and the three lodges shook very much, the poles almost being pulled out and the vine by which they were tied broken. Soon they heard a voice inside that asked why they were called, and the man told them that a girl was sick and that he wanted to know why she was sick, that no one seemed able to say. They heard some one say that the right one was not there yet, but that he was on his way. When this one arrived they asked him if he knew why the girl was sick, but he too did not know. Again they heard some one say that the right one had not come but that he would soon be there. Soon they heard another arrive, and the turtle asked him if he knew why the girl was sick, and the answer was, "Yes. I know. It is the moon who is making the girl sick."

The conjuror then asked the parents what they wanted him to do, either to ask the moon why he was making the girl sick or to let her go. So they said, "Ask the moon." Soon some of those strong animals left to go after the moon. The turtle was among those that went. The people said when these got to the moon it was dark and they could not see the moon. When they arrived at the moon, the moon asked them what they wanted. They told him they were coming after him. The moon was willing to come, but when they were halfway, refused to go any further, so they had to pull him along. The people heard the turtle tell the others, "Be strong; pull hard." Soon they got the moon in the little structure where the conjuror was staying. The man asked the moon, "Why do you make this girl suffer?" The moon said, "Why, when this girl was fasting, I blessed her, so she will have to suffer as long as she lives, for I am all the time suffering and she will be the same way." The man could do nothing with the moon so they let him go. So the girl suffered till she died. . . .

In other words these conjurors played an all-important rôle in the humdrum life of the village, being something of a cross between a fortune-teller, a judge, an arbitrator, a consoler and a general diagnostician. The examples we have given illustrate all these functions of his.

Here in these woodlands all trails gradually peter out completely. And thus does the glorious heritage of the south fade out in the woods and streams of this northern clime where Hare reigned supreme in the land of the living and where, so the legend of the happy-hunting-ground tells us, Chiapos, his brother, ruled over the land of the dead, welcoming to a life of undiluted pleasure all those of Hare's nephews and nieces, the human beings, who succeeded in crossing the dangerous stream that separated the living from the dead.

CHAPTER XVI

WHERE THE SHADOWS STOPPED

ALL things have an end. Though culture may be relayed from one tribe to another the light grows dimmer with every borrowing. Finally it ceases even to throw flickering shadows. We have seen the torch pass from the Mayas to the Toltecs thence to the Mound-Builders; we have seen an interesting renaissance develop among the Pueblo and some not altogether negligible experiments arise out of the attempts to preserve the débris of the Mound-Builders' civilization. Even on the Plains we could still discern something of the old vitality that inhered in the higher cultures. In the eastern woodlands the light is almost gone but not quite.

Yet even the eastern woodland tribes, especially those that were in more immediate contact with the Siouan and Iroquoian peoples, still possessed some of the old traits which had belonged to the higher civilizations although they did not always understand them. Along the Great Lakes a tribe like the Ojibwa could still achieve so relatively complex a ritualistic unification as the celebrated Medicine Dance. But this was the last flickering and may very well be of comparatively recent origin and due to their enforced contact with the Siouan tribes as they made their memorable journey from the Ohio valley northward to the great Plains. So thoroughly had practically all of North America south of the Great Lakes and west of the Rocky Mountains been saturated in varying degrees with the great impulses that had come originally from Central America that it is difficult to discover tribes where the light never penetrated. Yet they existed here in North America and in South America, too, where no suspicion of Peruvian influence was discernible. We find them just where we should expect to theoretically—in the Arctic North, in the recesses of the Rockies, in the impenetrable jungles of Brazil, in the inhospitable rain-soaked area of the Gran Chaco of Argentine and at the end of the world, on the pampas and monotonous plateaus of southern South America.

The tribes encountered there are of considerable interest and importance for the reconstruction of the history of aboriginal America, for they clearly represent protected survivals. Such as they, so we may assume all of America once was before the great civilizations had developed. There are, of course, differences, specializations, and even gradations among them and in some cases it might be said that the opportunity for a higher development had even presented itself but had never materialized. This was essentially the case for California. Even although the smell of the arid desert penetrated almost to the very coast and in that sense constituted at all times a covert threat, there were still enough places in that enormous area where one might have expected some blossoming forth of a higher culture. Yet it did not occur. Instead we find what has all the earmarks of an abortive striving which failed to materialize. We have apparently the beginnings of clans, the beginnings of dual organizations and the beginnings of ceremonial units. Something seems always to have stunted their growth midway.

What was it? There is no reason for assuming that the

Californians were intellectually inferior to any other tribe of North America. Such explanations will never do. We must seek elsewhere. Perhaps the explanation is not so difficult after all. California is really the end of the world. All the peoples from the north, the east and the south converged upon it. Even the northwest coast culture of Canada and the Pueblos of the southwest succeeded, although probably at a comparatively late date, in setting their impress indelibly upon certain parts of that state. But whatever higher elaboration they introduced was soon simplified and nullified by the barbarians who had from time immemorial lived there and the barbarians who had from time immemorial swarmed into the land from the Rockies.

The state was overrun by wild and nomadic tribes— Athabascans whose home was in the northern part of Canada; marauders like the Ute and the Paiute belonging to the Shoshonean group and numerous other equally simple and uncultivated peoples. No wonder, then, that the differentiation in language found here was so great that many scholars postulated the existence of twenty-two distinct and unrelated groups of languages, as different from one another as Hebrew is from English. We need not accept any such preposterous assumption and yet stand bewildered at the actual dialectic differentiation that existed there. There is no justification for attributing it to isolation. Only one adequate hypothesis seems justifiable; that invasions and migrations never ceased and that cultures mingled and combined, united and disunited, split up and were disrupted.

Everything is either at a loose end or in the process of becoming a loose end here. Whatever is stable, however, belongs clearly to the oldest stratum of aboriginal civilization in America. Witches and werewolves roam over the land and individual shamanistic practices that are never organized, dwarf everything else.

Yet, as is always the case, certain specializations occur and perhaps none is more perplexing offhand than the occurrence among these tribes, of remarkable creation myths. True creation myths are none too common in North America and superficially people have a tendency to associate them with the higher cultures. Yet here they are and developed to a really remarkable degree.

But we must not dwell too long on this region where the opportunities never materialized. To the west, in the recesses of the Rockies, lived innumerable tribes who had never even had these opportunities. They were proud of their unenlightenment and when they raided the habitations of the more highly civilized peoples they came back only with material booty. Possibly they may have been imbued with such a love of freedom that they felt instinctively that it was dangerous to have contacts of too intimate a nature with more sophisticated civilizations. They lived within easy striking distance of the prehistoric pueblos of Utah, Colorado and Arizona, and their ancestors must have lived in the Rockies at a time when some of this older Pueblo culture was still flourishing. But they refused to be inoculated. Perhaps vague rumors of what had happened to their distant kinsmen, the Aztecs, had come to them. Whatever the cause, they were content to let the old Pueblo civilizations crumble into dust and to dance in their deserted and ruined temples.

Not only in the Rockies were inaccessible recesses to be found. They existed in the Andes as well. And there among such recesses in the western part of Ecuador dwelt and still dwell a people who, although they were within striking distance of the ancient Peruvian civilizations, proudly preserved their ancient simple customs—the Jibaro.

They interest us for a number of reasons more particularly for two specific developments—the fairly well-marked organization of one of the oldest traits of aboriginal American culture, namely, the blood-feud, and a peculiar specialization of their own, the preparation of head-trophies. Let us turn to the organization of the blood-feud first.

When any important individual among the Jibaro dies the medicine-man drinks a certain preparation in order to determine whether his death has been caused by witchcraft and who the murderer is. It is incumbent upon the nearest male relative to take revenge. This revenge must be taken no matter how long it is delayed. On the deathbed of their father sons must make a solemn promise to fulfill this duty. To prepare for it the sons first consult the spirits in order to determine whether they will be successful or not. They retire to the forests and remain there for three days and nights, fasting. If they feel that the response of the spirits is favorable they make preparations for the attack.

Very frequently, and this is very important, such an undertaking is not left to one or a few individuals but the whole tribe takes part, that is, of course, if the murderer belongs to another tribe. In other words the private feud is merged into the corporate war expedition.

A very curious type of preparation is indulged in. Not only is the plan of war carefully prepared and the necessary instructions given but a formalized dialogue between two warriors must precede. This dialogue is rather stereotyped and epitomizes the whole undertaking. Take for instance this example:

First warrior: Let us speak loudly!

Second warrior: Let us speak words!

First warrior: What are we going to say?

Second warrior: Let us quickly assemble!

First warrior: Let us avenge the blood-guilt!

Second warrior: To-morrow we will sleep far **away.**

First warrior: Let us quickly take our enemy!

Second warrior: Quickly before he is told about it!

First warrior: So says the old chief!

Second warrior: Let us go, to return quickly, youths!

First warrior: Quickly, quickly!

Second warrior: We have been fighting!

First warrior: We have killed!

Second warrior: We have revenged the blood.

First warrior: Let us cut off the head of the enemy!

Second warrior: Let us carry it with us.

The actual obtaining of the head of the enemy is only the first part of the ceremony. Immediately upon their return the victors have to pass through a purification ceremony called "the washing off of the blood." The first slayer remains with his relatives until the trophy is definitely prepared. Then he makes his solemn entry into his own house. He is dressed like a penitent, his hair is untied and he wears no body painting or ornaments. At his side stands some old warrior who has a special function to perform here. Behind him the other warriors are arranged in a row. The slayer is first given the juice of tobacco and then he is allowed to disengage the trophy from the cloth in which it had been enveloped and it is hung around his neck. Followed by the others he now slowly and ceremoniously proceeds toward the house continually smoothing the hair of the trophy with his hand.

After a few preliminary dances the actual washing off of the blood takes place. The slayer takes his seat on a small round bench close to a vessel which contains the blood of a chicken. An old warrior, the director of the ceremonies, seats himself at his side. Around them the women form a semicircle. First the slayer is again given some tobacco juice. Then the director of the ceremonies grasps him by the hand, brings it down to the vessel containing the chicken's blood and lets him dip the index finger into it. Subsequently, he draws a broad line with the blood along the front side of one of his legs. Thereafter the slayer applies a similar stroke to his other leg. During this proceeding the women dance around him singing, "They have painted you with blood so that you may start the fasting." With this the blood-painting ceremony is finished. The wife of the slayer must also undergo the purification rites. Then when both have been purified they go to the river where they carefully wash their bodies.

The whole purpose of this rite is of course to purify the slayer from the blood which is attached to him after the killing of the enemy and to protect him against the spirit of the latter who is thirsting for revenge. It is believed by the Jibaro that the soul of the enemy is present in his blood.

A number of definite food restrictions are imposed upon the slayer subsequently, as well as many definite rules of action. Should he infringe these rules in any way the consequences would be fatal and disaster would overwhelm not only him but everything connected with him. All this would be caused by the spirit of the murdered enemy. The ghost of the murdered enemy is very revengeful, takes no rest, follows his slayer everywhere and always looks for an opportunity to kill or harm him. It is in dreams that the slayer believes that the murdered man comes to him.

It is only when all the rites are finished that the slayer may enter his own house again.

A fairly large number of ceremonies follow, the most important of which are the feast of painting with *genipa* and that called "the eating of the head." The feast of painting is given in order to bestow upon the slayer renewed protection against the spirit of the slain enemy and to promote his material wealth. The eating of the head has reference to the series of conjurations through which the spirit of the slain enemy is first trodden underfoot, mortified and enslaved.

Thus we see that the blood revenge ceremonial among the Jibaro is an artificial association of a number of distinct customs and rites all of which have been secondarily subordinated to the elaboration of a very generalized and simple custom. In a way, we are almost reminded of the conglomeration of rites found in the Sun Dance. The only difference is that here among the Jibaro it was not any impulse from the great civilizations of Peru that initiated the organization of the blood-feud, whereas the Plains tribes were simply making a new elaboration of elements that had come to them from the Mound-Builders.

Let us now turn to the rather gruesome individual specialization of the Jibaro, the preparation of the head trophy.

There are a number of ceremonies preliminary to the actual "skinning" of the head. Then when everything is in readiness the head is placed upon a large leaf. Upon the head itself is placed another leaf, one to which certain magical virtues are ascribed. This "seat" is reserved for the warrior who has cut off the head and it is while seated in this triumphant manner that he received the juice of tobacco which plays so important a part in all their ceremonies. It is blown through his nose by the chief.

Then the preparation of the head is begun. It is a long process. Along the back side of the head from the apex downward a long cut is made and the scalp of the skin slowly and carefully drawn off from the skull. The skinning of the face is said to be the most difficult part of this work, for here the skin has to be cut off from the flesh with a very sharp knife. When the complete skin has thus been detached it is immersed in a pot of boiling water and left for a while. Then it is taken out of the pot, put on the top of a stick and fixed in the ground where it is left to cool.

The actual reduction of the trophy now begins. As usual, first a magical ceremony has to be performed. People go down to the bank of a river and gather three small stones which are then heated at the fire. By means of a cleft stick one of the heated stones is taken up from the fire and put into the head through the opening at the neck. The head itself is kept in motion so that the heated stone rolls to and fro within it, burning off whatever blood and flesh happens still to be attached to the scalp. A similar procedure is subsequently undertaken with heated sand. The object of all this is only partly a practical one, for the real purpose is to mortify the soul of the slain enemy and to keep it at bay.

The reduction proper of the trophy is brought about by means of hot sand. Some very fine sand is taken from the bank of a river and heated over the fire in a piece of a broken clay pot. Then when it is sufficiently hot this sand is poured into the head so that it more than half fills it. The object is to remove whatever flesh is still attached to the skin, to make the scalp thinner and to reduce it in size. This is attained by pouring in the hot sand repeatedly. As soon as the sand in the head has cooled, it is taken out again, reheated and again poured into the head. After each time the scalp is scraped with a knife in order to remove what the sand has burnt off. The trophy thus dries and shrinks and as it does so, the face is cleverly molded with the fingers so that it retains its human features and comes to look like the head of a small dwarf.

The Jibaro are able by this treatment to gradually reduce the head in size until it is hardly larger than an orange, or about one-fourth of its normal size. At the same time it becomes very hard and dry. Through both lips, shrunk in proportion to the rest of the head, three small pins, painted red, and parallel to each other, are inserted and around these pins a string, also painted red, is wound.

In spite of this ritualistically organized blood-feud the Jibaro have a fairly simple culture like all South American tribes that have not come into contact with the ancient Peruvian civilizations. To the northeast and the southeast of them, however, dwelt far simpler tribes. So well had they hidden themselves in central Brazil and northern Argentine that even to-day we know very little about them. This much, however, we do know, that their social organization is very simple and that in the ceremonies they practice, the performers generally wear very fantastic masks, and that these masks, as well as quite a number of other traits, are strangely reminiscent of the Melanesians living in the South Sea Islands.

It is perhaps a far cry from the Amazon to Melanesia and yet we must courageously face the possibility that

Melanesians or at least strong Melanesian influences once penetrated into this humid and forbidding region. The case for an actual early Melanesian invasion has been considerably strengthened by the remarkable resemblances that have been discovered between the skulls of what was clearly the oldest race in South America, and the Melanesians proper. A distinguished French scholar, Dr. Paul Rivet, has even shown that these Melanesian-like skulls extend as far north as southern California. This, added to the numerous resemblances in the vocabulary of the Melanesian languages and Hokan, by far the largest linguistic unit in North America, has brought the whole question of the first peopling of aboriginal America to the fore.

It now seems more than likely that the earliest peoples to enter America were Melanesians. In that case, of course, the marked cultural resemblances between so many of the simple peoples of South America and Melanesia is of fundamental significance in any attempt at reconstructing the aboriginal history of the two Americas. . . .

Our journey is almost ended. As we proceed south from the Gran Chaco of northern Argentine toward the Pampas and thence to the Straits of Magellan to Tierra del Fuego, land, culture, everything, comes to an end. For a long time the Fuegians were regarded as among the simplest people of mankind. This is clearly exaggerated. But it is true, whatever may have been the cause, that the Fuegians possessed a very simple and undifferentiated culture. Perhaps this represents merely a degeneration. It is more plausible, however, to regard this tapering out of civilization as primary and to interpret the culture of the Fuegians as the last remnants of a very old heritage. Here too a recent contribution of Dr. Rivet is suggestive. He claims to have

discovered marked resemblances between the languages of
the Fuegians and the Australians. If his hypothesis should
eventually prove to be correct then we can postulate three
invasions of North America, all of which started from Asia:
an Australian, a Melanesian and a Mongolian proper. The
Mongolians, coming last and in greatest numbers, overwhelmed the first two so completely that only in a few
inaccessible regions of South America can traces of them
still be detected. Everywhere else the Mongolian impress
has been decisive.

CHAPTER XVII

THE HEEL OF THE CONQUEROR

THE Winning of the West meant the annihilation of the Indian. True, their annihilation had begun much earlier, with the first landing of the Spaniards. Yet strange as it may seem, the Spaniards, in spite of all their cruelty and lust for gold, did not eradicate the native population so completely as did the Anglo-Saxons. With the exception of the West Indies, Indians are to-day still living in large numbers throughout Spanish America and although they are nominally Catholics many of their old cultural possessions have been incorporated in the new civilizations that have arisen there. In fact, Argentine and Brazil excepted, Spanish America is racially Indian. The two greatest presidents Mexico possessed, Jaurez and Diaz, were of Zapotec lineage, the first a full-blood and the second a half-blood.

Not so where the Anglo-Saxons landed. The Pilgrim fathers, thorough in everything, fell upon their knees, and then, as the saying goes, upon the aborigines. Within a few years of their landing New England was pretty thoroughly freed from the harmless natives. The descendants of the South English who settled in the southeast of the United States among an Indian population that could have taught them quite a number of things, were almost as ruthless as the Puritans. The organized cruelty with which they exterminated the Creek is one of the most infamous incidents in a record that few of the Spanish *conquistadors* have equalled. The Spaniards and the French enslaved the natives but they never broke their spirit. That was reserved for the Anglo-Saxon. To the latter Indian warfare was essentially a man-hunt.

As the Indian populations were pushed westward across the Alleghanies and the Blue Ridge Mountains, they fought back as best they could. Although always defeated their spirit was unbroken for most of the United States was still open to them. The crisis came during the first few decades of the nineteenth century when the white invaders pressed them closely first in the valley of the Ohio and then throughout the old northwest territory. The circle became smaller and smaller; the leaders of the Indians more and more puzzled and desperate. What was to be done? Three possibilities existed: either to make one last stand and drive out the hated and destructive invaders, or incorporate what seemed best in white culture into their own culture, or finally, to give up their old culture and adopt that of the white man.

From the very beginning the leaders of the Indians seem to have realized these alternatives and were divided among themselves as to which was best. There were always Die-hards who insisted that no concession of any kind was to be made if they wished to preserve their old past and there were always others who felt that some sort of an adaptation, some sort of a compromise was imperative. Needless to say the number of those who advocated the complete giving up of their old culture was at all times small. One contingency existed that none of the Indians, even the wisest among them and there were many wise men among them, could possibly have foreseen, namely, that their own culture would break up and that they would adopt little from the

Whites except their vices. Yet this is exactly what has happened in the vast majority of cases.

As was to have been expected most of the energies of the Indians were expended in seeking for a compromise between their own culture and that of the Whites. Many prophets arose. One of the most famous was the Kickapoo Kanakuk. The speech that he delivered to General Clark shows clearly how willing the more intelligent and practical-minded Indian was to recognize that something in their old culture must have been wrong if they could be so easily exterminated, and that something in the white man's culture must be worthy of emulation if the white man could be so uniformly victorious. Naturally they did not know—they could not have suspected—what it was that made the white man successful.

Kanakuk even drew a picture of the journey to heaven which he had undertaken in order to have the Great Spirit enlighten his bewilderment.

"My father," he said to General Clark, "I will explain to you what the Great Spirit said to me, but to do so I must make some marks. The Great Spirit said to me you must start from a certain point. This is the point: I have marked it. Then we got to a point that I have marked B and finally to one that I have marked C where the Great Spirit said he would appear. At point B the Great Spirit gave his blessings to the Indians and told them to throw away their medicine bags, not to steal, not to tell lies, not to murder, and not to quarrel. He told them that if they did not do this they could not get on the straight way but would have to go along the crooked path. That path led to an abyss of fire. He told us to go to a place I have marked E, where there would be collected all the Indian chiefs and where there would be a great preaching. He told us that if we had not thrown away all our bad things by the time we got there, this place E would meet and become united with the abyss of fire and that then he would destroy everything and the world would be turned over; that if, on the contrary, we threw away our bad doings we would be able to cross this fire as well as the river which came next and finally come to a country where there was nothing but the prairie and on which nothing grew. There the sun would be hid from us by four black clouds. Then he would come and explain everything to us."

It is in such a strain that Kanakuk continues. He was a mild man, and a man of peace and a compromiser. He realized that much in the land situation could no longer be changed and he very cleverly developed a new theory as to the original ownership of the land. "Some of our chiefs," he told the General, "claim that the land belongs to us. But this is not what the Great Spirit told me. He told me that the land belongs to him and that no people own the lands and that I was not to forget to tell the white people this when I met them in council."

Yet of his old culture he was not willing to give up more than was necessary. Much of the old social organization and many of the religious beliefs were in the process of disintegrating even in his time. Particularly was this true of the personal guardian spirits and totems. So he makes the Great Spirit say, "Our old men had totems; they were good and numerous. Now you have scarcely any. If you follow my advice you will soon have totems again."

Compromise could go no further.

Kanakuk was only the first of a long line of prophets and compromisers, some of whom achieved notable if only temporary success. Only one, the great Handsome Lake of the Iroquois succeeded in forging a compromise religion that has lasted to the present day.

One of the last of these prophets, Wowoka, born in a little village in distant Nevada, was destined to initiate a new religion which would sweep over all the west, unite peoples who had known very little of each other, cause enemies to forget their grievances and which was finally to terminate in massacre.

Wowoka was a typical prophet. He had the most beatific of visions and his program was in part simply a variant of the dream that has always been dear to the human heart. "My young men shall never work," he said. "Men who work cannot dream and wisdom comes to us in dreams."

The religion which he founded was a mixture of old Indian beliefs and Christianity. Belonging to a non-agricultural tribe where the earth was regarded as sacred, he protested vigorously against the instructions that had been sent out from Washington.

"You ask me to plow the ground," he said. "Shall I take a knife and tear my mother's bosom? Then when I die she will not take me to her bosom to rest.

"You ask me to dig for stones! Shall I dig under her skin for her bones? Then when I die I cannot enter her body to be born again.

"You ask me to cut grass and make hay and sell it, and be rich like white men but how dare I cut my mother's hair?

"I want my people to stay with me here. All the dead men will come to life again. Their spirits will come to their bodies again. We must wait here in the homes of our fathers and be ready to meet them in the bosom of our mother."

The spiritual crisis of the Indians was getting desperate; they were beginning to lose their nerve. No wonder then that the doctrine of resurrection made a tremendous appeal upon them. There was little to be hoped for in this world and so they hoped for something better in another one.

Wowoka himself went to heaven to find out whether anything was still in store for the hard-pressed Indians. He came back with a message that the earth was getting old and worn out and the people bad, that he had been selected to renew it, make it what it used to be and make it better. Now when people feel that they must return to a pristine golden past that has long since disappeared, we can be sure that it is the beginning of the end. Let us listen to what Wowoka promised:

"The Great Spirit told us that all our dead were to be resurrected; that they were all to come back to earth and that, as the earth was too small for them and us, he would do away with heaven and make the earth itself large enough to contain us all; that we must tell all the people we meet about these things. He spoke to us about fighting, and said that it was bad and that we must keep away from it; that the earth was to be all good hereafter and we must all be friends with one another. He said that in the fall of the year, the youth of all good people would be renewed, so that nobody would be more than forty years old and that, if they behave themselves well after this, the youth of every one would be renewed in the spring. He said if we were all good he would send people among us who could heal all our wounds and sickness by mere touch and that we would live forever. He told us not to quarrel or fight or strike each other, or shoot one another; that the Whites and Indians were to be all one people. He said if any man disobeyed what he ordered, his tribe would be wiped from the face of the earth; that we must believe everything he said, and we must not doubt him or say he lied; that if we did, he would know it; that he would know our thoughts and actions in no matter what part of the world we might be."

All sorts of old beliefs, customs and even costumes immediately clustered around the new faith, and it spread with lightning like rapidity in every direction, north, west, south, taking on new aspects, new emphases, new interpretations. Wowoka's spiritual crisis found an echo in the breasts of thousands of Indians.

Far to the east the great individualists, the Sioux, welcomed it fiercely. Everywhere it aroused new hopes, led to new and hitherto unheard-of interpretations of the old past. Among the Arapaho it led to an intensification of their old mysticism. People danced till they fell exhausted to the ground.

The disturbances and the excitement among the Sioux finally grew to such proportions that the government decided to disarm the Indians preparatory to taking them to the agency. A conflict naturally broke out. An Indian is supposed to have fired the first shot. The white soldiers immediately replied by pouring a volley of shot directly into the crowd. Many Indians fell at the first volley. The survivors sprang to their feet and for a time there was a hand-to-hand struggle.

Soon the Hotchkiss guns trained on the camp, opened fire and sent a storm of shells and bullets among the women and children who had gathered in front of the tipis to watch what they thought was simply an unusual military display. The guns poured in two-pound explosive shells at the rate of nearly fifty per minute mowing down everything alive. The terrible effect may be judged from the fact that one woman survivor, Blue Whirlwind, received fourteen wounds. In a few minutes two hundred Indians, men, women and children were lying dead and wounded on the ground, some of the tipis were torn to pieces by the shells while others were burning above the helpless wounded. The surviving handful of Indians fled in wild panic to the shelter of the ravine pursued by hundreds of maddened soldiers and followed up by a raking fire from the efficient Hotch-kiss guns which had been moved into position to sweep the ravine. The pursuit was simply a massacre where fleeing women with infants in their arms were shot down after resistance had ceased and when almost every warrior was stretched dead, or dying, on the ground.

The white man had triumphed. From that time on the Indians were crushed. Their nerve was gone. Broken, disorganized externally and internally, they gave up the fight.

what they thought was simply an unusual military display.

CHAPTER XVIII

CAN THERE BE AN INDIAN RENAISSANCE?

THE last twenty-five years that have seen the breakup of
that European civilization ushered in so hopefully and op-
timistically in the sixteenth century, have also witnessed the
dawn of a new era. In the world that this new dawn prefig-
ures, cultural values which have been dominant for the last
five hundred years, will have to be partly discarded and
partly reorganized. Peoples and races whose course appeared
to have been run and lost only a generation ago can, in this
new reorganization, hope to play a new role both as givers
and recipients. What role then, can we assume the future
has in store for the American Indians?

In the first edition of this work I felt constrained to say
that the Indians had completely lost their fight, that their
nerve was gone, their fate sealed. The late Mary Austin
called me to task then both for my conclusion and my pes-
simism. Yet the future she envisaged for the Indians was
clearly a secondary and a marginal one, restricted almost
exclusively to the realm of the arts and handicrafts. It did
not presuppose the persistence of their languages or of any
of the social, ethical and economic values with which their
civilizations had always been so intimately and organically
connected. Nor did it assume the possibility of these Indian
civilizations being able to incorporate into their own life
the technological inventions of Western Europe and still
being able to retain many of their own unique traits and

viewpoints. Yet, if an American Indian rebirth is to mean anything, it must mean just this. Now what are the possibilities of its attainment?

The first requisite for such a renaissance must be a common homeland and a common tradition. Do these exist? In a broad sense they do. Certainly there is an unbroken stretch of territory from Central Mexico to Chile inhabited almost exclusively by Indians, thirty-five to forty million of them. In this area even the mestizo with little Indian blood feels, quite rightly, that he has only external connections with the cultural traditions of the European usurpers. Obviously, however, the thirty-five to forty million people here, Indians and mestizoes alike, have many different and distinctive cultures just as they speak many and mutually unintelligible languages. In view of all this, how can anyone speak of an Indian tradition common to all of them?

No; that is, scientifically speaking, out of the question. Yet, if today, we occasionally hear some members of the Indian groups speak glibly of transcending all these differences, cultural as well as linguistic, which have separated them so sharply in the past, this is forgivable. It is, after all, but an expression of the romanticism, the lack of realism and the lack of historical understanding, prevalent among all ruthlessly oppressed, disorganized and maltreated peoples. We do not have to go to the Indians to find examples of this. Moreover, this romanticism and lack of realism is far more prone to be found within the ranks of the benevolently disposed white overlords than among the Indians themselves. No Indian, from the northern reaches of Canada to Tierra del Fuego, who has given the matter any thought, doubts that a large portion of the white man's achievement must be included in this new reorganization of his old life.

That such an incorporation of numerous new technological devices and new viewpoints will make the past unrecognizable to many individuals is clear; that the die-hards in his own group will cry out in horror at such an attempt and try to hinder it at all costs, this, too, is self-evident.

Nor will this be the first time that Indian cultures have been completely transformed by new and alien influences. Let us glance briefly at the record. North of the Rio Grande, before 500 A.D., all the Indian cultures led the life of simple hunters and foodgatherers. Apart from Southwestern United States, they were still living in such a stage up to about 1100 A.D. Between 1100 A.D. and 1400 A.D., a good part of North America and, I make bold to repeat, a good portion of South America east of the Andes, were overwhelmed by so many new influences that it would indeed have been difficult, if not impossible, for a Siouan or an Arawak of the year 1000 A.D. to have recognized his culture, had he been reborn in 1400 A.D. It is of comparatively little importance that these earlier invaders belonged to the same racial stock.

Transformations, where the Indian culture still remained intact, took place on an equally impressive scale after 1492. The use of iron, the adoption of the horse and the impact of Christianity and of European culture in general, often produced new expansions of native culture that were rarely felt by the Indians themselves to be anything but legitimate extensions and growths of their own civilizations. There were and still are, in South America, a substantial number of such civilizations, quite apart from those areas that are exclusively Indian—Colombia, Ecuador, Peru and Bolivia.

In the United States proper the three outstanding examples of such new developments and recreations are the Iroquois, the Southwestern Puebloes and the Navajos. The three major traits we ordinarily associate with the last tribe —sheep-herding, silverwork and blankets—all represent borrowings from the Spaniards. Practically all the great rituals, so distinctive of their life today, come from other Indian tribes with whom they have come into contact indirectly through the intermediation of their white conquerors. And yet no Navajo would understand what an anthropologist or an historian meant if he pointed out that most of what he possessed today had come to him from non-Navajo sources.

For the Indian of today the only question of significance is whether one highly specialized type of civilization can be superimposed upon another without completely exterminating the first or, at least, without the members of this group feeling that their old distinctive pattern of life had perished irretrievably. Here the subjective evaluation is really vital and fundamental. The modern Egyptian *fellah* feels no connection with the Egyptian world of the ancient pharaohs any more than does the peasant of the Tigris-Euphrates with the past glories of Babylon or Assyria. But this has rarely, if ever, held true of the American Indian. And therein lies a highly significant cultural and spiritual fact which augurs well for the future.

As I stated before, the crux of the Indians' problem depends largely upon whether there still can be discerned, over and above their many cultural particularisms, a certain common culture with a legitimacy of its own which is worthwhile perpetuating. If the world that existed before the present war were to persist for an indefinite period of time, there would really be no point in attempting to discover whether such a common tradition existed or how legitimate or worthy of perpetuation it may be. The chances for an Indian renaissance would then be negligible. Fortunately, the old world order is clearly doomed. It is this fact, apparently, that seems to have given the more articulate and farseeing members of the various Indian nations the courage, the determination, and the optimism to seek out the common denominator and to attempt a new synthesis. Quite naturally they think in terms of such a new model as that furnished by the Soviet Union.

Indeed, it is only by reference to the social-economic achievements and values of the Soviet Union that they are in a position to properly evaluate what was permanent and worthy of preservation in their own past accomplishments. That these lay within the realm of government and flowed specifically from certain social-economic bases is clear.

What these bases were can be briefly stated. With the exception of the "imperialistic" civilizations of Central and Southern Mexico and Bolivia-Peru after 1300 A.D., all Indians—and this includes the Mayas—accepted as an axiom the inalienable rights of all the members of a given nation or tribe to food, shelter and clothing. Even in those parts of Mexico and Bolivia-Peru which were "imperialistic," restricted areas at best, this held true. The demand for such an irreducible minimum must not be regarded as a purely ideological one. On the contrary. It flowed directly from the nature of the Indians' social organization in which there existed no degradation of any part of the population, no stratified classes, no private property, no surplus values to be used for personal and anti-social purposes, and where women still occupied an equal position with men.

Thus, even to the Indians of today, in spite of the mental and physical degradation that their ruthless conquerors have forced upon them, the practical accomplishments and the future program of the Soviet Union constitutes no new revelation. They can see in it, on a new level of course, the continuation of a mode of life and a set of values, social, ethical and spiritual, with which they were at one time intimately acquainted and which they practiced within the limits of their technological achievements. The great problem that they must solve is how to throw off the influences of five hundred years of oppression and enforced degradation. And this, of course, they can only do, in most parts of North and South America, more particularly South America, with the help of the dominant white group.

In one country however, Mexico, they need no such help. That the Mexican Indians themselves recognize this seems to be borne out by the great strides that have been made there, in recent years, in recapturing a number of the more worthwhile elements of their ancient past and in the partial success they have achieved in integrating these elements with those aspects of the technology of the white man that must be perpetuated in the future. If any renaissance of Indian culture is possible, it should consequently have its center in Mexico. This is a fact that must be recognized and accepted by all Indians. Nor should the other Indian groups resent this too much. It does not constitute a criticism of them in any respect. It is simply a realistic recognition of certain accidental historical events, a recognition of the fact that it is in Mexico, after all, that the most mature and complete mingling of European and native American civilization has taken place without complete spiritual impoverishment of the aboriginal population. In no other part of Latin America have the Indians maintained their own so well, and in no other part of Latin America were the white invaders, from the very beginning, constrained to recognize so immediately and so persistently the cultural accomplishments of those they were attempting forcibly to "civilize."

It is no mean compliment to pay a conquered people, when the conquerors feel it necessary and even advantageous for their own interests to translate some of the plays of their most famous dramatists, Lope de Vega, into the native idiom. This was done in Mexico City within two generations of the arrival of the Spaniards. Nor is it an accident that when the true founder of modern Mexican literature, Fernandez di Lizardi, wrote his famous novel *El Periquillo Sarniento,* the Aztec words taken over into his vocabulary were numerous enough to justify a glossary.

For those who feel that it is too much to expect all the American Indians to look to Mexico for leadership and a common rallying-point, the answer must be that the only people who, by their success in integrating Spanish civilization with their own, could be taken into consideration, the Araucanians of South America, are too small in number and too far away from the major centers of Indian population in that continent, to constitute a true rallying-point.

Here in the United States the only hope for a continued survival of the Indian cultures would be if they were concentrated in some area within the United States contiguous to Mexico, and if they were given their own autonomy. This has actually been proposed by a representative group of Indians. The concentration of the Indian population of the United States in such an area is by no means a physical impossibility. The outcry against it, I imagine, would probably not come so much from the Indians themselves as from the whites. After all, fully half of our Indian population is already within striking distance of Mexico. The granting of autonomy is another matter. It would, perhaps, presuppose a fundamental transformation of the methods and thinking of our dominant class. For that, unfortunately, there is at present no warrant. . . .

And so we return to where we started. An Indian renaissance is quite within the realm of the possible and the attainable if certain conditions are fulfilled, if the Indians are permitted to determine what the renaissance shall be and if this is not left in the hands of well-meaning whites or romantic and unrealistic white governmental bureaus. Whether these conditions will be fulfilled still remains uncertain. However, if they are not, it is perhaps not only the Indians whose fate will then be sealed.

If they are fulfilled we will then be presented with the heart-warming spectacle of welcoming back into the fold of nations a people whose way of life and whose mature understanding of human relations should make it clear to everyone how iniquitous and contrary to all basic human values have been the so-called great civilizations of the world, from the advent of the ancient Egyptians and Sumerians to the present time. For the Indians it should consequently be a source of profound satisfaction to see so much of what they prized incorporated in the new civilization whose manifest destiny it clearly is to direct us toward the only road that can give us happiness, security and the proper sense of human dignity.

SELECTED BIBLIOGRAPHY

In the following bibliography I have selected popularly written descriptions wherever that was possible. When that was not possible I have given the most representative monographs.

GENERAL

Wissler, Clark. *The American Indian*, 1922. Although somewhat antiquated and written for specialists, this is still the only available general treatment of the Indians as a whole.

Kroeber, A. L., and Waterman, T. T. *Source Book in Anthropology*, 1931. This exceedingly useful work contains the following articles bearing on the American Indians:

Boas, F. *The Potlatch of the Kwakiutl Indians*, pp. 332, 338.

Boas, F. *The Decorative Art of the North Pacific Coast*, pp. 374-388.

Grinnell, G. B. *The Warfare of the Plains Indians*, pp. 367-374.

Nordenskiöld, E. *The American Indian as an Inventor*, pp. 489-555.

Sapir, E. *The Social Organization of the West Coast Tribes*, pp. 317-332.

Waterman, T. T. *The Architecture of the American Indians*, pp. 512-524.

Wissler, C. *The Influence of the Horse in the Development of Plains Culture*, pp. 505-512.

Radin, P. *Social Anthropology*, 1932. The following chapters of this book deal with the American Indians:

Chap. V. *The Iroquois.*

Chap. XII. *The Omaha.*

Chap. XVIII. *The Pomo* (Central California).

Chap. XIX. *The Central Eskimo.*

Chap. XXI. *The Kwakiutl.*

Chap. XXII.   *The Hidatsa.*
Chap. XXIX.   *The Arapaho.*

Murdock, E. P.   *Our Primitive Contemporaries,* 1934.   This contains the
following sketches on the American Indians:
Chap. VIII.   *The Polar Eskimo.*
Chap. IX.   *The Haidas of British Columbia.*
Chap. X.   *The Crows of the Western Plains.*
Chap. XI.   *The Iroquois.*
Chap. XII.   *The Hopi.*
Chap. XIII.   *The Aztecs.*

Forde, C. Daryll.   *Habitat, Economy and Society,* 1934.   This work
contains the following sketches bearing on our subject:
Chap. VI.   *The Paiute.*
Chap. V.   *The Blackfoot.*
Chap. VI.   *The Nootka and Kwakiutl.*
Chap. VIII.   *The Eskimo.*
Chap. IX.   *The Boro of the Western Amazon Forest.*
Chap. XII.   *The Hopi and Yuma.*

SPECIAL

Prologue

Radin, P.   *The Winnebago Indians.*   Thirty-seventh Annual Report of
the Bureau of American Ethnology.

Chap. I

Rasmussen, K.   *The People of the Polar North.*

Chap. II

Joyce, T. A.   *Mexican Archeology,* 1914.
Sahagun, Bernadino.   *A History of Ancient Mexico,* translated by F. Ban-
delier, 1932.

Spence, L. *The Gods of Mexico*, 1923. Good for the descriptions of the Aztec deities but exceedingly arbitrary in his interpretations.

1880. This is still one of the best resumés of the older Spanish

Bancroft, H. H. *The Native Races of the Pacific States*, 5 vols., 1875-sources.

Chap. III

The same sources as those for Chap. II.

Chap. IV

Means, P. A. *Ancient Civilizations of the Andes*, 1931. This contains a full bibliography.

Mead, C. W. *Old Civilizations of Inca Land*, 1924.

Chap. VI

The same sources as Chap. IV.

Chap. VIII

Shetrone, H. C. *The Mound-Builders*, 1930. Somewhat uncritical but the only available book on the whole subject.

Chap. IX

Swanton, J. R. *Indian Tribes of the Lower Mississippi*, Bureau of American Ethnology, Bul. 43, 1911.

Mooney, J. *The Sacred Formulas of the Cherokee*, Seventh Annual Report of the Bureau of American Ethnology, 1891.

Mooney, J., and Olbrechts, F. M. *The Swimmer Manuscript: Cherokee Sacred Formulas and Medicinal Prescriptions*, Bureau of America Ethnology, Bul. 99, 1932.

Swanton, J. R. *Social Organization, etc., of the Indians of the Creek Confederacy*, 42nd Annual Report of the Bureau of American Ethnology, 1928.

Chap. X

Goddard, P. E. *Indians of the Southwest,* 1927.

Kidder, A. V. *An Introduction to the Study of Southwestern Archeology,* 1924.

Parsons, E. C. *A Pueblo Indian Journal,* Memoirs of the American Anthropological Association, No. 32, 1925.

Parsons, E. C. *Hopi and Zuñi Ceremonialism,* Memoirs of the American Anthropological Association, No. 39, 1933.

Bunzel, R. *Introduction to Zuñi Ceremonialism; Zuñi Origin Myths; Zuñi Ritual Poetry; Zuñi Katcinas,* 42nd Annual Report of the Bureau of American Ethnology, 1932, pp. 467-1086.

Roberts, F. H. H. *The Village of the Great Kivas,* Bureau of American Ethnology, Bul. 111.

Stevenson, M. *The Zuñi Indians,* 23rd Annual Report of the Bureau of American Ethnology, 1901.

Chap. XI

Fletcher, A. C. *The Hako, a Pawnee Ceremony.* Twenty-second Annual Report of the Bureau of American Ethnology, 1900.

Dorsey, G. A. *Traditions of the Skidi Pawnee.* Introduction.

Chap. XII

Morgan, L. H. *League of the Iroquois,* 1904.

Chap. XIII

Wissler, C. *North American Indians of the Plains,* 1920.

Grinnell, G. B. *The Cheyenne Indians,* 1923.

Lowie, R. H. *Notes on the Social Organization, etc., of the Mandan, Hidatsa and Crow Indians,* 1917.

Deloria, E. *Dakota Texts.* Publications of the American Ethnological Society, Vol. 14, 1932.

Chap. XIV

Goddard, P. E.   *Indians of the Northwest Coast*, 1924.

Boas, F.   *Ethnology of the Kwakiutl*, 35th Annual Report of the Bureau of American Ethnology, 1921.

Hill-Trout, C.   *British North America*, 1907.

Chap. XV

Kohl, J. G.   *Kitchi-Gami*, 1860.   This is, in some ways, one of the best accounts of the Ojibwa Indians ever written.   Unfortunately it is very rare.

Radin, P.   *Ojibwa Ethnological Chit-Chat*, American Anthropologist, 1924, pp. 491-530.

Skinner, A.   *Social Life of the Menomini Indians*, 1913.

Chap. XVI

Kroeber, A. L.   *Handbook of the Indians of California*, Bureau of American Ethnology, Bulletin 78, 1925.

Chap. XVII

Mooney, J.   *The Ghost Dance Religion*, 14th Annual Report of the Bureau of American Ethnology, Part II, 1896.

INDEX

A

Algonquians, 30 ff., 273, 292.
Amazon, 165, 361 f.
Andes, 50, 122 ff., 137, 165, 355 ff.
Apache, 42, 45, 235, 251, 255, 292.
Arapaho, 292 f., 303.
Araucanians, 172.
Arch, 54 ff.
Architecture, 46, 52 ff.
Argentine, 50 f., 165.
Arikara, 291 f., 303 f.
Arizona, 41, 42, 234 ff.
Arkansas, 194, 200.
Art, 39, 42 f., 46, 50, 53 f., 56-59,
    142-149, 160-161, 200, 201, 333 ff.
Arauk, 166 f., 171, 173.
Astronomy, 71 ff.
Athabascans, 319.
Atortaho, Iroquois chief, 277 f.
Auguries, 157.
Aztalan, mound of, 198.
Aztecs, 46 ff., 82-120, 162, 187, 230.

B

Bear, worship of, 13, 343.
Beauracracy, 129 ff., 239 f.
Bingham, H., 139.
Black magic, 7-8.
Blackfoot, 292, 303-307.
Blood feud, 356-361.
Boas, F., 329.
Bolivia, 49, 165, 168.
Bourke, Capt., 313 ff.
Brazil, 166, 173, 353, 361.
Bridges, 138.
British Columbia, 45, 318-336.
Bronze, use of, 144.
Buffalo, rôle of, 32 ff., 291 ff.
Bundles, sacred, 262 ff., 303 ff.

C

Caddoan, linguistic family, 40 ff.
Cahokia, mound at, 192.

Calchaqui, 50, 173.
Calendar, 72-76, 158 f., 246 ff.
California, 42, 45, 234, 354 ff.
Cannibalism, 327 ff.
Canoe, 344-345.
Capitalism, 318-336.
Cardinal points, worship of, 61, 66,
    103.
Castañeda, 233.
Castes, 45, 97-103, 130-131, 157, 219-
    221, 322.
Cayuga, Iroquois tribe, 276 f.
Census taking, 131-132.
Central America, Indians of, 48 ff.,
    230.
Ceremonies and dances:
    (The arrangement is alphabetical
        with the name of the tribe in
        parenthesis following.)
    Age societies (Plains), 297-303.
    Blood revenge, ritual of (Jibaro),
        356-361.
    Cardinal points, ritual of (Maya),
        66.
    Condolence, ritual of (Iroquois),
        285-288.
    Coronation, Chibcha king (Chib-
        cha), 169 ff.
    Hako, ceremony of (Pawnee),
        256-259.
    Harvest, ceremony of (Creek),
        215-217.
    Huitzilopochtli, ceremony for (Az-
        tec), 85.
    Maize, ceremony for (Natchez),
        207-211.
    New fire rite (Hopi), 249-251.
    New year, ritual of (Maya), 66.
    Rain, ceremonies for (Puebloes),
        240-241.
    War bundle, ritual of (Winne-
        bago), 10-12.
    War feast (Natchez), 225-228.
    Winter ritual (Kwakiutl), 327-
        332.
Chapultepec, 89.

387